THE ROMANTIC REBELLION

By the same author

THE MEANING OF BEAUTY
THE ARTIST AND HIS PUBLIC
MASTERPIECES OF FIGURE PAINTING
CHRISTOPHER WOOD
EUROPEAN PAINTING AND SCULPTURE
INTRODUCTION TO EUROPEAN PAINTING
BRITISH PAINTING
STANLEY SPENCER
IN MY VIEW
TINTORETTO
THE ARTS OF MAN

THE ROMANTIC REBELLION

ERIC NEWTON

LONGMANS

LONGMANS, GREEN AND CO LTD
48 GROSVENOR STREET, LONDON W1
RAILWAY CRESCENT, CROYDON, VICTORIA, AUSTRALIA
AUCKLAND, KINGSTON (JAMAICA), LAHORE, NAIROBI

LONGMANS SOUTHERN AFRICA (PTY) LTD
THIBAULT HOUSE, THIBAULT SQUARE, CAPE TOWN
JOHANNESBURG, SALISBURY

LONGMANS OF NIGERIA LTD
W. R. INDUSTRIAL ESTATE, IKEJA

LONGMANS OF GHANA LTD
INDUSTRIAL ESTATE, RING ROAD SOUTH, ACCRA

LONGMANS GREEN (FAR EAST) LTD
443 LOCKHART ROAD, HONG KONG

LONGMANS OF MALAYA LTD
44 JALAN AMPANG, KUALA LUMPUR

ORIENT LONGMANS LTD
CALCUTTA, BOMBAY, MADRAS
DELHI, HYDERABAD, DACCA

LONGMANS CANADA LTD
137 BOND STREET, TORONTO 2

FIRST PUBLISHED 1962

PRINTED IN GREAT BRITAIN BY W. & J. MACKAY & CO LTD, CHATHAM

CONTENTS

ILLUSTRATIONS

NOTE

The illustration on p. 137 is reproduced from Oscar Wilde, *Salome* by permission of The Bodley Head Ltd; p. 156 from Goldscheider, *Donatello* by permission of Phaidon Press Ltd; p. 158 from Giselbertus, *Sculptor of Autun* (photo Franceschi) by permission of Trianon Press. Illustrations on pp. 30, 36, 39, 73, 81, 83, 84, 85, 90, 93, 95, 118, 140, 159 and 171 are from the Mansell Collection.

CHAPTER I

Romanticism in the Visual Arts

At an indefinable moment towards the end of the eighteenth century criticism became conscious that artists had tapped a new vein of inspiration. Philosophers and aestheticians, always on the look-out for the appearance of a 'tendency', began to analyse and discuss what they had discovered. What they said and what they wrote bears the mark of considerable excitement; and though today we can see how incomplete and often mistaken were their judgments, for that they were hardly to blame: they were working on insufficient data: the new mood in art had not yet had time to find for itself an adequate means of expression, nor had they yet succeeded in fully understanding it. What is important, however, is not that they were unable to arrive at a satisfactory definition, but that they realized that here was something that needed defining.

What they were attempting to define was something they eventually decided to call 'romanticism'. The word was not new. Nor indeed was the basic idea for which it stood. It is one of those words with an impressive family tree whose roots are embedded in the soil of hard fact, but whose meaning has steadily become more complex and less concrete, until what started as a label for a tangible phenomenon slowly turned into a metaphor and ended as a symbol of an idea.

Rome, Roman, Romance, Romanticism. The process whereby a noun gives birth to an adjective which, in its turn, gives birth to another noun is common enough. But the precise relationship of the adjective to the parent noun depends on an attitude of mind. The meaning of the word 'man', for example, is clear. No difference of opinion can arise as to what is or is not a man. But the meaning of the adjective 'manly' depends on what, at any given moment, seems truly characteristic of man in general. An analytical process—or at least a contemplative attitude of mind—is necessary before the essential man-ness of a man can be disentangled from all those attributes which he shares with the rest of the created world. Only when the disentangling process has taken place does the adjective 'manly' become necessary. But, once it has established itself, the abstract noun 'manliness' comes into being, and a slightly different set of values attaches itself to the word, for again a process of selection must take place. The question, 'What quality is common to beings who, in our opinion, deserve the epithet "manly"?' must be answered.

Seldom has a sequence of related words covered so wide a stretch of meanings as that which starts with Rome, the name of a city, and ends with the vague attitude of mind we now call 'romanticism'. Yet the steps between them are simple, and—until, in the nineteenth-century, German philosophers began to interest themselves in romanticism—logical. As early as the fourteenth century the word 'Romance' was applied to languages derived from Latin. Chaucer then uses it to mean tales of chivalry written in those languages. By the seventeenth century it had come to mean any prose fiction dealing with unusual or imagined events, and from then onwards it was vaguely applied to that class of literature in which fantasy predominated over probability.

Having established a generic meaning for the noun 'Romance', the seventeenth century then coined the adjective 'romantic', a necessary word as soon as the human mind had begun to inquire what were the qualities common to all literary romances. Pepys can write 'almost romantique yet true' and a contemporary of Pepys makes it even clearer what the word means to him when he speaks of 'the romantic and visionary scheme of building a bridge over the river at Putney'. At this date the word seems to contain within itself two ideas—'unpractical' and 'improbable' (extending in extreme cases to 'untrue'), to which, according to the temperament of the user, a third could be added, 'and therefore delightful'.

Not every man, still less every period, is capable of finding the unpractical and the untrue delightful, and the early eighteenth century, though quite conscious that the romantic mood could not be ignored, also felt that it ought to be challenged. It was, of course, the age-old challenge between emotion and reason, though the conscious opposition between Romantic and Classic did not appear till later. At first the reaction to whatever, in literature, was romantic took the form of a vague uneasiness—a sense that the rules of good taste were being threatened. Not until later was the word 'classic' produced as a stick to beat 'romantic' with—as though two mutually exclusive theories were being opposed to each other in the hope that one or the other, in some half-envisaged final test, would ultimately prevail.

It was probably the publication of Goethe's *Wilhelm Meister* in 1796 that stimulated certain German writers to an outburst of enthusiastic criticism of the new spirit in literature. Friedrich Schlegel's articles (in 1798) in the *Athenaeum* established the word 'romantic' in the sense that became accepted throughout the nineteenth century, but it was almost by chance that he adopted it. He had already made a distinction between the 'old' and the 'new' spirit in poetry by calling the former 'beautiful' and the latter 'interesting'; Schlegel regarded the 'beautiful' as 'objective' (on the ground that the laws of beauty are permanent and universal, and therefore independent of the personal temperament of the artist), while the 'interesting' was, in his view, 'subjective' and was the outcome merely of the artist's desire to express himself and his *vie intérieure*, regardless of 'good taste' or 'correctness'.

Schlegel, in his earlier writings, is a stout defender of classicism and good taste. But the defence would not have been necessary had he not realized that a new movement was on foot, that the sacred and universally valid laws of beauty were being broken, and that it was his duty as an aesthetician-philosopher to throw himself into the battle. It was only during the progress of the contest that he gradually became aware that there was much to be said in favour of the 'interesting', and that Shakespeare, the most massive figure known to him in the literature of the 'interesting', was as powerful a force as Sophocles, the type, for him, of the 'beautiful'. By the time that *Wilhelm Meister* was published, Schlegel was ready to announce his conversion to the new spirit, and to substitute for 'interesting' the more evocative word 'romantic'.

What happened, in fact, in the late eighteenth century, was not a discovery of romanticism, but a conversion to it. The awful threat of 'subjectivism', pushing its rude way into the objective serenities of classical art, breaking down the smooth walls of the old edifice, ended by seeming a positive blessing—an opening up of stuffy enclosures, a means, though perhaps rather a ruthless one, of introducing a breath of fresh air into their calm but stagnant atmosphere.

I have begun this book with a note on Friedrich Schlegel's writings on romanticism not because they are the core of the subject—they are not even a particularly good starting-point for an inquiry into the romantic spirit of art—but because they do at least attempt to examine certain manifestations of an internal struggle that had been going on since the dawn of civilization. Schlegel's starting-point was an interest in 'modern' literature, yet no sooner had he begun to examine it than he found himself tempted to trace its genesis to Shakespeare. He could, with a little more sympathetic intuition, have discovered the same elements in Homer and Dante. He could have noted that what formed the whole texture of the music of Wagner is discernible at critical moments in Bach, where its effect is all the more precious because, instead of being the whole texture, it shines like a jewel in its setting. He could have found in Racine and Pope sudden flashes of the same spirit which came so easily to Shakespeare. He could, in fact, have guessed that what seemed to him two mutually exclusive modes of thought and feeling were really two different attitudes of mind, each capable of enriching the other when fused together—each, indeed, producing an impoverished effect when isolated. What makes Bach greater than his contemporaries is his unexpected moments of mystery and nostalgia. What makes Wagner immortal is the formal pattern that underlies his magnificent hysteria. And had Schlegel widened his horizon to include the visual arts, he would have been surprised to find evidences of that same fusion of opposites in medieval architecture, in the whole of North European Renaissance painting, in Leonardo, in Giorgione and Tintoretto, in Rubens and in his own contemporary, Goya. It is certain that he would not have admitted into the romantic category all that we admit today, for he was on the look-out for extreme cases. It is only at a later stage in critical analysis that the idea of 'more' or 'less' romantic begins to occur. Our eyes and ears have become more finely adjusted to those interwoven threads, and we now detect overtones that once passed unnoticed. Behind the serene surface of Milton's poetry we begin to note the beat of an unexpectedly agitated pulse. Consequently we are driven to the conclusion that romanticism is a mode of feeling that can appear at any time in human history, but that only at certain periods and under certain conditions of cultural climate can it find a full and adequate means of expression. Romanticism is an attitude of mind in which any human being, at any time, may, by virtue of his humanity, indulge: but 'romantic' can only be applied with confidence to certain periods or races in which that same attitude of mind finds no hindrance to its means of expression.

But if romanticism is an attitude of mind which can find its expression in all the arts, one would have expected to find among critics and philosophers at least a general agreement as to its nature. In its extreme cases, the signs of its presence are easy to recognize; there is very little argument about which works of art show most signs of it, or about the presence of it in works of art that are, generally speaking, classic in form. Disagreement begins not when critics begin to point to concrete instances of the romantic or even of romantic elements in the classic. It is when they begin to describe the essence of the romantic attitude of mind that they become confused. It is, they agree, the cause of all kinds of stylistic symptoms which upset the balance, disturb the serenity, interfere with the time-honoured conventions of classic art. But though many attempts have been made to isolate and define this state of mind, the attempts have not been notably successful. One finds in analytical writings on romanticism too many categories and too little common ground between one category and another. The confusion is not surprising. One would expect an ingredient that can be traced through most of the art of the world to be the reverse of simple. But if it is an ingredient in the true sense of the word, it must have a common essence, however complex it may be and however many subdivisions it may be resolved into.

It is not, of course, necessary to find a *perceptible* common ground between a painting by Altdorfer, a Gothic cathedral, a nocturne by Chopin, and a poem by Alfred de Musset. Even though an agreed vocabulary could be found that would establish correspondences between the different media that artists use, the differences of temperament between any two artists, even working in the same medium, would account for utterly different ways of expressing the same general attitude of mind. It is not in the kind of sounds or relationships of form and colour conceived by the artist that one would expect to find the common factor, but in the state of mind that prompted the artists to conceive them. Surely, one would think, where a recognizable effect appears a moderately satisfactory definition of its origin could be found. Even if a hundred critics, each with his own preconceived idea of what romanticism really consists of, have produced a hundred different accounts of what, in their view, is the nature of the disease behind the symptom, surely some level-headed analyst could then co-ordinate those hundred different accounts and discover a formula that would prove them all to be different aspects of the same basic disturbance.

Such a formula has, as far as I know, never been discovered, and I am inclined to think that the reason why the discovery has not been made is that, though the common factor between different 'categories' of romanticism does, in fact, exist, it is not quite the kind of common factor that philosophers have been looking for.

I suspect that abstract thought, as such, is an impossible ideal, and that behind all attempts to envisage an abstract idea there must be a concrete image, which, by its very nature, limits the freedom of abstract thought. The opposition, for example, between romantic and classic is real and inescapable, but only by envisaging a specific *kind* of opposition does it become possible to describe either the nature of the two opposing forces or the relationship in which they stand to one another. In their search for such descriptions I believe that aestheticians have had before their minds the image of the seesaw, in which, if one end is in the air, the other must be on the ground; classic and romantic must then appear as rivals, each capable of triumphing by virtue of its own inherent weight (which, for some reason, varies from time to time) in relation to that of its opponent, yet both capable of achieving a precarious and short-lived balance whenever their weights are roughly equal. Such an image allowed philosophers to watch the behaviour of romantic and classic movements throughout history with a good deal of acuteness, but it limits them because they can only succeed in understanding the development of both movements in so far as each happens to triumph at the expense of the other.

In many ways the seesaw image has proved itself serviceable, but I believe that it presents a fundamentally misleading picture of the romantic-classic opposition in that it compels the theorist to think of the two as mutually exclusive. It is the main purpose of this book to substitute for the seesaw another image, which seems to me to correspond more closely to the historical facts and therefore to be more serviceable in explaining them. Meanwhile, a moment's thought will make one suspect that the seesaw image has misled the theorists in their search for a formula that would unite the various categories of romanticism by finding for them a common denominator. The weight on the romanticist end of the seesaw must owe its potency to some factor that binds all the theories of romanticism together into a compact unit conveniently placed at one end of the plank. If no such factor can be found—if, in fact, there seem to be romanticisms of various kinds and even of contradictory kinds—then there is no sense in arguing that they are all not only in opposition to classicism, but that by adding their separate but unrelated weights to the non-classic end of the seesaw, they are all in the *same kind of opposition* to the apparently homogeneous weight of classicism at the other.

A word that has been so recently promoted and given a more or less technical status in order to fill a gap in the existing vocabulary ought not to present this kind of difficulty. The problem of defining romanticism would hardly exist if we could be content to use it in the sense which Schiller and Schlegel had in mind in the late 1790s. But since their day two factors have complicated the issue—firstly, our growing suspicion that romanticism may not be, in any obvious sense, the antithesis of classicism, but rather that it resembles a flavour that can occur in any classic dish in any proportion, so that it may be at times only faintly perceptible, and at others so powerful that it destroys the basic flavour of the dish; and, secondly, if romantic is a relative and not an absolute term, a quality liable to crop up at any moment in any place and at any pitch of intensity, then there is little likelihood that a simple definition of it can be easily found. Too many racial temperaments, too many varieties of the *Zeitgeist* have been at work for a single, recognizable kind of romanticism to emerge in every country or at any period. Classicism, on the other hand, is generally recognized as something less variable, and it would seem more profitable to consider what the word 'classic' means, or is generally supposed to mean, before examining the innumerable attempts to explain the true essence of the romantic.

It is not easy for the contemporary mind to grasp a set of principles that must have seemed axiomatic at certain moments in the history of art. Nor does one find anywhere a reasoned and complete statement of those principles during those moments, for when agreement is universal there is no need to state a creed. It is only at moments when the basic principles are threatened that such a statement becomes necessary: and, as always happens when basic principles are threatened, the resultant polemics are tinged with passion and overstatement. A petulant note can be heard that too often turns an argument into a quarrel. It is only when one has made allowances for the special situation caused by an outbreak of hostility that one can fairly judge what principles are involved and to what extent they are in danger.

Yet there is no doubt at all that, in Schlegel's mind, 'principles' were at stake, and that even though no precise definition of them could be discovered, a given work of art could be judged by its conformity to them. Evidently the principles of classicism were founded on a conception of beauty: the artist's first obligation was to produce something recognizably 'beautiful'. But to recognize beauty is one thing, to define it is another; and if classicism insists on the application of rules, it must of necessity start with definitions.

Yet when one turns back to the writings of those Greek philosophers who were mostly concerned with beauty, and who were certainly interested in the art that surrounded them—an art which, in every one of its manifestations, we would all agree to call 'classic'—the strange fact emerges that there is no attempt to link the two. Beauty, for the Greeks, was a quality to be found in the created world, and, since Hellenic man was the measure of all things, its most obvious example was the human body. Plato, with his perpetual search for root causes and first principles, was driven to the theory that behind these examples of beauty in the material world there must be a set of archetypal forms—specimens of 'absolute' beauty which he could only envisage in terms of mathematics.

Art, on the other hand, was no more than the activity whereby man imitated the created world. Its only connexion, in the minds of Plato and Aristotle, with beauty was the assumption that a work that imitated 'beautiful' Nature must itself be beautiful, and that if Nature produced objects that could be regarded as varying in their content of beauty, then the artist would be well advised to select the most beautiful objects and especially the most beautiful men and women as models for his mimetic art. Such a theory implied a standard reducible to mathematics, a formula for human beauty that could exist in the mind of the painter or sculptor and thus save him the trouble of selecting and discarding models when he came to carry out the mimetic process.

This attractively simple theory brought in its train a good many unanswered and unanswerable questions. It seemed to explain the sculptor admirably, the painter rather less so. But the poet and the dramatist fitted in rather badly, and the composer of music seemed to escape entirely from the mimetic net. However, since the concept of 'the Arts' as means of communicating between an artist and his fellows does not seem to have occurred to the classic philosophers, the search for a formula that would link them together was not pursued very far. There were separate arts, since different kinds of human skill were involved in the carving of a statue and the composing of a poem or a melody, but there was no need for such an all-embracing term as 'the Arts'.

More difficult was the question of the purpose of 'the Arts'. The Greek mind, with its healthy, intelligent curiosity about function, was a little troubled by this. Was art's purpose merely to represent? Surely not. Wasn't it rather to admonish, to educate, to improve? And if so, was the imitation of 'beautiful Nature' the only means of doing so? Does the secret of art's desirability lie in some kind of equation between the Beautiful and the Good? But—it is Plutarch who first hints at this puzzle—why do certain imitations of the unbeautiful strike us as having in them something akin to beauty? Medea's slaying of her children is surely not a beautiful incident, yet a representation of the scene might be—mightn't it?—well, perhaps not exactly beautiful, but certainly moving, memorable—a thing one would *want* to contemplate in the way one wants to contemplate beauty. How odd that it should be so!

And yet, if art is to instruct the mind as well as to delight the eye, how inevitable!

It is at this point that the complexity of the artist's problem begins to trouble the Greek philosopher. The artist, he assumes, is particularly concerned with the Beautiful, even if only to the extent of recording its appearance and giving it more or less permanent form in paint or marble. But to record appearances is not a sufficiently complete programme. It is not even a sufficiently interesting programme. The artist must also sometimes tell a story, and even though his medium may not be quite as suitable as that of the poet or the historian for the telling of stories, he can never quite escape from the obligation to add action to appearance. And once action has been introduced an entirely new set of judgements comes into being.

A statue whose only meaning is 'This was the appearance of Medea' can only evoke in the spectator a response to her physique, and since we may be sure that the sculptor, obsessed by the idea of physical beauty, would limit himself to no more than three categories of human physical perfection—adolescence, maturity, and early middle age—we can be equally sure that his Medea was no more ('no less', perhaps he would have said) than an idealized representation of feminine maturity. Of Medea's character we should be told little or nothing. But when the statue's meaning is extended to 'Thus Medea slew her children' we are confronted by the same idealized woman—still 'beautiful' in any normally accepted sense of the word—engaged in an action whose moral implications are ugly, however rhythmically satisfying to the eye that action might be.

Here, in its simplest form, is Schlegel's dilemma—the discovery that to the 'beautiful', that perfection at which Nature so often hints but which she so rarely achieves, can be added the 'interesting', which has no apparent connexion with perfection, and that the result of this addition, far from detracting from the value of the work of art, may considerably enhance it.

Doubtless Plutarch did not see the dilemma in the same terms as Schlegel. To Plutarch it seemed puzzling that a desirable woman engaged in an undesirable action should, when translated into art, be a satisfying object of contemplation. But he could not resolve the puzzle. Perhaps it did not occur to him that the physical and the moral belong to different categories, or that the act of slaying could be rhythmically pleasing to the eye but morally repellent to the mind. If it had done so he would certainly have been tempted to consider more closely the relationship between form and content in art, that problem which has so intriguingly preoccupied later writers. He might even have concluded, as Schlegel had already begun to conclude in 1800, that form could justifiably be modified by content and that the power of a work of art whose content was a morally undesirable action might actually be increased if the form of the actors was envisaged by the artist as physically undesirable.

Such a notion, even if it could have occurred to an artist nurtured in the classic tradition, would have been instantly rejected. Even to the sculptor of the Laocoön group, the fact that the central subject-matter of the group was fear, pain, and imminent death was never allowed to interfere with the form. What had to be produced was a representation of two beautiful youths and one beautiful bearded athlete in attitudes which, despite violent muscular action, were still harmonious and graceful. Consequently these visual harmonies make it impossible to regard the group as a serious attempt to represent agony in its intensest form; for the true classic artist is never in any doubt, when visual harmony and emotional intensity are at odds, which must be sacrificed to the other. The Laocoön sculptor could permit himself, perhaps, to twist the bearded athlete's lips into the conventional pattern of pain or to carve one or two conventional furrows in the brow, but to allow that agony to dictate terms to the whole body, still less the whole group, was unthinkable.

To Schlegel, on the other hand, writing in the dawn of a romantic period, the 'interesting' depended on something more than subject-matter. It could not be achieved without a complete abandonment of 'beauty' whenever 'beauty' conflicted with the interests of 'expressiveness'. If cruelty is the essence of the artist's message, then the formal equivalent of cruelty must be sought for in the very shapes and colours he uses. A negation of grace, an insistence of harshness, is justifiable. The artist's function, as Schlegel saw it in 1800, was not to imagine formal perfection but to communicate emotion and to do so as intensely as possible.

It is not surprising that Plutarch and Schlegel solved their dilemmas in different ways. During the seventeen centuries that separate them certain revolutions in human values had occurred, the most far-reaching of which had been Christianity, whose challenge to accepted pre-Christian modes of thought changed the whole texture of civilization and with it the whole history of art. It is a commonplace to say that Christianity taught men to despise the material and to value the spiritual world. The generalization is certainly not true. Pagan man was as conscious of the reality of his soul as the Christian, even though he differed from the Christian in his account of how to behave for his soul's good. And Christian man was as conscious of his physical environment as any Greek—indeed, in many ways his appreciation of the material world was more complete.

What separates the two is not a transfer of loyalty from the material to the spiritual, but a different way of relating them and, perhaps more significant, of using them as ingredients in the desirable life and particularly as subject-matter for art. The Hellenic tendency to divide the arts into an elaborate system of watertight compartments, each with its presiding genius resident on Mount Parnassus, was a result of a frank acceptance of the limitations imposed on each branch of the arts by the nature of its medium. Sculpture's natural concern was with the human body, and, since the Greek was a self-conscious perfectionist, it was with the body's physical perfection that the sculptor busied himself—not merely by closely observing it and by deducing from its manifold variants an 'ideal' which has since imposed itself on the whole of subsequent Western civilization, but also by reducing that ideal to a canon and by founding on it a theory of visual proportion just as applicable to the abstract art of architecture as to the mimetic art of sculpture.

The natural concern of literature, on the other hand, was with the *vie intérieure* of the individual, the destiny of the race, the relationship—always delicately balanced and often strained to breaking-point—between man and his gods. Each of the arts had its proper field, and the artist's business was to define that field, enlarging it if possible, but not, unless driven, allowing it to encroach on the territory of neighbouring arts. To the true Hellene, the modern habit of searching for common ground between the arts and triumphantly noting the hidden correspondences between them would be unintelligible. Architecture that could be thought of as frozen music, music of which the composer himself could say 'There Fate knocks at the door', would lack that purity which architecture and music should strive to attain. True, for each kind of artist there must always be temptations. Homer is compelled to describe the shield of Achilles and he does it with evident relish even though such a description would be better handled by a painter than a poet. The sculptor of the infanticide Medea trespasses, and not unwillingly, on the tragedians' domain. But such minor trespasses are inevitable. They should be, and in Classic Greek art they are, reduced to a minimum.

But Christianity threw all the arts into the melting-pot so that their frontiers are no longer inviolate. Systematized purity gives way to a complexity in which it is not easy to discover a system. Architecture behaves like a tangled forest, man's body shrivels and gesticulates in an attempt to reveal man's soul, poetry begins to rejoice in the seen, painting in the unseen. And with this melting of the frontiers of the arts, Plutarch's dilemma disappears. If the serenity of physical perfection is no longer a sculptor's main preoccupation, why should not Medea slay her children, Judith assassinate Holofernes, the Romans torture their Christian victims? Agony is no longer shameful because it contradicts beauty. Agony, given the right situation, *is* beauty, not only for the dramatist, but for the painter. Beauty is no longer an absolute. It takes its value from its context. And its context is no longer man in conflict with his gods, but man endeavouring to identify his own will with the will of his God. In that endeavour the arts lose their separateness. Christian man is imperfect: he is no longer the central fact of the created world or the measure of all things with the gods made in his image. Therefore the ideal is no longer to be sought for or found in him; and even if the arts of sculpture and painting still regarded themselves as mimetic, to imitate imperfection would be a waste of time. But sculpture and painting are no longer mimetic. They can, at best, imitate the seen; but since the seen has become unworthy of imitation, what they now require is a set of symbols for the unseen.

It is not long before the new point of view finds its expression in aesthetic philosophy. Surprisingly early, Plotinus (A.D. 203–270), still obsessed, as were his Greek predecessors, by the idea of 'beauty' and the need to define it, produces an entirely un-Greek definition and in doing so discovers that beauty in art is not the automatic result, as the Greeks had assumed, of copying beauty in nature. Beauty in a work of art, says Plotinus, is the direct outcome of divine inspiration. He goes further, and, by a process of reasoning thoroughly in tune with today's ways of thinking, notes that since inspiration is purely subjective, and since the spirit of the artist passes into his work of art, beauty is a fragment of divinity that has found its way, through the artist acting as medium, into the thing he has made.

Here, for the first time, is the conception of art as communication, and, at its best, as the communication of an exceptional state of mind, a heightened emotional condition. Gone are all the pre-Christian attempts to reduce beauty to a formula, or to extract the essence of it from the physical world. If the artist can by-pass the whole of visual experience and short-circuit straight back to divinity, there can be no question either of rules or of realism. Plotinus is, of course, a little too simple in his account of the creative process. He rightly insists that the visual arts can deal with the unseen, but he fails to realize that a work of visual art can only come into being when the artist has translated the unseen into the seen, that in doing so he cannot communicate his meaning except by symbols understood by the spectator, and that such symbols must take the form of references to the material world—not necessarily close copies of it, but, at least, remembered images sufficiently explicit to be recognizable. None the less, in substituting inspiration for observation as the artist's method, and emotion for beauty as the artist's chief stimulus, he changed the whole pattern of aesthetic theory, and in doing so made the first spoken plea for romanticism.

CHAPTER 2

Central and Centrifugal

The study of aesthetic theory is by no means the surest introduction to the understanding of works of art. A glance at the Parthenon sculptures in the British Museum or at the illuminations in the Winchester Bible is sufficient to reveal the limitations of Plato and Aristotle on the one hand and of Plotinus on the other. We can see well enough that the Greek sculptor of the age of Praxiteles was doing something far more difficult and far more important than merely to copy in marble the physique of the idealized human body: and the medieval painter depended for his success on something rather more practical than inspiration. It is certainly revealing to know what Aristotle thought were the proper aims of the Greek sculptors of his own age and of the generation that preceded him, or how Plotinus defined the problems the medieval Christian artist was called upon to solve. To listen to their voices across the intervening centuries is our only means of guessing at the opinion of the Hellenic or the medieval world about its own art. But writers are notoriously prejudiced about the art of their own time. They see in it only what they are looking for, and what they look for is limited by the cultural climate of their age, in which they are as closely involved as are the artists about whom they write. They have an inescapable *parti pris*.

If we are to understand the essence of romanticism in the visual arts by first establishing what is meant by the word 'classic', we must turn not to Aristotle but to Pheidias, and, later, not to Félibien, the mouthpiece of the French Academy, but to Poussin, and, later still, not to Winckelmann but to Canova and Ingres.

As soon as we do so, the arguments of the exponents of classicism are seen to be sadly thin and incomplete. Classicism, as they explain it, is either too simple or too pompous to be satisfying. Pheidias, Poussin, and Ingres were neither simple nor pompous. Yet they have, one feels, a common factor. They were immensely concerned with beauty, which they regarded as an absolute, and they were certainly concerned with representation: but they did not, like Aristotle, confuse the beauty of the representation with the beauty of the object represented. What is at once apparent in golden age Hellenic art, and in each of the self-conscious revivals of it in the early sixteenth, the mid-seventeenth and the early nineteenth centuries, is an endeavour to purge beauty of irrelevances and complications, to present it with the maximum of what they would have agreed to call 'nobility' as regards content.

Such a programme is necessarily a limited one, for to purge beauty of irrelevances is to reduce its range to a few selected types: and the artist who confines himself to nobility automatically cuts himself off from all those moods of restlessness and strain, unsatisfied desire and troubled ecstasy, that have proved so potent in the hands of artists who have rejected or ignored classic theory. Everything that is dubious or tentative or obscure in life must be completely resolved by the classic artist. He has chosen, out of the infinite vocabulary of form presented to him by his experience, only those forms towards which Nature always seems to be pointing in her attempt to solve her own problems. From the average he deduces the ideal, and classic art is only saved from stagnation by variations between what one artist and another regards as the ideal.

What applies to form also applies to the behaviour of form. If the human body can be represented in art, not as it is, but as it would be if only Nature could be dissuaded from experimenting and producing an infinity of variations from an unstated norm, so also can it be thought of as purged of unnecessary variations in behaviour. It must be free from the taint of eccentricity. In action, however violent, it must be generalized. In repose, however complete, it must not suggest sloth. The struggles between centaurs and lapiths in the Parthenon metopes make no attempt to discover the attitudes taken up by the human body in its desperate attempts to overcome its adversary. Nor is the recumbent Dionysus of the pediment completely at rest despite the extraordinary sense of serenity and well-being that it communicates. Power can be suggested, but always with more power in reserve.

Yet limited though this search for the norm and this hatred of the extreme or the eccentric may be, without it art would have no starting-point to move from and no standard to measure itself by. In a world whose very existence depends on a struggle between opposed imperfections, here, in classic art, are certain samples of perfection. Without them we would never hear that completely serene and satisfying final chord to which the curious and often tortured harmonic progressions of life always seem to be leading, but which life itself can never achieve. For life cannot afford to arrive at perfection: if it did it would cease, since it would bar the way to its own development, the only irrefutable evidence we have that it is not an illusion.

It is not easy to realize the hypnotic power that this Hellenic set of standards has exerted and still exerts on the cultural habits of mind of Western Europe, and in particular on our conception of mankind. Despite our knowledge to the contrary, we are still convinced that the Hermes of Praxiteles and the Medician Venus are norms from which each individual is a regrettable variation. Again and again attempts have been made to escape from the devotion to the Greek ideal. On at least three occasions during the past five centuries neo-classic movements have attempted to reinstate it, each time with an increase of pedantic defiance, but each time in the full conviction that only by returning to the norm could the sanity of art be preserved. It was only to be expected that such attempts should be short-lived. Nothing could be more difficult than to achieve the perfect balance and the golden clarity of true classic art or to remain for long just at that central point of perfection where nothing is overstated and yet nothing is lacking in vitality. Whatever has the questing vitality of the parochial must be avoided. Classic art, in its search for the norm, must ignore whatever is local. It must concern itself with the generic rather than the specific. And it must attempt to discover the timeless instead of identifying itself with what is characteristic of the period to which it belongs. It is, of course, an impossible ideal. Between Praxiteles and Canova and between Raphael and Poussin there are important differences—and no wonder, since no individual can free himself from the fetters of his own personality and his own generation, however conscientiously he may try to merge himself with the depersonalized and the timeless. He attempts to discover the true centre—the 'still point of the turning world'—but even in theory he can never succeed.

What matters, however, is that the classic artist consciously makes the attempt to establish laws for those ultimate harmonies. It is true that as long as he is interpreting the organic world of men and animals and landscape he is baffled by the constant process of growth, change, and decay. But when he approaches the non-mimetic arts—particularly that of architecture—he is on firmer ground. It is easier for a Vitruvius to produce the canon of perfection in a column than for Polycletus to discover the canon of perfection for the human figure, though even here Vitruvius is compelled to offer four alternative samples of perfection—Doric, Ionic, Corinthian, and Tuscan—each with its own virtues, none of which can lay claim to ultimate or absolute perfection.

Yet even if we admit that the ultimate and absolute of formal harmony is undiscoverable by man, it is an undoubted fact that certain men, at certain periods, have deliberately devoted themselves to a search for idealized harmony and that others have equally deliberately rejected such a search. That being so, the image of a seesaw is less appropriate, perhaps, than an image that resembles a wheel, in which classicism finds itself somewhere near the 'still point' of the axle, and non-classicism attempts to move outwards along the spokes towards the circumference.

At this stage, although one can assume that romanticism is in some sense a protest against the search for a fixed set of laws, it is by no means certain that all such protests are romantic or that every centrifugal movement is necessarily a romantic movement. But at least, we begin to suspect, the image of a wheel is more likely to be useful than that of a seesaw in that it contradicts the idea of mutual exclusiveness and of the triumph of one party at the expense of the other. It contradicts, in fact, the notion of a two-party system. By visualizing centifugal movements not only in any direction but also prepared to halt any distance from the centre, we may be led to discover a multitide of protests of different kinds, all of them prepared to be extremist in different degrees. That, in fact, is what we do at once discover.

If we begin our inquiry empirically by drawing up two lists of painters and sculptors about whom there is general agreement as to their wholehearted classicism or romanticism, it becomes apparent at once that certain major figures appear on neither list—another strong argument against the seesaw.

Any list of classic artists would certainly include all Greek sculptors from Pheidias to Praxiteles (though a doubt arises in the case of Scopas), Raphael between 1500 and 1509, Piero della Francesca, Poussin, Ingres—with reservations in the case of his portraits—Canova, and Thorwaldsen. The list of unquestioned romantics is longer. It includes, in the fifteenth century, Piero di Cosimo, Botticelli, and Leonardo, continues with Giorgione and Altdorfer; about the seventeenth century we are doubtful; in the eighteenth century Watteau and Guardi; in the nineteenth Turner, Delacroix, Daumier, and Rossetti, Rodin, and Van Gogh; and in the twentieth Graham Sutherland. Architecture, in which there is no confusion between form and content, can be more easily classified. All Greek building of the fifth and fourth centuries B.C. is, by any test, classic; all North European Gothic from the beginning of the thirteenth to the end of the fourteenth is romantic. In literature there is little question about Pope and Racine on the one hand, Shakespeare, Shelley, and Keats on the other. In music Handel and Mozart may stand for the classic point of view, Wagner and Liszt for the romantic.

Such lists of opposites are easily made, but having made them one is faced with the fact that Masaccio, Michelangelo, Caravaggio, Velasquez, Rembrandt, Courbet, and Cézanne will fit comfortably into neither list. Nor will Byzantine architecture, nor Chaucer, nor the later Beethoven.

If our wheel simile is to help us, we must first ask whether the true essence of romanticism depends on the distance or the direction from the centre, and the answer is surely that it depends on direction. Taking, for the sake of argument, Raphael as a typical representative of the classic position, and Caravaggio and Altdorfer as rebels who protested against it, it seems plain that their movement, if it could be described as centrifugal, was not only away from the centre but away from each other. Caravaggio and Altdorfer differ from each other even more than either of them differs from Raphael. In neither of them do we find that 'nothing too much' which is the negative motto of classic art. Each of them has decided to pursue his own genius as far as it can and will lead him: and the idea of anything that appealed to their vigorous impulses being 'too much' could never have occurred. To Altdorfer, no tangled forest, no symbol of claustrophobic growth, no image of man threatened by the forces of Nature could be intense enough. Caravaggio, too, was an extremist, though the direction of his extremism is by now so familiar that we hardly realize how far he had pushed away from the classic, the classic: love of clarity, the search for the ideal behind the real, the generic behind the specific, the avoidance of whatever is not serene or noble. All these qualities are as alien to Caravaggio as they are to Altdorfer. None the less, even before we have tried to put the meaning of 'romantic' into words, we know that Aldorfer is a wholehearted Romantic and that Caravaggio is not.

This is not quite the place to analyse the difference between them, for if at this stage we attempt to make deductions from the comparison between two painters we run the risk of confusing form with subject-matter. Already, by mentioning Altdorfer's tangled forests, we have allowed subject-matter to intrude—as though a tangled forest were, in itself, a romantic object, and any painting which tackles one as its main theme must automatically be a romantic picture. The deduction may be true in so far as the word 'tangled' takes precedence over the word 'forest'. But it would be foolish to attempt to trace the roots of romanticism to the subject selected by the artist rather than to the form taken by his work of art. Certainly, subject-matter cannot be ignored, and when it becomes necessary to return to our comparison between Altdorfer and Caravaggio it will also be necessary to consider whether what they painted is not as potent a factor as how they painted—though both 'how' and 'what' must ultimately meet and have a common origin in the mysterious creative levels of the artist's mind.

Yet, since there *are* non-representational arts which cannot deal with subject-matter in the specific sense that painting can, and since they, too, can be unmistakably classic or romantic, it is evident that the true roots of romanticism must be looked for in the representational arts *below* that point at which style and subject meet, and that in the non-representational arts style alone furnishes the only available evidence.

One may as well begin with the least representational and the least functional of all the arts, namely music. Probably no one has ever satisfactorily explained how it is that music by its very texture, its melodic intervals and harmonic progressions, can evoke moods which we instantly recognize and label 'nostalgic', 'serene', 'angry', and so on. The verbal expression marks in a musical score take it for granted that the average performer and the average listener alike see the connection between the music itself and words like *'dolce'* or *'agitato'*. Such words may be the equivalent of 'tangled', but not of 'forest'. So that music offers us as pure a laboratory specimen as can be found if we are attempting to trace the roots of style, though its disadvantage is that, having traced them, we cannot put our finding into words that have any precision.

No better example could be found of a composer brought up in a classic tradition but constantly liable to make romantic excursions from it than Brahms, and no clearer example of both classic form and classic mood could be found in his music than the opening statement of the *Andante* of his First Symphony.

It has all the clarity, the explicitness, the dignity characteristic of classicism in whatever medium it is expressed. The same phrase appears later, almost casually, after a long development section, in the following form

syncopated, restless, diffuse, and accompanied by dark mutterings in the bass—surely the musical equivalent of Altdorfer's tangled forests, yet richer in emotional content, if only because music, existing as it does in time, can afford to develop romantic growths out of a classic germ. Painting cannot perform this miracle. It is not by accident that when Turner set himself to challenge his predecessors he chose to emulate Claude. He could not have taken Poussin even as a starting-point, for Poussin's system of composition was something he could not understand. In Turner's mind, no formal melodic line invented by Poussin could ever germinate into a romantic variation. And, indeed, even in music, perhaps the romantic variation on the classic theme could only occur naturally at that moment of transition occupied by Brahms.

In music such contrasts of mood can not only alternate but grow out of each other and intensify each other. In architecture they are mutually exclusive. It may be an accident that the columns of a temple immediately suggest to the mind the upward thrust of forest trees, and if one is considering architecture as a set of purely formal inventions, such an association of ideas must be rejected. But 'tangled' and 'growth', words that never occur to the mind in connexion with the exterior of the Parthenon, can hardly be resisted when we enter a Gothic structure. The very fact that a Greek temple is essentially an exterior while the Gothic church draws us into its interior is part of the contrast. The classic building is a beautifully made box to contain and protect the god: the Gothic is an enclosed space whose exterior is the inevitable result of its inner function. And since the complex ritual of worship and self-identification with the Divine Will for which the Gothic church was built is, in itself, an attempt to attain to Plotinus's 'inspiration', Gothic architecture contains all those restless, dynamic overtones which the classic mind rejects. It gropes for what can never be completely known. Hence it cannot be governed by law or reason. Each example of it, instead of being an application of fixed Vitruvian principles, is a fresh attempt to discover a new channel of contact between earth and heaven, with the architect as intermediary. Its only constant principle is a vertical rhythm—the natural visual symbol of 'upwardness'—and its only constant mood is that of dynamism and growth. A Doric column suggests no such mood. It is the immovable support for a set of immovable, self-sufficient horizontals. It multiplies itself in a series of arithmetical progressions easily grasped by the eye. The slightest irregularity in that simple mathematical sequence would be intolerable. Such an irregularity in a Gothic church would certainly be noticeable, but it would not be intolerable. One would assume that it was the result of some non-mathematical necessity whose explanation was not to be found in Vitruvian laws of proportion but in the nature of the ritual which man had evolved to draw his strength from God.

If then the essence of romanticism in the non-representational arts is a refusal to look for absolutes of law and harmony in the outer, material world and an attempt to discover, empirically, any means that will serve to symbolize the inner, spiritual life, it follows that romanticism in any of the arts is always characterized by experiment—attempts to discover new formal devices whose only requirement is that they shall be appropriate to the mood to be expressed. Such experiments can lead the artist into hazardous paths. Only the most inventive and confident minds can make them successfully. Hence the aesthetic ineptitude of so much that is romantic in the arts. To fling away the crutches of established law and rely on inspiration or intuition is to court disaster. Classic theory may produce, and often has produced, art that is devitalized and boring because of its refusal to be personal. Romantic theory is apt to produce art that is invertebrate, slipshod, and impotent because it relies so completely on the quality of the mind in which it was conceived.

One can distinguish, therefore, between classic and romantic by saying that classicism seeks for the impersonal ideal in the physical world and thus aims at a perfection which should in theory be reducible to a set of acknowledged laws, while romanticism disregards the physical world in so far as it provides a set of symbols for the spiritual or emotional life of the invididual: and that therefore the possibility of discovering or applying anything resembling law cannot enter into it.

But these two points of view, even though they seem to contradict each other, are by no means mutually exclusive. Nor, having stated them, have we covered the whole field. It has already been pointed out[1] that some of the greatest artists, notable among them Velasquez, neither search for a material ideal nor do they disregard the physical world.

Michelangelo, Athlete
Sistine Chapel, Rome

If at this point we return to our comparison of Altdorfer with Caravaggio, it will become evident that (1) not all centrifugal movements are romantic, and (2) painting, unlike architecture, can choose its own centrifugal *distance*.

No painter before the year 1910 can be considered merely as an architect of form. He owes an obligation to subject-matter: his picture must of necessity refer to his own specific experience of the visible world. Raphael's Madonnas, Altdorfer's forests, and Caravaggio's bald-headed old men and elegant boys, even the apocalyptic creatures

[1] See p. 26.

in Gothic illuminations, are all derived from retinal images of the thing seen, even though those images, in their final form, may be distorted almost beyond recognition. Whatever the quality of their creators' imaginations, none of them could have been produced by

Caravaggio, Amore Trionfante
Kaiser Friedrich Museum, Berlin

blind men. What distinguishes one painter from another is the use he makes of his visual experience. It is evidenct that Caravaggio neither simplifies and ennobles like Raphael nor does he search for the complex and sinister overtones so dear to Altdorfer. His search is for visual truth of a kind that we are now accustomed to call photographic. Manifestly what he looks for is not *the* visual truth but *a* visual truth, for there are as many kinds of visual truth as there are pairs of eyes to see. Caravaggio deliberately selects those aspects of visual truth that are revealed by the impact of light. To call such a selection 'realist' is no more than a convenient way of avoiding the issue, for light and shadow conceal just as much of the truth as they reveal. The torsos of Michelangelo's 'athletes' in the Sistine Chapel contain more purely visual information about the structure of the human body, its muscular tensions and relaxations, than the torso of the boy in Caravaggio's *Amore Trionfante*. What Caravaggio has done is to suppress anything that did not belong to the particular case seen under specific conditions of light. To call the method 'photographic' is fair up to a point, for the camera, by its very limitations, achieves easily what Caravaggio did with considerable effort, namely a complete acceptance of the momentary optical effect.

This habit of eye, so natural to the camera, so unnatural to the human being, is what makes Caravaggio's painting so oddly arresting. It has an immediacy that had never been seen before. Not 'Thus it was' but 'Thus it presented itself to my unusually observant eye' is Caravaggio's method, Consequently everything depends on the nature of 'it'. Had Caravaggio confined himself to the painting of the commonplace happening, the insignificant object, he would have been the least interesting of painters. His famous still-life in the Ambrosiana in Milan is remarkable only for its *trompe l'oeil* vividness. But what makes him memorable is the disquieting contradiction between his vision and his subject-matter. To take infinite pains to present us with the objectively seen, to insist that between the image on the retina and the image on the canvas there is no difference at all: and then to create for us a set of intriguing happenings of dramatically chosen personages, of haunting presences—that is the secret of Caravaggio's power. His method is precisely that of the twentieth-century Surrealists, who painstakingly invent images of what is logically impossible seen through the passionless, objective eye of the colour-photographer. The rendering of what is emotionally provocative—sometimes erotic, sometimes sadistic—in a manner that betrays no emotion at all is Caravaggio's discovery. He is, one might say, the Hemingway of painting. Once the method had become familiar it spread instantly to those countries that could understand it, particularly to Holland and to Spain. The young Velasquez snatched greedily at it. It was, in fact, an artistic invention of the first importance, and Caravaggio, by carrying it to extreme lengths, took up his position very near to the circumference of the wheel.

But extremist though he was, his attitude is the very reverse of the romantic attitude: that becomes evident as soon as we compare him with Altdorfer, whose vision was violently personal but whose subject-matter was taken from the phenomena of everyday life. In Altdorfer's

Altdorfer, St George (detail)
Alte Pinakothek, Munich

art the forest is haunted by demons and the very clouds are apocalyptic: in Caravaggio's there are no forests, for they could not be assimilated into his style, but the Northern Demons, translated into the Bacchic minor deities of Hellenic mythology, are painted without surprise, as though they had deceived the painter into thinking them street-urchins.

Here, surely, is the key to the *direction* of romantic deviations from the centre. They are deviations undertaken by sensitive, agitated minds that automatically translate natural phenomena into personal terms, heightening their meaning, often distorting their shapes in an attempt to establish a mood rather than to record an appearance. Altdorfer becomes hysterical at the sight of an oak-tree. Caravaggio remains unperturbed in the presence of a decapitation.

It is perhaps surprising that the imperturbable artists, an impressively large and powerful body, have never been given an agreed label by art historians. They certainly need one. The word 'romantic' performs an indispensable service in linking together artists as stylistically unlike each other as Blake, Turner, and Grünewald. Yet no word exists that would perform the same service for Masaccio, Velasquez, Courbet, and (I add the name with some hesitation) Rembrandt. To call them realists is not merely superficial. It is misleading. Such men contribute far more than imperturbability. That is merely the negative side of their temperaments. They are not only imperturbable. Their materialism springs from a conviction so strong that it becomes a faith. Yet every kind of faith can be abused if it is served by the head rather than the heart. Caravaggio positively parades his heartlessness so that it becomes a little alarming. Masaccio and Velasquez do not. They have more serious things to do than to produce that kind of *frisson*. For that reason their stature is larger than Caravaggio's, though it is more difficult to express in words. Masaccio has been extravagantly and justly praised, but the emphasis behind the praise has too often been on the fact that he was a pioneer. Velasquez was no pioneer. Critics are lost in admiration of his achievement, but when they try to explain why that achievement amounts to genius they are at a loss. No artist whom posterity has agreed to place in the first rank has so puzzled his admirers. Merely to praise him for his wizardry in the manipulation of paint and his unerring eye for the unity of tone that creates, in its turn, pictorial unity, is to put him high in the second rank of artists to which Franz Hals and Fabritius belong. Yet every receptive eye feels intuitively that he cannot be put into their category. Despite the lack of obvious excitement, and the absence of poetry—the lack, in fact, of romantic overtones—he is, inexplicably, a giant. Such judgments cannot be based on an agreement that he was imperturbable, that he took the world as he found it, never idealizing it into perfection, never underlining its imperfections, or his own excitement about its strangeness. From Schlegel's point of view, he is surely the least 'interesting' painter in history.

His greatness, therefore, must be explained without reference to classic calm or romantic excitement. It depends, I think, as does that of Masaccio, on an innate sense of the dignity of man and an unquestioning acceptance of him in his environment as the proper ingredients for pictorial art. Such an attitude of mind is rarer than one might suppose. There is a vast difference between this broad acceptance of the visual world and the camera's factual record. The camera *cannot* interfere with the facts. Velasquez could, if he chose, but *will not*. He may simplify, reorganize, omit, or subtly emphasize. (And part of his inexplicable genius lies in his power to do all these things so persuasively that we are not aware that he has done them.) But he will never allow his own tone of voice to come between the image in his picture and the spectator. The hysterical tones of an Altdorfer would seem to such a man both unnecessary and insincere: the serene 'idealizations' of a Raphael would strike him as a veiled insult to the created world—a world which, in his eyes, asks neither for exaggeration nor reform, but merely for understanding.

It is characteristic of such artists that the farther they stray in their subject-matter from the created world towards the world of the spirit, the less capable they are of persuading us that this solemn worldly wisdom is enough. Velasquez's comment (and despite his imperturbability it *is* a comment) on the Spanish princesses assembled in that great gaunt room with their attendant dwarfs and dogs *must* be accepted. But his comment on the boy Bacchus and *his* attendants will not work the same miracle. Once Bacchus has taken the place of the Infanta we are moving in a world that is *not* entirely the world of the senses. Wisdom and imperturbability will no longer suffice. We begin to long for that impassioned tone of voice that will persuade us that this is a god and not a Spanish boy decked for the occasion with a wreath of vine-leaves, and surrounded by grinning peasants who have momentarily stopped their work in the vineyards in order to sit for their portraits. Velasquez's marvellous understanding of sun and soil, tanned faces and earthenware jugs, makes him incapable of interpreting either religion or myth. In the Bacchanalian scene in the Prado we are back at the point to which Caravaggio led us, but the intention is

Velasquez, The Topers
Prado, Madrid

different. Caravaggio, like the Surrealists, wished us to be surprised and perhaps a little shocked. Velasquez had no such wish.

In Courbet's case that same superb acceptance of the physical gives us exactly the same confidence in him whenever his theme requires no more than acceptance, and the same embarrassment whenever something more is required. Courbet differed from Velasquez in that he was anxious to explain himself. He began to count as a painter at the very moment when the classic *versus* romantic controversy was at its height in Paris, and he wished to make it clear that he belonged to neither party. In his attempt to find a label to describe himself, no better word than 'realist' presented itself, but he knew its inadequacy. 'Names', he wrote in his 1855 manifesto, 'have never at any time given a true idea of the things they stand for', and he added, 'To translate the manners, the ideas and the outward appearance of my age as I perceived them . . . such is my aim.' And in 1861: 'Painting . . . can consist only of the representation of things both real and existing. . . . Imagination in painting consists in finding the most complete expression for an existing thing, never in imagining or creating this object itself.' And even more specifically: 'Once the beautiful is real and visible it contains its own artistic expression. The artist has no right to enlarge upon this expression.'

Such words would be more convincing if they had been uttered by Velasquez. But Velasquez had no need to utter them, while Courbet in his endeavour to escape from the alternative tyrannies of Ingres and Delacroix was forced to utter them. Coming from him they sound a little too defiant. Both Delacroix and Ingres could have replied with some justification that artists have not only a right but a duty to enlarge on anything that seems to them important, even though they might choose to quarrel about what *was* important.

Courbet's defiance defeats its own object. In his anxiety to confine himself to the 'existing thing' and to find the 'complete expression' for it, he dramatizes his own natural earthiness, and that very 'enlargement' he is so anxious to avoid creeps in despite himself. Instead of accepting the visible facts of life as Velasquez had done, he over-emphasizes them, and the romantic overtones that are the sure sign of emotional over-emphasis can be plainly heard whenever he suspects that his 'realism' will be too 'ugly' to please the classic party and too pedestrian for the romantics. His dictum, 'The beautiful is in Nature: once it is found it belongs to art', should have given him courage. In his best work it did so. Whenever he tackled a theme whose beauty he had himself 'found' and had made it 'belong to art', his own sincerity carried him through to a triumphant conclusion. Such a theme was the great *Burial at Ornans*. It is painted with all the dispassionate honesty of Velasquez. It has the solemn gravity that is hardly ever absent when an artist is obsessed by a presence or an event that belongs naturally to his own environment. It corresponds exactly to Velasquez's *Las Meniñas*. Both pictures are sober and searching accounts of happenings that were an integral part of the artist's life. When Velasquez attempts mythology or religion he is on unfamiliar ground and he fails us because his very faith in earthy commonplaces blinds him to the deeper meanings of myth. Courbet was never tempted to this kind of failure; his temptations led in another direction. They led him to a precipice not of earthiness but of vulgarity. He held to his definition of 'Imagination' as 'the complete expression of an existing thing', so that he was saved from the mistake of trying to paint a god. But when he made the even worse mistake of searching for whatever, among 'existing things', was most immediately and superficially emotive, his failure was far worse than that of Velasquez.

The raw harmonies of a sunset, the blatant eroticism of a nude, the superficial pathos of a dead stag in the snow, the grandiose vanity of his big picture of himself in the studio surrounded by his admiring model and obsequious friends—these are not beauties that need to be 'found' by an artist. They are the highest common factor of basic human experience, and when they are presented to us undigested without insight and without the benefit of careful translation into formal harmony they become a little nauseating: they are, in the most literal sense, 'vulgar'. When Courbet yields to this kind of temptation his vaunted realism is overlaid by a false romanticism—false because the heightened emotionalism of the painting springs not from the artist's own exceptional emotional equipment but from the intense but banal emotiveness of the 'existing thing' portrayed.

When we compare these two 'realists' with a third, Masaccio, we find ourselves in the comforting presence of an artist who was never tempted to the edge of any precipice. Masaccio knew exactly what he wanted to do. He, too, drew his strength from an unshakeable faith in the 'existing thing'. He 'found' beauty without even knowing that he was looking for it.

It happens that Masaccio was born at the very moment when Florentine painting was waiting for a signpost and a guide. As a pioneer he is a figure of the first importance. But his greatness would have been apparent at any moment in history, for he belonged temperamentally to the category of Velasquez. He alone among Florentines has Velasquez's penetration into the essence of the 'existing thing'; his power, like that of Velasquez, depends on rigorous selection, and like Velasquez he never distorts in order to intensify his own comment. That could be said of neither of his great contemporaries, Fra Angelico and Jan van Eyck. The latter, delighted though he was with the magnificently honest statement of fact, was incapable of rigorous selection. The former was uninterested in the 'existing thing' unless it could provide him with a symbol of holiness or divinity.

For Masaccio neither the symbol nor the factual report mattered. What he did supremely—and he could have done it with the same confidence at any moment in the history of civilization—can be realized by examining a single detail from the Brancacci chapel frescoes. In the *St Peter and St John Distributing Alms* in the Brancacci chapel in Santa Maria del Carmine, Florence, the central figure is a peasant woman holding her baby on one arm and stretching out the other to accept St Peter's gift. The figure is one of the most profoundly observed in the history of painting. Stylistically, of course, it belongs to the early years of the fifteenth century, but as a human document it is timeless. Its monumental quality, its density and weight, are unforgettable, but in addition it has an immediacy that is not to be found again in painting until Degas solved the problem of seizing on the sudden impulsive gesture and suggesting its momentariness and its unexpectedness without giving it the 'frozen' effect of a snapshot. Masaccio's woman, one *knows*, has just shifted the weight of the child she

Masaccio, St Peter and St John distributing alms (detail)
Sta Maria del Carmine, Florence

carries into the crook of her right arm in order to balance her own weight as she leans forward, eagerly, but not at all impulsively, to receive the gift. She gazes earnestly at the saint as she does so, but one knows, too, that she will pocket the gift, shift her balance on to the other foot and attend to her baby the moment the complex gesture has been completed. The 'meaning' of the sudden gesture is intensified (again a device that Degas might have used) by the way in which her arm, in its eagerness to take the proffered gift, cuts across the face of one of the onlookers. One is momentarily prevented from seeing something one wants to look at. Such effects happen often in the art of the cinema. In painting they can only be achieved by a man who is obsessed not only by the 'existing thing' but also by the sequence of 'existing effects' as the drama unfolds itself.

This brief excursion into the nature of realism was necessary if we are to clear the ground for an examination of the romantic protest. It is not the only kind of protest against the position taken up by idealists like Raphael and purists like Mondrian. If the simile of the wheel is to be serviceable, we must first admit that only one half of the spokes lead outwards in the direction of Altdorfer and Turner. The other half belong to Masaccio and Velasquez. And even for these centrifugal movements there is a central position. As we move round the wheel's circumference from realism to romanticism we arrive at a point where the two merge. The artist's point of view can find its appropriate position at any distance and in any direction from the centre. Hence the critic's conviction that Velasquez is a 'central' realist, Altdorfer a 'central' romantic; but hence, too, his doubt in the case of Rembrandt.

CHAPTER 3

Distance and Direction

Art history is in the habit of grouping artists by periods or schools. In the previous chapter I have ignored both in order to stress an equally valid grouping by temperaments. In doing so the usual art historian's categories, based as they are on style and subject-matter, must be replaced by a different categorization, and a terminology borrowed rather from the psychologist than the historian. The word 'realist' calls up a mental image of a style but hardly, or only by implication, of an attitude of mind; it fails to point to the common factor between Masaccio and Velasquez. The word 'extrovert', on the other hand, provides common ground for both. Courbet, had he lived in an age that was as familiar as our own with the vocabulary of psychology, would surely have welcomed such a description of himself. The artist who is primarily interested in the world of the senses—whose interest in it may, indeed, be passionate—but who refuses to brood upon it or to use it as a stimulus to his own emotional reactions, is familiar enough. It may be that such a temperament will usually lead him to a mode of painting that is 'realist' in essence: but 'realism' is the name of a symptom rather than a temperament. Moreover, it could be more appropriately used to describe a subdivision of the 'extrovert' category than the category itself. 'Realism' is something less than a preoccupation with and a delight in the 'existing thing'. It is a concentration on the appearance rather than the essence, and I suspect that the distinction, so clear to us today, between appearance and essence has been considerably sharpened by the invention of photography.

The camera's account of phenomena, based as it must be on the appearance of a given object at a given moment and therefore largely conditioned by the impact of light at that moment, is not one that comes easily to the contemplative eye of the artist. 'Realistic' in the sense of 'photographic' has two meanings. It can be applied to the kind of painting that attempts to reproduce the impact of light at the expense of colour or structure—the Caravaggesque vision. But it can also be applied to the artist who not only deals exclusively with the 'existing thing' but also never 'imagines or creates' the object portrayed or imposes formal distortions on it. Before the invention of photography only this second sense of the word had a valid meaning. I propose, therefore, to use the word 'extrovert' in the chapter that follows instead of 'realist'.

I do not suggest, however, that the word 'romantic' should be displaced by 'introvert'—'romanticism', unlike 'realism', has already acquired all the psychological connotations it needs. It can be applied equally to a human temperament and to a mode of expression. It is therefore useful in focusing the mind not merely on a mood—or a large family of related moods—in the arts, but also on the relationship between those moods and the men who give expression to them. Introvert they certainly are, but their brooding inwardness is usually of a special kind. I have already pointed out that the romantic artist's emphasis on his personal reaction to experience forces him into a perpetual series of attempts to discover the appropriate form for the expression of that reaction; and that when he fails to discover this form, his failure as an artist is lamentable. His self-appointed task requires wings. If his wings are not strong enough to lift him he remains rather foolishly earth-bound, unhappy that he cannot fly, yet ill adapted to live a pedestrian existence. Or when, Icarus-like, his home-made wings do perform their function but break loose from his shoulders, he plunges headlong into a sea of bathos and is destroyed. No such fate awaits the extrovert, who is never tempted to leave the solid earth. I shall therefore continue to use the word 'romantic' to mean the introvert whose wings are not mere symbols of a desire to fly, but useful and efficient implements that do, in fact, enable him to leave the earth behind.

The distinction between the extrovert and the romantic is one of degree rather than of kind. Art cannot exist at all until the artist's personality has been stimulated by his environment, and until his environment has passed through the sieve of his personality. There is no such thing as art that makes no reference to fact: for even the rigid rectilinear compositions of a Mondrian are based on visual experience: they could never have been conceived without visual knowledge of the vertical tree-trunk and the horizontal horizon. And there is no such thing as art in which fact has not been transformed by personality. Even in Altdorfer we find a real forest: even in Velasquez a personal mood, and though there is no difficulty in discovering extremes of objectivity and subjectivity, as we move round the circumference of our wheel we

Mondrian, Composition with Red, Blue and Yellow

In the possession of Mrs Basil Gray

eventually reach a point where the two are fused in more or less equal proportions. Somewhere between Altdorfer and Velasquez we find a point of balance, and somewhere near that point is Rembrandt, surely the most remarkable example of a temperament that is neither imperturbable nor hysterical. That fusion of two extremes partly accounts for Rembrandt's greatness. It also accounts for the impression he almost always conveys that he is not only great but *normal.* Beside him both the wholehearted romantic and the wholehearted extrovert seem extremists. In his presence we become aware that though romantic excitement and extrovert detachment may both generate memorable works of art, the artists who possess either of these qualities to the exclusion of the other to such a degree that we can speak of them as geniuses, must be slightly unsatisfactory as human beings. Altdorfer, we may be sure, was too neurotic for comfort: Velasquez too content with his environment and too engrossed in his craftsmanship to be anything but a bore when he was not engaged in painting.

But Rembrandt, by virtue of his balance between the two extremes, is, for most of us, the supremely satisfactory artist, the man who never makes us uncomfortably aware that he is an exception even though his skill as a technician is exceptional. He is profound without being remote, and he accepts the world of the senses without being prosaic. He possesses a sturdy pair of wings, but will not use them merely for the sake of performing aerial acrobatics.

It will be useful, therefore, to pause for a moment to examine this magnificently normal creature who, in occupying the central position where the romantic and the extrovert meet, sheds so much light on both.

What strikes us at once is the immense range available to him by virtue of that central position. If, by a considerable effort of memory, one calls to mind a representative series of his works—paintings, drawings, and etchings—it becomes evident that hardly any fragment of human experience, however important or however trivial, however universal or however momentary, is outside his range. I do not mean 'beyond his powers of expression in a given medium', but 'outside his interest in a given situation'. As one examines any set of representative mixed drawings by him one may, at last, become so fascinated by his handwriting—his power to control the movement of the reed pen at whatever speed it passes over the paper, so that the swiftest scribble is exactly where he wanted it to be to a hundredth of a millimetre— that one begins to think them monotonously similar, even monotonously masterly. It is only when one looks not at the handwriting but at the intention behind it that one realizes how completely he was equipped to tackle almost everything that his visual environment offered or that his brooding spirit imagined. The mother furiously snatching up her screaming child whose shoe falls off as he hangs helpless in her awkward clutch is as 'momentary' a record as any artist has ever produced, not excepting Degas. Yet the pen that produced a *Supper at Emmaus* moved at precisely the same speed. The difference lies in the tempo of the mind.

It is only when one begins to compare this power to move effortlessly from spiritual to material, from symbol to fact, from philosophy to anecdote, that one realizes that no other artist can perform so remarkable a feat. Every other artist, when he moves away from his chosen field, tends to become bored and restless and therefore helpless and incompetent. At no moment in his career was Rembrandt either helpless or incompetent. If one groups artistic temperaments under the three main categories of classic, romantic, and extrovert, each of which is capable, in varying degrees, of absorbing some of the characteristics of the other two; and if one places Rembrandt precisely at the point of the circumference at which romantic and extrovert meet, it becomes evident that he is at the farthest possible point from the classic temperament. He has neither the will to imagine nor the desire to portray an ideal world. The mother who snatches up her child can never be the ideal mother. The two disciples who gaze so intently at the radiance of the vanishing Christ are still Dutch peasants though they are also symbols of humanity amazed by the supernatural. Basically they are as anti-classic as the little scene of domesticity. Nobility of form, grace of movement, the conscious avoidance of ugliness and the conscious pursuit of harmony, those constant obsessions of the classic artist, can never be part of his programme. Yet Rembrandt is as capable of creating nobility as Raphael, though for different reasons. Where Raphael is noble because nobility is for him an intrinsically desirable quality, Rembrandt is noble only when nobility is appropriate to his theme. In the drawing of the exasperated mother it is so inappropriate that nothing could have induced him to tranquillize any of those sudden linear modulations that give the drawing its urgent character or to introduce that suaver set of rhythms which Raphael would have imposed on to the drawing even of a thistle. The *Supper at Emmaus*, on the other hand, positively demands nobility of an unusually solemn kind, and Rembrandt has no difficulty in expressing it. In his hands it becomes even more powerful precisely because his obsession is not with what is noble but with what is appropriate to the theme of the moment. But since it is never the *only* appropriate element in his theme, one searches in vain through his work for even a faint echo of Raphael. In the Emmaus drawing nobility is overlaid with a double overtone of mystery and immediacy. Consequently that extraordinary pen line travels across the paper even more impetuously than in the mother-and-child drawing. In the interest of mystery the golden clarity of classicism must be jettisoned: in the interests of immediacy those suave descriptions of physical perfection based on the Hellenic ideal must be abandoned.

These stern refusals to use the normal vocabulary of classicism are common both to the extrovert and the romantic artist. Yet, except at

Rembrandt, Naughty Child
Kuppferstich Kabinett, Berlin

the perilous point where the two meet, they have nothing but that refusal in common. Velasquez and Altdorfer are as antipathetic to each other, by virtue of their central positions, as both are antipathetic to Raphael by virtue of his. Rembrandt, on the other hand, can use at will the vocabulary of both Velasquez and Altdorfer and by doing so can double his range. He can share Altdorfer's excitement, but has no need of his hysterical modes of expression. He can equally share Velasquez's steady, objective grasp of the material world, but he can endow it with emotional overtones that are outside the range of Velasquez.

Consequently, when one compares him with the 'central' artists one becomes aware that whereas his greatness is largely dependent on his freedom of movement round two-thirds of the circumference of our imaginary wheel, theirs, however remarkable their genius, depends on the limitations imposed on them by their lack of freedom. The range of expression denied to the complete romantic, the complete extrovert or the complete classic artist is enormous.

Call to mind any great artist and ask not the sensible question 'What aspect of life did he make precious for us by intensifying it?' but the unintelligent but none the less revealing question 'What aspect of life or what department of human experience was barred from him by reason of his temperament?' Faced with that question the limitations of greatness at once appear. Raphael is incapable of mystery, Velasquez of any kind of idealism; Michelangelo, that master of structural form, fails to provide an environment for the race of human beings he creates; Rubens cannot conceive of tranquillity; Piero della Francesca is incapable of suggesting tumult; for Renoir the world is always soft and cushioned; for Mantegna it is always hard and metallic; El Greco does not know the meaning of the word 'weight'; Ingres and Poussin are unaware of the atmosphere that softens and modifies all solid objects; Monet is so obsessed by it that he has little interest left for their form.

Such limitations are only serious if one is looking for breadth rather than intensity. Naturally they are the basic factors in determining each artist's style, for style is the outward expression of temperament. But they determine far more than style. It is true that they cannot determine subject-matter, which, until the nineteenth century, was usually imposed on the artist by his patron, but they may easily make an artist incapable of penetrating to the true meaning of the subject-matter to which he is committed. The brothers Pollaiuolo, commissioned by their patron to paint the martyrdom of St Sebastian, find it impossible to express the essence of martyrdom because they are temperamentally uninterested in, and therefore incapable of portraying, the outward manifestations of suffering. None the less they produce a magnificent altarpiece because, being passionately interested in muscular action, they are admirably fitted to paint a picture whose theme is not martyrdom but archery. Left to themselves they would have selected themes whose keynote was action for its own sake, and in the famous engraving of *The Battle of the Nudes* that is exactly what they did; just as Degas, left to himself, selected subjects involving momentary gesture, which he could so easily find on the racecourse, in the *corps de ballet* or the laundry. Being a great draughtsman, he could, if occasion demanded, paint an adequate portrait, but the best of his portraits still show unmistakable signs of his instinctive search for gesture at the expense of character. It is the attitude rather than the personality of his sitter that counts, even though he is sufficiently penetrating, at times, to express personality in terms of gesture.

But as soon as we detect the kind of opportunism in an artist that can *substitute* archery for suffering or gesture for personality, we begin to suspect that we are no longer in the presence of a 'central' temperament. Degas and the brothers Pollaiuolo are situated somewhere near the frontier between two temperaments, and for that reason they can expand their range beyond that of the central artist. If their subject-matter has been dictated to them they manage, as it were, to accept the letter of the dictation but to alter its spirit to suit themselves. They can slip quietly across the frontier without too obviously betraying their trust. Everyone has heard the apocryphal story of how Rembrandt accepted a commission to paint the portrait group now known as *The Night Watch* and how he substituted chiaroscuro for portraiture. For him the journey from the extrovert to the romantic category presented no difficulties.

If, in a given case, it proves possible for these two categories to intermarry and thereby to become more universal (though not necessarily more intense) than either could be in isolation, what about the other two frontiers? Is intermarriage possible between the classic and the romantic artist on the one hand or between the classic and the extrovert artist on the other? Are the three main categories in any sense mutually exclusive? Is it not imaginable that some artist could so combine the extrovert's satisfaction with reality, the classic search for the ideal and the romantic emphasis on a personal reaction to both, that he could conceivably occupy the central point at which the three temperaments meet?

One of my objects in writing this book is to suggest that such a fusion of temperaments *is* possible, that such a central point does, in fact, almost succeed in occupying it. From the middle of the first decade of the sixteenth century, during a period of nearly twenty years Titian managed to achieve a balance in which the real and the ideal are interwoven and given a heightened flavour that can only be called romantic.

If the reader will, for the moment, accept this estimate of Titian's position in the general pattern of artistic temperaments, he will see that my image of a wheel with classicism as its centre and the centrifugal forces of romantic and extrovert painting forcing their way outwards from it towards the circumference will no longer serve. Perhaps it is childish to insist on an image at all when manifestly no image—or at least no two-dimensional image—will exactly fit the extremely complex relationship between temperament and style. But since I feel it important to prove that the old seesaw image in which classic and romantic become mutually exclusive is not only incomplete but misleading, and since the opposition between centre and circumference, though adequate if we divide artistic temperaments into two, ceases to be helpful when we add a third, I suggest that the accompanying diagram may help us to grasp the manner in which such temperaments can interact and strengthen each other.

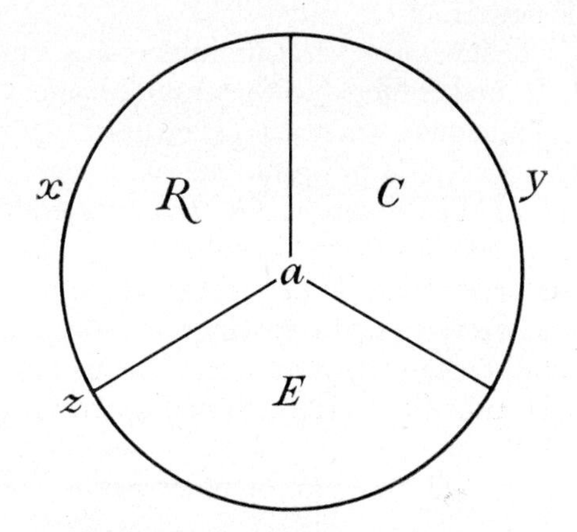

Our circle remains. Its circumference is still inhabited by the extremists. But classicism is no longer its centre. It is now divided into three by lines meeting at that central point where, as I suggested, Titian is to be found during the 1520s. Each of the three areas, Classic, Romantic and Extrovert, shares a frontier with the other two, so that it is now possible to place any artist, according to his temperament, at the appropriate *distance* and the appropriate *direction* from the centre.

We have decided, for example, that Rembrandt must be placed somewhere on the line that separates R from E. His distance from the centre will then depend on the amount of classicism he can absorb into his romantic-extrovert temperament. If the reader agrees with me that the answer is 'None at all', then we must place him on the circumference at the point where R and E meet.

To have constructed a diagram which will enable us to 'place' any artist according to the kind of message he is capable of communicating is not a very honourable or illuminating achievement. It makes no pretence of increasing our enjoyment or understanding of his work, for though it can indicate his position on the map of artistic temperaments it cannot differentiate between genius, talent, and mediocrity. That central point where our three fundamental attitudes of mind meet may be occupied by Titian, but it may equally be the point chosen by a hundred insignificant artists who, lacking the conviction to evolve a style of their own, have gravitated to the centre through sheer indolence or tired eclecticism. And that perilous point on the circumference where we have placed Rembrandt is now available to any art student who can paint more or less what he sees and then, by a little stylistic intensification, add some of the romantic overtones he has learned from his betters.

But there is, I believe, a general usefulness in such a diagram as I have suggested. It makes possible that preliminary sorting out and putting away into pigeon-holes that must be done before specialization can begin. Our concern is going to be with everything that can reasonably be placed in category R. And since we know that category R will eventually need a good deal of subdividing, there is no harm in so arranging our artists within that category that they begin, like politicians, to develop right and left wings and a centre party. And if, in addition, their distance from the centre can be taken as indicating the degree of their antipathy to the two main parties to which they do not belong, so much the better.

For example, to put Rembrandt at point *z* is to 'place' him as far as possible from the central classical position. It would not be difficult to think of artists equally fitted to endow that reality with all kinds of emotional intensifications, but who are, none the less, far more sympathetic than he to the unadulterated classicism of Raphael. They would occupy appropriate positions along the line *za*. Raphael himself would, of course, be stationed somewhere near point *y* and, perhaps, Altdorfer at point *x*.

Our diagram, then, makes it easier for us to sort out the heterogeneous collection of works of art with which this book is concerned—the works that can reasonably claim a place in that segment of our circle we have labelled 'Romantic', but which differ from each other in their capacity to assimilate elements borrowed from the other two segments. If that preliminary sorting can be done the diagram will perhaps make it more possible to examine and define the different kinds of romanticism with which this book is concerned. I have no intention of referring the reader back to it whenever a work of art or an artist has to be related to others of his kind. But it may be useful to bear it in mind as a guide to some of the complexities of style and vision that are encountered whenever an artist attempts to express his personal experience in terms of the accepted traditions of his period.

CHAPTER 4

Romantic States of Mind

One hopes to find in the dictionary precise definitions. These in their turn should be the result of a lexicographer's deductions from the often imprecise common usage of speech or literature. In the case of technical or scientific terms such definitions can achieve a certain completeness, for the usage on which they are based is generally that of specialists or trained thinkers who have invented the word in order to cover a fairly narrow and definable set of meanings. But in certain vague areas of human experience which are neither narrow nor definable precision is no longer possible. Definitions, whose purpose is not only to explain meanings but also to establish the exact frontiers of those meanings, break down.

The word 'romantic' is an extreme case. It is easy to explain in words just what 'oxygen' is or is not. The frontier between 'oxygen' and 'not-oxygen' is sharp and inviolable. Not so the division between 'romantic' and 'not-romantic'. Yet the dictionary definitions of both 'oxygen' and 'romantic' can only be arrived at by examining the context in which both words are commonly used. No analysis of romanticism can be of the slightest value unless it is based on an examination of those contexts. The Third Edition of *The Concise Oxford Dictionary* defines romanticism in seventy words, and if that definition were entirely satisfactory this book would be useless except as a catalogue of concrete instances of the qualities referred to in the dictionary.

Those seventy words are worth quoting in full, for presumably they have been arrived at after a careful study of contexts. They are an attempt to discover the common ground covered by a vast number of such contexts and to divide that common ground into smaller sub-sections without attempting too much detail.

'Romantic,' says the *C.O.D.* (which limits itself to 'current English' and is therefore not concerned with those gradual slight shifts of meaning that every word must suffer in its evolutionary stages), 'a. and n. Characterized by or suggestive of or given to romance [the *C.O.D*'s definition of 'romance' concerns itself almost entirely with forms of literature and is not very helpful], imaginative, remote from experience, visionary (*a romantic story, scene, adventure, girl*); (of music) subordinating form to theme, imaginative, passionate; (of projects etc.) fantastic, unpractical, quixotic, dreamy; (of literary or artistic method etc.) preferring grandeur or picturesqueness or passion or irregular beauty to finish and proportion, subordinating whole to parts or form to matter.'

I do not envy the lexicographer. He is committed to a degree of brevity which is almost bound to make his definition obscure. One can guess that it has been arrived at by answering the question 'To what kinds of object, person or situation can the adjective be most appropriately applied?' And the answer is 'To a story, a scene, an adventure, a girl; to music; to projects,' etc.; and to literary or artistic methods, etc.' (I deplore his use of 'etc'.) But it is still necessary to inquire just what quality turns a story into a romantic story, a girl into a romantic girl. In the case of music the answer is given, but I find it difficult to understand. 'Music that subordinates form to theme' is, to me, a meaningless phrase. If by the 'theme' is meant what programme notes usually call the 'subject', I cannot conceive of a theme that is not communicated to the listener by means of its form. 'Imaginative' (also applied to music) as a synonym for 'romantic' is to me equally obscure. Music, of all the arts, must be *'imagined'* whether it is classic or romantic, whereas in painting it could be argued that to 'copy' appearances does, in some degree, relieve the painter of the need to imagine them. 'Passionate' music, on the other hand, I think I recognize when I hear it. Then comes the category 'projects, etc.' I have already referred to a seventeenth-century use of 'romantic' as applied to a project for building a bridge over the river at Putney,[1] and it is natural perhaps that practical men should use the adjective in a derogatory sense, to suggest that a given project will not 'work', but I doubt if the automatic exclamation on hearing of a projected journey to the moon would now be 'How romantic!' Perhaps, since this entry in the 1934 *C.O.D.* was written, 'fantastic' projects have ceased to strike us as 'romantic'. Lastly comes the category 'literary or artistic method etc.' Here the *C.O.D.* becomes a little careless; 'preferring grandeur, picturesqueness, passion or irregular beauty to finish and proportion' is less a description of a method than of an intention, even though, as must always happen in considering works of art, it is the method that betrays the intention. 'Passionate' as applied to the emotional content of music could surely have been equally applied to the content of both

[1] See p. 10.

painting and dancing. The assumption that a distinction can be drawn between intention and method or between content and form (never a very useful assumption in art criticism) becomes increasingly meaningless, especially when applied to painting, as painters become more insistent on the idea that the *act* of painting is largely a means of releasing subconscious impulses. '*Tâchisme*' as a method we now think of as an index of an intention or a temperament; 'passionate *tâchisme*' we assume to be the visible expression of a passionate nature.

So much for the dictionary definition. If we find it inadequate it must be either because the author of those seventy words had not read or listened to a sufficient number of people as they exclaimed or wrote 'How romantic!' or else had not been sufficiently acute in his analysis of what prompted them to make the exclamation.

One is forced, therefore, to turn one's back on the *C.O.D.* and begin to listen and read for oneself, compiling a little list of the kinds of occasions on which 'How romantic!' was spoken or written. At the top of such a list must come not the written but the spontaneous spoken word—usually uttered by the average man in the presence of a sudden stimulus. And the stimulus, for the average man, is not often a work of art: still less often is it a 'project'. It is usually a situation or an experience that prompts the exclamation.

'How romantic!' he says as the moon rises over the lake or is glimpsed through the foliage of the forest. The same lake, the same forest, at midday provoke him to no such excited remark—least of all 'How classic!'

Mountainous scenery, especially when well provided with precipices, ravines, and torrents, is romantic: plains, except under certain conditions of light, are not. Ambitions or ideals attained in the face of adversity (e.g. the 'escape' chapters in *The Count of Monte Cristo* or the seduction of Felton and the death of 'Milady' in *The Three Musketeers*) are more romantic than success stories from which the element of struggle, the danger of defeat, are absent.

Love, especially when reciprocated but thwarted, and particularly if it involves elopement, is always romantic: marriage never. To supply the story of Romeo and Juliet with a happy ending would seriously interfere with its romantic power.

Short though it is, that simple list is enough to furnish us with what we need in the way of clues. Three major qualities emerge: mystery, abnormality, and conflict. Each makes its massive contribution to the romantic mood, and I doubt if any one of the three can be omitted without considerably diminishing the impact of the mood. The romantic artist I propose to define, for the time being, as the artist who is exceptionally sensitive to those types of experience that involve mystery, abnormality, and conflict, who can most vividly translate such experiences into a mental image, who can most effectively discover the formal equivalent of that image, and who can evolve a purely technical means of making that formal image both intelligible and eloquent in his work of art.

Inevitably this description of the creative process, though I believe it to be essentially true, is misleading in its implication that the four stages involved—the initial experience, the formation of the mental image, the discovery of its formal equivalent and its final manifestation in the chosen medium—are, in fact, divisible. As every artist knows well enough, they interpenetrate each other and the last three even modify each other during the process of creation. The 'mind's eye' image of the picture an artist is going to paint will probably only faintly resemble that picture in its early stages. It will become more precise and definite, it may even undergo radical modifications, during the act of painting. Yet without it the act of painting could never have begun.

The 'mind's eye' image has, in fact, a very precise 'flavour' derived from the quality of the artist's experience, but regarded as the picture's prototype it is far from precise. For that reason I have ventured to suggest that there is an intermediate stage between the imagined picture and the painted picture—a stage which is concerned almost entirely with the organization, the purely architectural aspect, of the artist's work. That organizing process, which is all-important to the classic artist, tends, as we shall see, to become a little slipshod and careless in romantic art, but it cannot be dispensed with. And just as it may modify the mental image as it evolves, so it, in its turn, is modified by the behaviour of the medium. The artist—in every branch of art—may choose whatever medium seems to him most appropriate for the statement he is to make, but it will always assert itself, and it will often lead him in a direction he is reluctant to take. The composer, for example, may feel that his melody will be more intelligible and eloquent if it is given to the human voice rather than to the violin, but during the creative process there may easily come a moment when the human voice will not be able to express what has been germinating in his 'mind's ear'. He will then be compelled to choose between modifying what he wants to 'say', abandoning his chosen medium for another, and making demands on his medium with which it is hardly capable of complying.

The visual artist is equally at the mercy of his medium's behaviour and must equally choose between forcing it to misbehave and modifying his first intentions. Usually he compromises between the two. The medium of oil paint, so wonderfully capable of rendering the subtle play of light on surfaces, so ill adapted to spinning an arabesque of line, must always be misused by the artist whose mental image is essentially linear. Or, if his artistic conscience will not allow him to misuse it, he must alter the whole 'flavour' of his mental image and produce, in the end a more 'painterly', a less linear, picture than was suggested by his mental image.

This struggle between the flavour of the artist's vision and the stubborn refusal of his medium to communicate that flavour is often one of the most notable characteristics of romanticism in all the arts. For the extrovert the struggle hardly exists. That unruffled state of mind that belongs to the keen but unimaginative observer is usually best served by traditional methods based on the behaviour of the medium itself, and in the hands of a great craftsman like Velasquez or Manet our impression is of a man who can make his medium obey the subtlest dictates of his will. Velasquez, at his best, is a wizard. Nothing he has to communicate is beyond his powers of expression. Mind and hand seem to have worked together in a miraculous collaboration. In this case one cannot conceive that any problem arising from the manipulation of paint could have interfered with or modified his 'intentions'.

But the romantic with his more personal and more urgent intentions may find it necessary to evolve an entirely new set of technical procedures in order to externalize those intentions. His success will then depend on his capacity to invent a new range of technical methods. Hence the failure of so much romantic art when the artist is too impatient or too distracted to experiment and attempts to express a new content by traditional means. And hence its astonishing power when a new set of technical possibilities has been opened up. One has only to think of the new pianistic possibilities discovered by Liszt when it became evident that the traditional pianistic techniques would not serve his romantic state of mind.

All art begins with a state of mind and ends with a work of art, and the process whereby the former is translated into the latter is always as I have just described it, an attempt on the artist's part to discover the formal equivalent of a state of mind, in which the attempt itself may to some extent modify the state of mind.

My concern, in the present chapter, is with romantic states of mind rather than with romantic modes of expression, but since we are faced with the awkward fact that only when a mode of expression has been found can a state of mind be deduced, even in this chapter it will not be possible to discuss the state of mind without constant reference to the mode of expression, whether it be the simple exclamation 'How romantic!' or the elaborate statement contained in Shakespeare's *Romeo and Juliet* or Turner's *Fighting Téméraire*. The difference between the exclamation and the play or the picture is merely one of greater precision and added detail. The artist who, seeing the great three-masted vessel towed down the Thames to be broken up against the pageantry of a sunset, decides to paint a picture of the dying ship and the dying day, is not more *sensitive* than the onlooker who is content to make an exclamation. His state of mind is not more romantic, but his capacity to translate emotion into pigment is more highly developed, his willingness to explore the perilous possibilities of such translation is infinitely greater; so is his skill and his preparedness to undertake a great deal of gruelling manual labour. Not the intensity of his feeling but the precision of his expression makes him remarkable.

None the less, the man who has neither the skill to translate nor the willingness to work can be equally moved. His exclamation may even be a surer index of his state of mind than the romantic paintings or dramas of artists whose skill and capacity are inadequate for the task they have undertaken. How often have I listened to the mediocre artist explaining the romantic profundity of the emotions that give birth to a deplorable work of art! Without knowing it his explanation was more indicative of his feelings than the painting in which he had tried to express them.

It is therefore not necessary, for the purpose of the present chapter, to look at Turner and Altdorfer, to read *Romeo and Juliet* or to attend a performance of *Giselle*. We know that they are successful expressions of a set of emotions in which mystery, abnormality, and conflict are fused in various proportions. We know that if we are on the look-out for their opposite characteristics of clarity, normality, and serenity we shall be disappointed. The means whereby romantic states of mind discover their formal equivalents and give birth to recognizable and classifiable romantic styles must be left to a later chapter.

If we return to that short list of obviously romantic experiences—moonlight, torrents and precipices, love in adversity—it will surely strike every reader that a world composed entirely of such experiences would be intolerable. The mystery of moonlight may be a stimulus to the imagination for no better reason than that the amount of illumination available is insufficient for man's practical needs. No serious work can be done in moonlight, since nothing is completely revealed. The tree-stump might be a man, everything has a double meaning. Action is suspended: imagination is awakened. Moonlight must stand as a type of those central universal experiences that are impressive because of their mystery. Romantic poets have discovered in it one of the more useful keys to unlock the door that leads into the nostalgic mood. 'In such a night as this' is a magic phrase for the release of humanity from the pressure of present events. It must be followed by 'Troilus, methinks, mounted the Troyan walls' or 'Stood Dido with a willow in her hand'. As soon as the present moment is allowed to intrude with 'Did pretty Jessica, like a little shrew, slander her love' the dream is shattered, the romantic mood evaporates. Present events demand adequate illumination. If a tree-trunk might be a man the mind is at once enmeshed into an adventure of delicious doubt: but doubt is only delicious to the romantic. To the extrovert, who insists on examining the exact nature of phenomena, doubt is abhorrent. A man is a man and a tree is a tree: it is his chief task to distinguish between them. To the classic who seeks for the generalized ideal behind the particular phenomenon it is useless. A man points the way to one set of ideals, a tree to another. If doubt arises idealization becomes impossible.

Mystery—less obvious but more potent—is inherent in mountain scenery. The level plain yields up all its secrets at a glance. The mountain conceals its hidden side, the eye cannot penetrate into the recesses of the gorge and cannot grasp the architecture of the perpetually moving torrent. Again, what is hidden must be imagined, what is restless cannot be compelled into a precise image.

Love is not quite so mysterious. Its symptoms, even at their most intense, are familiar and predictable. If its course runs smooth from the lovers' first meeting to their final union it holds no interest for the amateur of romantic sensation, but its very intensity makes smooth running unlikely. Its current is continually interfered with by cross-currents, Montague-Capulet feuds, social conventions, even the normal demands of everyday life. Doubt as to the ultimate outcome, the capacity of love to overcome interference, adds its own quota to the mystery. What makes the Romeo-Juliet story romantic is not merely its tragic ending (which, after all, is the result of no more than a series of unfortunate misunderstandings) but its continual suspense—the doubt as to the ultimate issue of the conflict between the lovers' will to be united and the resolve of their enemies to separate them. Had a classic author tackled the same plot the doubt would have been suppressed. The conflict would still have been there, but all things would have moved steadily towards the inevitable, predictable, unmysterious appointed end.

Mystery and abnormality have points of contact. Or rather, once mystery becomes normal it becomes irritating. A world of perpetual moonlight would be an impossible world to live in because it would be a world in which doubt was normal. A world of mountains and torrents would be equally impossible: it would be a world in which all the normal actions and events of life would become difficult and dangerous. A world in which love was for ever at fever-heat and was constantly having to surmount obstacles would be a world in which emotional tension would perpetually interfere with the even tenor on which civilization depends. The romantic, unlike the extrovert, can never rejoice in the normal. What interests him must be the exceptional. What the *C.O.D.* in this connexion describes as 'remote from experience' is, on the contrary, always well within the limits of experience, but it must be experience that is memorable because it is exceptional.

Moonlight is less normal than daylight. One remembers that sudden change of tone in *Paradise Lost*[1] as twilight falls, the world empties itself of activity and silence and the brooding night take charge 'for Beast and Bird, they to their grassie Couch, these to their Nests were slunk, all but the wakeful Nightingale', and the moon 'rising in clouded Majestie, at length apparent queen unvailed her peerless light'. The romantic note depends on the pre-established sense of silence and emptiness. For man, at least, night is abnormal. Blake uses exactly the same device:

> The birds are silent in their nest,
> And I must seek for mine,
> The moon like a flower
> In heaven's high bower
> In silent delight
> Sits and smiles on the night.

Mountains make a welcome contribution to the romantic frame of mind as much for their abnormality as for their mystery. Love, though practically universal as a human experience, becomes abnormal by being isolated and intensified. It provides the best possible romantic material for literature, especially lyric poetry, and almost the worst

[1] IV, 599.

possible for the visual arts. E. M. Forster in his *Aspects of the Novel* aptly compares its position in literature with its importance in life: 'How much time does love take? The question sounds gross but it bears on the present enquiry [the relation between real life and the life lived by the average hero or heroine of fiction]. Sleep takes about 8 hours out of 24, food about 2 more. Shall we put down love for another 2? Surely that is a handsome allowance.' We can agree with Mr Forster that *homo fictus* and *homo sapiens* differ considerably in the amount of time and emotional energy they have to spare for love, but as *homo pictus* is hardly affected by it we can safely leave that aspect of romanticism to the literary critics.

A taste for abnormality, however, in the strict sense of a liking for departure from the average is one of the chief characteristics of romantic art. While the classic artist carefully omits the abnormal on the ground that it is the sworn enemy of the ideal, and the extrovert is uninterested in it since it forms so small a part of that totality of experience with which he is prepared to deal, the romantic artist can only exercise his full power when he is surprised or excited by the unfamiliar. That surprise and that excitement are, in fact, his stock themes. How many portraits painted by German artists at the very period when idealistic portraits were being produced in Italy go out of their way to proclaim that the sitter's features are so oddly individual, his character so curious and exceptional, that he may, without offence, become positively ugly! He may indeed be a more stimulating subject for an artist *because* of his ugliness.

Schlegel was right when he suggested that the 'interesting' was in some basic way incompatible with the 'beautiful'. I do not imply that all departures from the normal are departures from beauty. But it is surely true that to seek out and isolate the particular, the personal, the quality that belongs to the given case and to no other, is to be indifferent to beauty, or at least to regard it as unimportant compared with 'character'. The romantic artist neither pursues nor avoids beauty. He ignores it, since it has no place in his programme. 'I am surprised and excited' is the very core of his message. 'This experience is what surprised and excited me' is a secondary consideration. In some cases, faced by Grünewald's *Crucifixion*, for example, we may reply 'But I find it repulsive', to which he will answer 'Possibly, but the quality of my intense response to it is surely more important than its inherent and possibly repulsive nature. You confuse my comment with my subject-matter.' In others we accept it. We, too, have responded to the same precipice, the same sunset, though we would never have expressed our response so violently. 'I like sunsets but surely you have exaggerated' is the thought which was put into words by the lady who remarked 'I have never seen a sunset like that, Mr Turner.' The reply 'Don't you wish you had, madam?' is the inevitable romantic's reply, and he makes it with considerable satisfaction. Had the same lady ventured to say 'I have never seen King Philip in quite that way, Mr Velasquez,' the painter would doubtless have been distressed by his failure to persuade her that he had stated the facts correctly and convincingly. In other cases—Van Gogh can be our example—there is no search for the abnormal stimulus. The tree, the cornfield, the rush-bottomed chair, are part of the furniture of everyday life. But in that case the surprise and the excitement must be intensified. The abnormality of the response must compensate for the normality of the subject.

Thirdly, the quality of conflict, which I believe to be at the root of romantic states of mind.

It could, of course, be argued that the whole of life is based on the resolution of the struggle between opposing forces, and that if conflict ceased one force would permanently gain the upper hand and the balance of nature would be upset. From the struggle between gravity and centrifugal force which keeps the universe in a condition of strained equilibrium to the struggle between the negative and positive charges of electrical energy within the atom, the whole of nature is perpetually engaged in a violent struggle in which no single force is allowed to gain more than temporarily the upper hand, lest ruin should ensue by the release of energy that could not be controlled. Man is too puny to interfere with the dynamic balance of the universe, but to the extent that he can and does interfere with the structure of the atom he upsets that delicate balance, that tug-of-war which remains stationary only because neither of the immense opposing forces can gain more than a momentary advantage over the other. We know well enough what price we have to pay in human fear and unhappiness because of that comparatively slight interference with the physical structure of matter.

The opposing forces of body and soul, laughter and tears, self-indulgence and asceticism, love and hate, energy and inertia, are surely what make life inexhaustibly interesting. And when man exercises his choice by preferring one set of opposites to another the shallowness that always accompanies incompleteness invariably results. If Greek sculpture elevates the perfection of the body and ignores the soul, the result, we feel, has its own perfection but also its own emptiness. If medieval art elevates the soul at the expense of the body the resultant imperfection may become a positive virtue, but again we feel that an important contribution to the fullness of life has been omitted. We wait patiently for a Michelangelo to restore those spiritual tensions that make the body eloquent without destroying its material beauty, and we feel grateful that the perilous balance has at last been restored. When the eighteenth century places too much reliance on reason its art ceases to be more than charming, and when the mystic laughs at reason and attempts to put intuition in its place, again we become conscious of the limitations that belong to extremism.

Without denying the perpetual struggle, the classic temperament delights in the equilibrium that results from it. The extrovert is unconscious of or uninterested by what is taking place, while the romantic continually underlines the struggle behind the equilibrium.

I am inclined to think that the advent of romantic movements is a by-product of the decay of humanism. When man is the measure of all things he places himself at the exact centre and contentedly regards his environment as something that must contribute to his well-being or else be ignored or detested if it does not. Hence his hatred of precipices and gorges. Picturesque they may be, but they threaten the suave progress of civilization. In classic drama there is hardly any landscape and what there is is only vaguely related to man. In Shakespeare, King Lear is as severely assailed by the elements as by the ingratitude of his daughters, so that the two become at length indentified in his unbalanced mind. Macbeth is haunted by darkness: the drowsy hum of the shard-borne beetle seems to him to ring night's yawning peal. In *The Tempest* it is the enchanted island that sets the romantic tone of the play. In *Romeo and Juliet* dawn, symbol of hope, is always breaking and jocund day stands tiptoe on the misty mountain-top.

This consciousness of Man *versus* Nature or Man absorbed into the mood of Nature is a romantic discovery, and it always results in Man being displaced from his central position as the measure of all things and being involved once more in a struggle from which he may or may not emerge victorious, but which always belittles him. His victory or defeat are unimportant as compared with the hazardousness of his adventure. And that hazardousness creeps into art as soon as Man turns his back on his fellows and begins to explore his environment. The humanist fifteenth century gave birth to a few temperamental romantics who will appear later on in these pages, but it is only when a Leonardo begins to make drawings of the warfare between rushing water and the static rocks that oppose them that romanticism can speak with its full eloquence.

If the balance that results from struggle is the classic obsession and the struggle that underlies balance is what delights the romantic, we can easily see how closely the two can come to each other. It is not a difference of vision but a difference of emphasis and a resultant difference of preferences. The idealized Madonnas of Raphael never find themselves in an environment that threatens or disturbs their peace. The equally idealized Madonna of Leonardo's *Virgin of the Rocks* is half buried in a dark grotto that symbolizes the uneasy conflict between Nature and Man.

The preoccupation with landscape that is not regarded as a background to Man's life, but as a half-personified set of forces that can dominate him, is essentially a romantic preoccupation. It gives birth to landscape painting as such, since Nature, to the romantic eye, is self-sufficient and need no longer justify herself by being regarded as an 'environment'. This shift of attitude that begins, in romantic periods, to rejoice in the struggle between Man and his environment affects every branch of art. It is not only seen in the rearing and snorting steeds of Delacroix and Géricault but in the very layout of gardens. Man must not be allowed to tame Nature. A sweet disorder, a wildness in which Nature is positively encouraged to oppose herself to the ordered geometry of classic gardening, becomes essential. Here the *Oxford Dictionary* hits the nail squarely on the head in pointing the opposition between 'picturesqueness or irregular beauty' on the one hand and 'finish and proportion' on the other.

Man must, of course, intrude into unspoiled Nature, but when he does so he need not dominate. It is not by chance that the figures in paintings by obviously romantic artists tend to appear on a reduced scale. The two figures in Giorgione's *Tempestà* must have seemed surprisingly small to a generation brought up on Raphael. Watteau's figures are almost invariably dwarfed by the trees or the palaces in which they find themselves.

No wonder, then, that the romantic eye finds a special satisfaction in mountainous scenery, in which Man always has the sense of being dwarfed or of having to struggle to assert himself.

It is an easy step from the struggle with Nature to the conflict with other forces of adversity. King Lear himself knows that. There is no essential difference between his conflict with his daughters and his battle with the elements. Conflict is still the theme, and because the romantic makes it his central theme we have come to regard it as being as valid and satisfying as the classic insistence on the final resolution of conflict.

Is there a common factor that unites our three characteristics of mystery, abnormality and conflict under a single large heading? I think there is. Each of them is an aspect of the rebellious temperament that dislikes whatever is law-abiding, whatever conforms to a pattern.

The feeling that somewhere there are laws of beauty that can be tabulated, golden sections that must be introduced if aesthetic appetites are to be satisfied, orders of architecture that can be described and obeyed, rules of composition that must be followed, is typical of the classic mind.

The romantic appears at first sight to be a temperamental law-breaker. But what actually happens is that he refuses to acknowledge the existence of law as applied to self-expression. If the classic architect can construct the perfect temple by following the instructions of Vitruvius, then the less artist he, for by doing so he resigns some of his rights as an individual. He submerges himself in a category that he is bound to obey, and obedience is a denial of the romantic creed.

Obedience, the acknowledgement of an accepted code, is repugnant to the man whose only loyalty is to himself and whose only duty is to express himself. 'Thou shalt be exceptional and follow that which is exceptional' is his only commandment.

This attitude of proud individualism does, I think, unite the three qualities I have selected as being basically romantic.

Mystery evades the law by its very refusal to be specific, its preference for the dubious, its insistence that the man may be a tree or the tree a man.

Abnormality is the negative of law. Its very existence depends on its refusal to conform to law-abiding behaviour. The precipice rears itself up in defiance of the laws of gravity. The Gothic cathedral makes nonsense of the law of Vitruvius. The eloping couple become significant because they defy the laws of society.

Conflict evades the notion of a law that can claim obedience, since its essence is the unresolved struggle between opposed laws.

The 'grandeur or picturesqueness' referred to in our dictionary definition are basically symptoms of conflict. The conflict between the amiability of classic 'beauty' and the *terribilità* which is its opposite, result in the grandeur of what we now know as 'the sublime'. Picturesqueness is almost invariably the result of a conflict between Man the creator and Time the destroyer. The once flawless building attacked by that destructive hand becomes, as a ruin, automatically picturesque.

Romanticism claims full freedom of individual expression, it asserts that heightened personal emotion alone is worth expressing, that the means of expression must be forged in every case to fit that heightened emotion, and that to follow tradition or to imitate what has been done in the past is to destroy the uniqueness of the individual.

Yet despite the romantic protest against the discipline of law we know well enough that without obedience to law and the traditions that enshrine law no human creative act can be intelligible or eloquent. The wildest garden must be *designed*, or it becomes meaningless because chaotic. This is the romantic dilemma. How, without discipline, is chaos to be avoided? How, if each man is to be a law unto himself, can he make himself understood by his followers? How can anything assert itself except by constant reference to clarity? How exalt the abnormal without reference to the normal? Or conflict without a knowledge of serenity? How is the romantic to discover, without a profound consideration of the problem of form, pattern, and design, the formal, considered design that alone will make him intelligible?

Intelligibility demands intelligence, and however deeply the romantic mistrusts the intellect he is lost if for a single moment he loses touch with it.

CHAPTER 5

The Romanticism of Mystery—Pre-Nineteenth-Century Romantics

The last chapter was concerned with states of mind, based on certain types of experience which common parlance agrees to call 'romantic'. It is only because of our need to isolate in our minds such experiences and such states of mind that the word 'romantic' has come into being, and it is only by noting the context in which the word is commonly used that we can discover its various meanings in ordinary speech.

But a word coined to cover a set of emotions which are familiar to us, even though only at rare intervals do we experience them with any intensity, may not turn out to be quite so simple or so easily defined when they become ingredients that have passed through an artist's mind and found their expression in a work of visual art. In this and the following chapters we shall no longer be concerned with what the average man regards as a romantic experience, but with what the artist produces when he attempts to find the visual equivalents of such experiences. If the term 'romantic art' has a meaning it must be discovered by noting how my three main catagories of romanticism—mystery, abnormality and conflict—can be translated into visual terms.

If we consider, for example, the well-known tremor of excitement that accompanies the doubt, mentioned in the last chapter, as to whether an object seen by moonlight is a man or a tree, we can easily see how such doubts can engender a positive *frisson* of pleasure. But for the purpose of the artist, mystery of so commonplace a kind is hardly mystery at all. It amounts to little more than vagueness. And no art worthy of the name has ever been based on vagueness. The distinction between clarity and mystery in art is far more fundamental than the distinction between what is clearly seen or depicted and what is blurred or incomprehensible. For the artist, clarity and mystery are not merely attributes that depend on bad or good eyesight or strong or weak illumination. The clarity of Raphael is the result of a passion for the ultimate incontrovertible statement. It is the clarity of the classic artist whose chief desire is to announce his discovery of the ideal family of forms at which Nature is always hinting, but which she will never reveal.

The mystery of the romantic artist, on the other hand, is clearly related to mysticism, which is equally intolerant of doubt, but for a different reason. Classicism discovers the invisible ideal that lurks behind a thousand visible variants on or departures from it. Romanticism discovers that the invisible is all that really matters, but that it can only be communicated by inventing its visible equivalent. The mystic is in no doubt as to what he must say, but he knows that it can only be said in terms of metaphor. And the essence of metaphor is that it clarifies something that is, in itself, hardly expressible. Sunrise as a phenomenon, for example, can be recorded in paint, and the Impressionists, obsessed by the urge to record phenomena, made such records with success. But they were concerned with appearance rather than with essence. The state of mind engendered by sunrise cannot be communicated by means of visual records. The essence of sunrise can only be expressed by personifying it, and even by selecting details from the personification. Homer's formula for it, 'rosy-fingered', rescues it from the extrovert and hands it over to the romantic. The mystery involved in so doing is the mystery of the relationship between an experience and the metaphor chosen by the artist—between the felt and the seen.

It is tempting to describe this use of metaphor as symbolism, but to do so would be an oversimplification of the situation. The device which we recognize in all the arts, but especially in the visual arts, as symbolism is no more than a sub-category of what I have called 'mystery'. Symbolism certainly has a part to play within the general framework of romanticism and it must be discussed later, but the romanticism of mystery *need* not employ symbols, though it cannot avoid the use of equivalents, and those equivalents may be, and frequently are, as clear-cut in form though not as explicit in meaning as anything we can find in classic or extrovert art. Homer's rosy-fingered maiden is not a symbol, but an attempt to express one of Nature's moods in humanistic terms.

One remembers the temperamental antipathy between Blake, the romantic, and Sir Joshua Reynolds, who could best be described as a classic extrovert. It drove Blake to make those exasperated comments in the margin of his copy of Sir Joshua's *Discourses*: 'Grandeur of Ideas is founded on Precision of Ideas'; 'Vision or Imagination is a representation of what actually exists, real and unchangeably'; 'A spirit and a vision . . . are organized and minutely articulated beyond all that Mortal and Perishable Nature can proceed'; 'All the copies of nature from Rembrandt prove that Nature becomes to its victim nothing but blots and blurs'.

These are the explosive utterances of a romantic who had the misfortune to be born into an age when romanticism itself needed both explaining and defending, but who lived long enough to see the full-blooded romanticism of the nineteenth century established and to acquire disciples who had no longer any need to protest against the eighteenth-century modes of thought.

For that reason it is easier to note the essence of Blake's romanticism than that of Turner, for the true flavour of a new attitude of mind is most easily isolated when it least belongs to its context, and when it not only makes its appearance as a protest against the contemporary spirit but also has to forge a new language to express the protest.

During the Periclean age any sculptor who wished to express any of those abnormal, mystical or restless states of mind referred to in earlier chapters would have been compelled to swim against the current of classicism and to twist the accepted idioms of his time out of recognition. And we know that only Scopas, in that single-minded confident age, attempted to do so. There is more to be learned, therefore, from the faint neurotic overtones we can detect in Scopas than from the whole of Rodin, for Rodin had no need to swim against the stream. The sculptural language he inherited was exactly the language he could use with a certainty that it would be understood.

Similarly, there is more to be learned by looking for an isolated romantic in Italy in the last decades of the fifteenth century, or from a Dutch romantic in the middle of the seventeenth, than by reviewing the whole corpus of nineteenth-century painting in England, France, and Germany.

During Raphael's lifetime—a generation obsessed by the search for formal perfection—there may have been plenty of artists who brooded on the problem of the strange and the mysterious, but only the most daring among them could evolve a means to express themselves. And during the lifetime of Pieter de Hooch it must have been even more difficult to conceive an art that would express something more than a general contentment with the pots and pans, the trees and meadows and cattle, of Dutch everyday life.

For that reason this chapter will occupy itself with a search for romanticism among non-romantics. And since the least romantic of all periods in the Christian era is surely to be found in Italy at a moment when the Renaissance was approaching its climax and the word 'classic' implied not only a reverence for Greek and Roman culture but an attitude to art that was rapidly perfecting that extraordinary instrument, the style in painting and sculpture that led into the High Renaissance, we may as well begin our inquiry at that moment, by looking for an artist who used the inherited pictorial idiom of his time and yet extracted meanings from it that seem to run counter to the spirit of his time. Botticelli, for example, has no apparent difficulty in using the tight, descriptive contour that was the common heritage of all Italian painters in the third quarter of the fifteenth century in a way that has unmistakable mystical implications, whereas his contemporaries, Ghirlandaio or Lorenzo di Credi, have no such magical power.

It will be remembered that Wölfflin[1] compares a nude by Botticelli with one by Lorenzo di Credi by noting that they are 'as radically and unmistakably different . . . as an oak from a lime'. To say no more than that is surely to miss the real difference between them. It is not merely a difference of personality—the one radiant and energetic, the other flaccid and nerveless. Both seem to Wölfflin equally convincing as statements about the human figure, but it would be truer to say that whereas Lorenzo di Credi is an extrovert who describes an object, Botticelli romantically evolves a mood. What is remarkable is that Lorenzo di Credi, for all his lack of tension, is using the visual language of his period for the purpose for which it had been evolved, while Botticelli gave it a set of meanings that none of his contemporaries had ever thought it capable of conveying.

Certainly Botticelli discovered a shape for his Venus which must have seemed to him 'idealized' and therefore purely classical in intention, while Lorenzo di Credi's extrovert eye was firmly tied to the shape of the model before him, yet nothing could be less classic in effect than the shape which Botticelli's Venus finally assumes. Hers is not the form that Nature hints at but never achieves. She is, on the contrary, attenuated and almost invertebrate, rhythmically based on curves that echo each other, anatomically weak and unconvincing. Botticelli certainly idealizes when he distorts, but his distortions are not, as were those of Raphael and Ingres, attempts to discover a generalized norm. They were efforts to discover the formal equivalent of a mood. His Venus bears the same relationship to the concept 'woman' as does Turner's *Interior at Petworth* to the concept 'light'. The two artists are inspired by the same romantic purpose. The difference between them

[1] *Principles of Art History*, pp. 2 and 3.

lies only in the vocabulary of form and style they inherited. Like Blake, Botticelli was a temperamental romantic living in a classic period. Had he not had the good fortune to be understood by one of the most enlightened of all patrons, Lorenzo the Magnificent, recognition might not have come to him during his lifetime.

Even more striking, as an example of romanticism struggling to express itself in an unromantic age, is the case of Leonardo da Vinci. Leonardo, like Turner and Wordsworth, was a temperamental pantheist, constantly amazed and awed by the forces of Nature and constantly attempting to express his amazement in terms of 'equivalents'. But for Leonardo there was an additional complication to be solved. Not only did he inherit the classical linear language of his Florentine predecessors, but he also inherited the scientific belief that the world could be understood and explained by observation, experiment and the deduction of natural laws from the data observed and collected. This inner conflict between the scientific method and the romantic frame of mind very nearly prevented Leonardo from becoming an artist at all. It also enabled him, in moments of exceptional inspiration, to produce works of art in which the two contradictory sides of his nature achieved a hazardous fusion. Much of Leonardo's work is a paradox in which intelligent, rational curiosity and blind creative intuition are at perpetual war with each other, sometimes finding themselves in unconvincing juxtaposition, but occasionally reinforcing each other.

In the well-known preparatory drawing for the *Adoration of the Kings*, after making one of those elaborate perspective layouts that the Florentine mind found so congenial as a demonstration of applied optical science, Leonardo must have been overtaken by a sudden impatience with Florentine pedantry. The carefully contrived space with its vanishing-point and its ruler-and-compass precision is suddenly invaded by agitated ghostly figures, plunging horses and a recumbent camel. Only the camel could have any connexion with the arrival of the Magi. The rest of the mysterious, restless crowd is unrelated, either as narrative or as mood, to an Adoration. Not only are the Virgin and the Infant Jesus omitted, but there is no available space in which they could seat themselves amid the general confusion.

This is an extreme example of Leonardo's split personality at work, and it almost suggests a man suddenly turning on himself in mocking disgust at his own pedantry. But there is hardly a drawing in the whole long sequence in which romantic impulses are not just below the surface. Even in the anatomical studies they are implied: even the engines of war and peace in the purely mechanical demonstrations of engineer-

Leonardo da Vinci, Cloudburst
Royal Library, Windsor
Reproduced by gracious permission of H.M. The Queen

ing are often served by a race of men summoned from a world in which machinery plays no part.

It is in that remarkable series of drawings that scholars, searching for an adequate title, call 'cloudbursts' and 'deluges' that Leonardo's romantic interpretations of natural forces take full charge, unfettered by any obligation to describe or idealize. They were done between 1510 and 1514, in his late fifties and early sixties. One recognizes in them the same rough translation of Nature's latent energy into purely formal terms that is to be found in so much of Turner. Like Turner, Leonardo could discover visual equivalents of Nature's power and Man's insignificance that were never even suspected in early sixteenth-century Italy, and never adequately envisaged by any other artist in early nineteenth-century England. These drawings of Leonardo's are, in the strictest sense of the word, as abstract as anything conceived by Turner, even in his most apocalyptic moments. Turner's waves, clouds, mountains and storms may mingle almost inextricably, but they are still, in origin, observed phenomena. But the rhythmic, swirling lines in this series of drawings by Leonardo are nothing of the kind. They may contain echoes of his earlier researches into the rhythms of flowing water or of rock formation, but they are essentially lines of force, as little dependent on what the eye can see as the diagrams that explain magnetic fields in a treatise on electricity.

These are the final expressions of a man who could rarely prevent the creations of his subconscious mind from interfering with the researches of his conscious intelligence. But it is noteworthy that once he had done them a change came over his creative processes. After 1504 there are records of his 'doodling' with geometric games or making ambitious toy dragons. It would seem that he had outgrown the Florentine intellectual discipline so that he no longer wished to fall back on it; and at the same time the springs of his romantic imagination had dried up. Under such conditions the romantic temperament loses its power. At the best it becomes invertebrate, at the worst merely silly.

Blake and Leonardo, condemned to work in periods when their contemporaries were bound to misunderstand them, were also forced to invent new modes of expression, twisting available traditions into directions that were equally misunderstood. Such artists may easily acquire, in their own lifetime, immense prestige, but usually for what seems to us the wrong reason. Vasari's praise of Leonardo is wholehearted and enthusiastic, yet it leaves out of account almost everything that makes him seem to us a genius and therefore a misfit. To Vasari he was a professional Florentine painter of immense competence who finally rendered the *maniere secco* of his predecessors obsolete, an artist who, but for the personal eccentricities that continually distracted him, would have been the equal of Raphael and Michelangelo. To us, the nearer he approaches to either of his great contemporaries the less interesting he becomes. There are strong Raphaelesque characteristics in the *Mona Lisa*, but what makes the portrait significant for us is precisely that element in it that Raphael could never have detected—the romantic overtones that break through the classical design. The *Mona Lisa* was painted in 1503. It must have seemed to Raphael so satisfactory a solution of the problem of design that he almost 'quoted' it in his portrait of Maddalena Doni in the Pitti Palace, of 1505. Yet despite the formal resemblance between the two portraits the romantic ingredients in Leonardo's picture—not only the famous half-smile but the fantastic landscape background and the lights that flicker along the folds of the sleeves—are what first attract our eyes; Raphael's portrait

Leonardo da Vinci, Mona Lisa
Louvre, Paris

Raphael, Maddalena Doni
Pitti Palace, Florence

contains no such ingredients, yet, because they are absent, we can regard it more easily as a superb example of classical clarity. The two pictures are products of the same Florentine tradition, yet Raphael's strikes us as being firmly based on what was seen—in short, on his sitter's appearance and personality—Leonardo's on an imaginary creative process to which the Florentine girl who was—who must have been—his sitter made an almost negligible contribution.

In Leonardo we admire not only what he achieved but the struggle involved in the achievement. And that struggle can be seen through the history of art at every turning-point in the development of style. The extrovert artist, struggling to assert himself as a realist at a moment when classicism or romanticism are in the ascendancy, has exactly the same need to invent a new and unfashionable set of technical procedures. The mannerist idioms of the sixteenth century had to be reshaped before Caravaggio could say what he had to say. Courbet had to invent a new way of painting before he could make his full protest against the romanticism of Delacroix. Seurat, completely classical in temperament and intention, inherited the broken brush-stroke invented by the Impressionists for the purposes of objective recording, and turned it into *pointillisme*, a technical process whose very nature makes objective recording almost impossible.

These technical innovations that grow out of and yet protest against the established tradition are inevitable whenever the *Zeitgeist* approaches one of those points in which we feel that a corner is being turned rather than a climax reached. It is, in fact, only by means of such innovations that the corner can be turned at all.

Such stylistic experiments always strike their contemporaries as surprising and slightly shocking. Apparently it is less easy to accept new means than new ends. Yet new ends positively demand new means, and it is only during the period just before the surprise and the shock have died down that the new ends can have their full impact. What inevitably occurs at such moments is that what began as an experiment becomes in the end an acceptable convention. What was once surprising passes into general currency and thereby severs its connexion with the purpose for which it was invented. Once that has happened it loses that special flavour that it once evoked and can be used indifferently in any context. Blake's sauve articulation, Turner's mysterious opalescence, will both serve equally as the tools of the academic artist half a century later who is no longer driven onwards by an urgency or purpose that forces him to invent a new set of painterly idioms. The technical discoveries of a Rubens become the stock-in-trade of an Etty. The divisionism of Monet degenerates into a device for giving a spurious breezy look to an otherwise tired landscape of today.

It is characteristic of the romantic temperament that without a constant self-renewal by technical experiment it loses its eloquence. For, to a far greater extent than the extrovert or the classic artist, the romantic *must* renew and enlarge his vocabulary of formal expression. By definition he avoids the generalized and seeks the exceptional. Being a rebel and an individualist there are more and larger areas for him to explore: there are more ways of defying law than of adhering to it.

Technical departures from tradition are therefore the most easily recognized sign of the romantic temperament. And even though we may subdivide romanticism into expressions of mystery, abnormality and conflict, each demands that the artist should make his own set of adjustments to the pictorial language he has inherited before he can fully express himself. It is by these adjustments that the romantics draw attention to themselves: and it is by noting them and the use made of them that we can read the message of the artist who used them.

Watteau, La Gamme d'amour
National Gallery, London

Examine, for example, the surface of a painting by one of the most obviously romantic of all great painters, Antoine Watteau. Perhaps no other painter has so successfully used the seen as a starting-point for a journey of exploration into the unseen. That starting-point—the trivial extract from a flirtation, the young man playing a guitar or snatching a kiss, the young girl practising a step in the gavotte or the minuet—is invariably as banal as in any Dutch *genre* painting of a music-lesson or an exchange of pleasantries over a glass of wine. As a documentary description of an unimportant event there is nothing to choose between a conversation in the parlour by Pieter de Hooch or Terborch and one in the park by Watteau. Yet in their deeper meanings the difference is profound. And the difference depends on the surface of the painting—the mysterious caress of a brush that listens to the commands of the mind rather than the eye. The result—on such seemingly trivial causes are massive effects based—is that where Terborch tells us of a happening, and, even then, of the appearance of a happening, Watteau presents us with the visual equivalent of a sigh. The tremulous passage of light over the satin surface of a sleeve is not, as it would have been even in Rembrandt, the result of an acutely observant eye, though Watteau's

Terborch, The Guitar Lesson
National Gallery, London

eye was more alert for expressive little inflexions of gesture or facial expression than any of the *genre* painters of Holland. But what marks Watteau as a romantic artist is that it never occurs to us to think of him as a recorder of the comedy of manners at the Court of Versailles. Torborch both records and comments on the event. 'Thus it was' and 'How satisfactory!' are his two messages. No picture by Watteau contains the implication of 'Thus it was': and his comment is not on the event but on life, which is invariably elegant and yet invariably sad. A heartbreaking nostalgia pervades his pictures. The exquisite puppets engaged in their endless round of gallantries against a background of soft music are caught up in a tragedy from which they cannot escape. All unmindful of their fate his puppets play the parts assigned to them, and play them with such careless perfection that their fate and not themselves becomes the key to Watteau's meaning. No artist can extract such unexpected meanings from such unlikely subject-matter without deliberation or calculation. It is never true to assume that the romantic artist is a thoughtless creature who trusts to luck and intuition when he begins to translate his *vie intérieure* into pigment. One of the most potent of Watteau's compositional devices—the relation in scale between his figures and the total area of the canvas they occupy—is certainly a deliberate one. With the exception of certain famous paintings by Giorgione (which have almost exactly the same emotional effect) no other paintings, except those by Watteau's imitators, show just this ratio of mankind to his environment.

Where figures are contained within a landscape there is seldom any doubt as to whether the artist has painted a 'landscape with figures' or 'figures in a landscape'. The distinction is more important than it sounds, nor does it invariably depend on the physical size of the figures. In Giorgione's *Tempestà* the soldier and the woman with her baby are insignificant in size, and they are forced almost brutally into the lower corners of the canvas. Yet the picture would lose more than half its meaning if they were eliminated.

It was a Giorgionesque discovery that the human being could be given an added significance by being dwarfed by Nature. The soldier and the woman are no mere devices for furnishing a foreground. Watteau, no less of a humanist than Giorgione, uses the same means to intensify the nostalgic mood of his pictures by reducing the size of his figures so that the little spinneys in which they wander and the trees that overarch them invariably belittle them dramatically as well as physically. They move in an environment less civilized but nobler than themselves, and the contrast between the elegant puppetry of man and the untamed generosity of Nature adds one more level to the romantic comment whenever Watteau leads his actors out into the open air. It is always in the park rather than the palace that Watteau's bitter-sweet pathos is most potent. As might be expected from this most reticent of artists, the Man-versus-Nature device is never exaggerated. Nature never threatens to engulf, as she does in Altdorfer (who is equally anxious to belittle humanity by reducing its physical size). No threat is ever allowed to develop. Watteau's humans are never presumptuous ants at war with forces more powerful than themselves. They are merely made to seem pathetically trivial. The contrast, for him, requires no emphasis.

It is this power to extract profound emotional overtones from the commonplace event that is the mark of the romanticism of mystery. Watteau's contemporaries and imitators, Lancret and Pater, seized avidly on what they took to be a foolproof formula—elegance and frivolity served by a caressing brush-stroke—and achieved charming pictures that doubtless mirror the age but omit the sigh, the pathos. As for Boucher's make-believe nymphs and goddesses, they are unmindful of everything but their own physical desirability. No music echoes round them and no fate can overtake them. No stylistic inventions were needed in order to paint them. Had Boucher attempted to borrow from Watteau he would not have known what to make of his borrowings.

This necessary parenthesis on the romanticism of Watteau, which, though deeply rooted in him, might almost be traced to a set of painterly devices, has interrupted this rapid survey of those early evidences of romanticism which we have traced in Botticelli and Leonardo.

They are not the only Florentine artists in whom new and fundamentally romantic overtones can be heard in an age that, on the whole, ignored them. It is difficult to think of Uccello's *Hunt in the Forest* as a true product of the age that produced it. It seems to everyone who sees it for the first time to contain all the nostalgic implications of Alfred de Vigny's *'Dieu, que le son du cor est triste dans les bois'*. As for Piero di Cosimo's masterpiece, *The Death of Procris*, no Italian painting of the fifteenth century is so packed with the essence of nostalgia. There is no symbolism here—or if there is it does little to account for the haunting melody of the work. Piero di Cosimo, conscientious student as he was, in common with so many of his contemporaries, of classical mythology, produced one of the least classical references to it imaginable. The tenderness and pathos of the fawn, the deliberately ungainly figure of the dead nymph, lying crumpled on the meadow, the lonely shore and its odd fauna—all these ingredients would surely have appealed to the medieval mind and might have been painted by a medieval artist had one existed with the requisite science and skill. Piero's meadow is carpeted with flowers that remind one of a tapestry woven in Touraine; the dogs and the waterfowl on the shore are lifted from a medieval bestiary.

Florentine romantics of the fifteenth and early sixteenth centuries are admittedly rare. It was inevitable that they should be, for Florentine intelligence was based on a philosophical turn of mind, and Florentine art was obsessed by formal problems that were closely related to those of mathematics. In Venice, where poetry was more congenial than philosophy and music than mathematics, the hard crust of Renaissance classicism was more easily broken. The sensuous flavour which developed steadily in Venetian art from the earliest of Bellini's Mantegnaesque essays, done while he was still a youth in Padua, to the last of Titian's great symphonic pictures was not in itself romantic, but it could easily be used for romantic ends. And when Giovanni Bellini's father, Jacopo, filled the two sketch-books which his sons inherited at his death (one of which is in the Louvre, the other in the British Museum) with outline drawings in each of which small figures are contained in an environment that evidently interested him as much as, or more than, the figures themselves, he laid the foundations of a new relationship between man and his surroundings. That relationship became the foundation on which Venetian romanticism was built. It was the same relationship which Watteau rediscovered and used for the same purpose two centuries after Giorgione, the most romantic of all Venetians. Both artists are convinced that Man is dominated by Nature, yet both somehow suggest that in the day-dream world that they create in their canvases Nature herself is part of the dream.

None of Watteau's immediate predecessors prepared the way for his romanticism. Giorgione, on the other hand, must have noted the constant recurrence not only of romantic devices, but of romantic *meanings* in the work of his master, Giovanni Bellini. The dream-world, the pantheism in which Man is no more than an aspect of Nature, the delight in enigmas, and, in his early work, when Mantegna's austerity was still the main votive force in his art, his capacity to intensify emotion by a sudden unexpected emphasis that is never to be found in Mantegna himself—these were the foundations built by Bellini for the later romanticism of the Venetians. Giorgione, despite his personal brand of mystery, owed his awareness of it to Bellini.

These elements are worth examining separately, for they combine in various degrees to produce, in the end, Venice's unique contribution to romantic art, the *poesia*, the picture without a subject or, at least, the picture whose avowed subject is of so little importance compared with the mood it evokes that we are forced to think of it as lyrical rather than dramatic or narrative.

The day-dream, at the end of the fifteenth century, was a new invention—if 'invention' is the right word for the kind of imagery that the mind's eye conjures up when it banishes intellectual processes and allows itself to accept whatever the unconscious levels of experience offer to it. We have seen how, despite Florentine self-discipline, one or two Florentines could make tentative approaches to such a frame of mind. But for the average Venetian artist a creative process that could banish intelligence was less difficult to achieve.

In Bellini's long career the day-dream alternates with the heroic or the monumental: and in his old age he discovered a formula for uniting the two. In the London National Gallery's early *Agony in the Garden* the cold dawn that strikes across the low hills and picks up the white houses on their crests, the empty valley with its winding paths, the distant straggling procession led by Judas, the ghostly angel in the sky, seem, by some odd Venetian magic, to be images conjured up by the dreams of the three sleeping disciples, while they themselves, untidily and even unskilfully scattered in the foreground, are no more than incidents in the drama that requires their presence. The *St Francis* in the Frick Museum in New York is an extension of the same theme. The saint has stepped stiffly out of his dark cave to find himself suddenly overwhelmed by the wonder of the bright morning sun in the foothills of the Veneto. What matters is not the saint himself but his ecstatic communion with every vivid detail of his environment. The donkey, the meadow, the castle, every pebble on the path, every bush on the hillside, every leaf and tendril on the vine above his head, is seen with an intensity of enjoyment because it is seen and enjoyed *by him*. The picture itself is *his* day-dream. Ostensibly St Francis is receiving the stigmata: he should be unconscious of his surroundings in his mystical communion with the symbols of suffering. In fact, he is, like Rimsky-Korsakoff's heroine, singing a Hymn to the Sun.

The five little allegories in the Accademia in Venice are too obviously romantic in this sense to require commentary, and to submit them to the kind of analysis that the professional iconographer would like to indulge in would be to destroy them.

Again and again, in his later years, that favourite Venetian theme the Sacra Conversazione recurs, and each time the conversation becomes more and more an integral part of Nature. In the *Earthly Paradise* (Florence, Uffizi), the mystery deepens. Dreams of such haunting complexity can doubtless be explained, but only by an exploration of the subconscious levels of the mind that would turn the romantic artist into a plaything for the psychologist and thereby make him powerless to approach us on *our* subconscious levels. When the iconographer tackles such problems he can only do so on the level of romanticism itself.

As for Bellini's sudden concentration of emphasis, a single example will suffice—the *Pietà with St John* in the Brera Gallery in Milan. Here,

Giovanni Bellini, Pietà with St John
Brera Gallery, Milan

in a comparatively early work that uses all the metallic surfaces and forced contours he had inherited from Mantegna, the magnetic power depends entirely on an expressiveness that was quite beyond Mantegna's range. Other artists could conceivably have imagined the pathos of the three heads, but only Bellini could have painted the striated sky and the glimpse of the hillside behind the Virgin's cloak. But the essence of the tragedy is contained in the four hands that occupy the picture's centre. The right hand of the Virgin and the left hand of St John are bony, tense and rigid. The limp right hand of the dead Christ is more expressive than the drooping head, but the culmination of the picture's meaning is contained in his left hand—the helpless weight of the knuckles that rest on the hard white marble slab that acts as a barrier between the three unapproachable figures and ourselves.

Giorgione was never quite capable of such intense concentrations of meaning. Yet the handful of paintings by which he is remembered are pervaded by an enigma that is essentially Venetian and yet only occurs in Giorgione. Even in those paintings that Titian produced during the first few years just after Giorgione's death, notably the *Sacred and Profane Love*, in which he seems to have caught the spirit of Giorgione by direct contagion, the ultimate secret has not been grasped. The mystery is there, the *poesia* is fully developed, but they offer too obvious a temptation to the iconographer. The enigma of *Sacred and Profane Love* could be solved without destroying its fragrance. Not so the *Tempestà* or even the Dresden *Venus*.

The *Tempestà* has often been called the first 'landscape with figures', yet none would dare to say that if the two figures were to be removed it would remain a masterpiece or that with a less interesting background the figures would be memorable in the way that so many of Raphael's figures are memorable. Like the sleeping disciples in Bellini's *Agony in the Garden*, Giorgione's soldier and the mother suckling her child are unaware of each other, yet it is their combined day-dream that calls the landscape into being. The trees, the sequence of towers shining against the blue-black sky, the flash of lightning and the idiotic broken columns (perhaps they more than all), are the stuff that dreams are made on, and the dreamers have retired to the lower corners of the canvas in order to leave the vista between them as an open invitation to us to creep in between them. They ignore us as completely as they ignore each other. And, as though he could foresee that one day the scientist would defeat the iconographer, Giorgione has left, underneath the soldier, a woman bathing for the X-ray photographer to discover. An artist who could improvise in the very act of painting could be neither classic in temperament nor narrative in purpose. Such an acceptance of second thoughts could only happen if he were quite deliberately attempting to be evocative for evocation's sake. Edgar Allan Poe's analysis of the creative process that produced his poem *The Raven* is the only kind of analysis that will explain the *Tempestà*.

Just as Poe decided, in cold blood, that the word 'nevermore' would produce the reverberating echo he needed, so Giorgione must have evolved the forms that *he* needed by a process of trial and error. It is a process that must often happen in the evolution of a poem. It is interesting, for example, to know that Keats's Giorgionesque lines

> . . . charmed magic casements opening on the foam
> Of perilous seas in faery lands forlorn,

appear in the first draft as

> Charmed the wide casements opening on the foam
> Of Keelless seas in faery lands forlorn,

and it is typical of the romantic that he can regard his own words and his own forms as incantations. Keats listens to 'forlorn' and succumbs to it. Like the word 'nevermore' it is not a descriptive adjective, but becomes a bell to toll him back from his subject to himself. This kind

Giorgione, Madonna
Castelfranco, Veneto

of art is hardly promising material for the iconographer; however potently it may lure him on, it can only lead him to a point where his equipment is useless. He might as usefully attempt to analyse the molecular structure of a perfume.

This effect of the dreamer enclosed in his own dream is the key to many of Giorgione's paintings. In the *Tempestà* it can hardly be

Giorgione, Venus
Dresden Gallery

missed. In the *Three Philosophers* it is disguised, in the *Sleeping Venus* the insistent classicism of the single figure distracts a little from the hidden 'meaning'. In the Castelfranco Madonna Giorgione's acceptance of the conventional formula for a symmetrical altarpiece almost blinds one to it. Yet of all his paintings this is perhaps the most striking example of pure classic form used as a vessel to contain romantic enigmas. The impossible height of the Madonna's throne not only separates her from the two saints below her but induces a vague wonder as to how she managed to achieve her inaccessible position. She belongs to the wide landscape behind her—a conventionally serene stretch of a country such as Raphael might have imagined, yet by some magic it becomes a Turneresque pastoral. It, too, is part of a dream, and one reason for its becoming so is Giorgione's odd device of the high wall that forbids us to enter it and imprisons the two languid saints in a paved courtyard. They too, like the soldier and the woman in the *Tempestà*, are unaware of each other.

In the whole range of the romanticism of mystery there is nothing quite so unemphatically mysterious as these delicate Giorgionesque understatements. We are hardly aware of the means whereby Giorgione casts his spells, for there is nothing in them that does not belong to the

Titian, Venus
Uffizi Gallery, Florence

language of the Venetian tradition. When Titian painted his recumbent Venus in the Uffizi he quoted Giorgione's Venus line for line, with the exception of the goddess's lowered right arm. Yet the spell has vanished. She is still a goddess, but she no longer occupies forbidden ground. She has opened her eyes and is aware of our admiration. She is also aware that she deserves it. Her two handmaidens who rummage in the chest for her garments are part of her waking life and not of her secret dreams. By contrast with Giorgione's whispered incantation Titian's masterpiece is earthbound. It is even a little banal.

Mystery can take many forms, for when the unseen is made visible it reveals a variety that the seen can never have. Giorgione's version of it, like almost all Italian versions, has a serenity and a sweetness that would be regarded as cloying and characterless north of the Alps. Italy had inherited from Greece a reverence for the classic formulas for beauty that persisted even in the dream world. Nothing that could destroy these formulas could be admitted. Tragedy was admissible, but not brutality. The whole of the emotional range from the sinister to the fantastic, from the macabre to the grotesque, was alien to the Italians

Dürer, The Knight and Death (detail)
Print Room, British Museum

of the late fifteenth and early sixteenth century. A few half-hearted attempts—the skulls and bones that surround Carpaccio's nursery dragon, for example—to suggest such moods are laughably inept when we compare them with their Central European equivalents—the monsters of Grünewald or the horned beast in Dürer's engraving of *The Knight and Death.* Doubtless Dürer had to consult Verrocchio's *Colleoni* before he could achieve the Knight, but his companions and the landscape through which he rides could never have been conceived in an Italian mind.

Yet hints of the sinister and the forbidding did make their way into Italy from the North. Tintoretto seems to be one of the few Venetian painters who positively welcomed studio assistants from Germany or the Low Countries. Hans Rothammer, Martin de Vos, and Paolo Fiammingo all worked under him; it is quite evident that their North European mannerisms must have been sympathetic to him and must even have encouraged him in the development of what we think of as his 'San Rocco' style, so different from the blithe optimistic style of the four allegories in the Ducal Palace or the *Origin of the Milky Way* in the London National Gallery. In these last there is no hint of Germanic or Flemish influence. They are purely Venetian in their acceptance of physical perfection and sunshine. But when Tintoretto abandoned golden-age mythology and turned his attention to the New Testament, a set of dark, uneasy tensions, entirely non-Italian, pervaded his work. And in extreme cases—particularly in the two nocturnes in the lower hall of the Scuola di San Rocco, the *St Mary of Egypt* and the *St Mary Magdalen in the Desert*—a lurid Northern light glitters among the foliage, the tangled roots of the trees and the dank undergrowth. We find ourselves, surprisingly, in a land of melodramatic, moonlit romanticism that seems to herald the Teutonic gloom of the late eighteenth century and even the picturesque glamour of Scott.

The threatening silhouette of Melrose Abbey would hardly be out of place against the lurid sky of the St Mary Magdalen panel.

These are the most obvious examples of Tintoretto's romantic mood, but it recurs again and again in San Rocco—in the fitful light that plays among the hills in the background of the *Flight into Egypt*, in the ghostly procession seen through the open door in the *Adoration of the Magi*. And in one of his last pictures, the *Last Supper* in San Giorgio, probably painted in the year before his death in 1594, the same phosphorescent light turns the whole picture into a dream.

This infiltration into Italy of North European romanticism has its own Italian flavour, for not even Tintoretto nor, after him, Magnasco, that specialist in the *bravura* of mystery, could tolerate the complete emotional apparatus of the typical German artist. Mystery, as such, was acceptable to the Italian temperament, but the alternation between frank brutality and an almost cloying ecstasy was never allowed to appear in Italy.

German romanticism tends to stress one or other of two moods, cruelty and sweetness, and in both cases what strikes us is a quality of excess, of overstatement. To the Italian eye, tuned to the tremulous understatements of the Giorgionesque *poesia*, emphasis of the kind one associates with Grünewald and Altdorfer must seem unnecessary and, in extreme cases, repellent. To the British eye, the frank German preoccupation with refinements of cruelty and ecstasy and its resulting flavour appears to be lacking in 'taste' in proportion as it is exaggerated in character. Almost all the German romantics of the Renaissance and of the period that corresponds to the Italian High Renaissance are basically realists, close observers of the world of phenomena, who have romanticized that world by ignoring its serenities and exaggerating its tensions. This, with a vengeance, is a pursuit of what Schlegel, in search of a descriptive word, decided to call 'the interesting' as opposed to 'the beautiful'. Had he been an Italian it would not perhaps have occurred to him that the beautiful was lacking in interest or that the kind of strangeness he discovered in the German literature of his time was not the only possible kind of 'strangeness'. The difference to him between, say, Cranach and Botticelli, had he cared to examine it, would have been the difference between a witch's incantation and a lover's sonnet. We, with our more acute sense of the emotional overtones of pictorial art, tend to make a finer distinction between them. Both artists, we would admit, are poets: both are immensely concerned with aspects of femininity—Cranach with the self-consciously seductive, Botticelli with the self-consciously chaste—and both, in their deliberate exaggerations, are equally romantic in intention. The important difference between them—and it is one that Schlegel, with his inherited Teutonic assumptions, would have missed—is that Botticelli's romanticism was a revolt against classicism, Cranach's was a revolt against the extrovert temperament. Botticelli's Venuses were variants on an original by Praxiteles, those of Cranach refer back to engravings by Dürer. The two artists approach each other, but from opposite directions.

Cranach's formula for the female nude, especially towards the end of his career, in the 1530s, was a response to a demand for mildly aphrodisiac art. The sweetness, so often latent, behind or side by side with the savagery in German art was something for which Cranach had a particular genius, but it was also something for which his Court patrons had a special appetite. Despite the obvious erotic devices Cranach uses—the heavy necklaces and enormous hats that emphasize the nakedness of his Venuses and his candidates at the Judgement of Paris—it is not easy to describe how he achieved his odd effect of fastidious frivolity. No other artist has managed to give his creatures quite that effect of vulnerability, and when, in the *Judgment of Paris*, the three goddesses are being inspected (no other word seems appropriate) by two bearded gentlemen in heavy armour in a landscape filled with towering crags and pine-trees, the effect is of delicate fruits threatened by thistles.

Cranach's calculated excess of sweetness could only be German, but it is personal rather than typical, and there is more than a hint of decadence in it. To find the romantic elements in German art at their most intense one goes, of course, to Grünewald. The Isenheim altarpiece contains everything from the purely sadistic to the embarrassingly ecstatic. Fantasy and horror, saccharine and vinegar, alternate in this extraordinary potpourri of exaggerated emotions, and only Grünewald's undoubted genius could weld them into a unity.

The Isenheim altarpiece (now in the museum at Colmar) is a structure of unusual complexity, possessing two sets of movable wings hinged at the outer edges and opening from a centre line. It consists of two fixed outer panels (St Anthony on the left, St Sebastian on the right) flanking a Crucifixion. Below is a Lamentation in the form of a predella panel. When the two panels that form the Crucifixion are folded back they reveal, on the reverse side, an Annunciation on the left and a Resurrection on the right, while in the centre—again divided down the middle and hinged at the outer edges—is what would have been, in Italy, a Nativity, but which, with the North European symbolism

Lucas Cranach, Judgment of Paris
Karlsruhe Museum

and mysticism added, must be called an Incarnation. Again the central panel can be swung back on its outer hinges to reveal a carved centrepiece (ordered from and completed by Nikolaus von Hagenau before Grünewald had begun work on the paintings) and the two outer panels. On the left St Anthony and St Paul the Hermit converse, on the right St Anthony is tortured by evil spirits.

Grünewald, Isenheim Altarpiece: Virgin and Child (detail)

Colmar Museum

It is characteristic of all romantic art that subject-matter should dictate terms to the artist, giving him the opportunities he is always seeking for those exaggerations that will give emphasis to his personal comment. And when, as in German art, the comment itself turns to violence, the subject is of unusual importance. Apart from the two saints that flank the Crucifixion in the Colmar altarpiece, each of Grünewald's subjects (whether they were chosen by him or specified by his patrons hardly matters) offers an exceptional opportunity for an emphasis on physical pain or spiritual triumph or on the macabre or sinister. One can well believe that even had the opportunity been denied him, he would still have imposed his favourite moods on these paintings. Indeed, in the Annunciation, a subject which almost every Italian except Tintoretto had regarded as demanding the maximum of quiet, unstrained reverence, Grünewald has insisted on an agitation and

Grünewald, Isenheim Altarpiece: Head of Christ (detail)
Colmar Museum

a tension that seem, at first, inappropriate. But in the other panels Grünewald insists that we should either recoil in horror or be swept off our feet by sharing the ecstasy. The division between the two extremes is so sharp and the relation between them so obvious that there is surely no need to point out the *descriptive* means Grünewald has employed in order to make certain of his effect on the spectator. The body of the crucified Christ, every square inch of which is lacerated and wounded by thorns, is painted with an insistance that is surrealist rather than pre-Raphaelite, as though the appallingly repetitive pattern of wounds were a symbol of physical suffering, cunningly disguised as a description. The crown of thorns, enlarged into a monstrous bush, could only be thought of as a symbol of unbearable torture. That translation of symbol into description is, of course, the mark of the romantic and is no different in kind from the firebox that Turner insists on placing between the buffers of the locomotive in *Rain, Steam and Speed.*

But more important than Grünewald's realistic treatment of symbols is his invention of formal devices to fit the awful intensity of his chosen mood. It is never easy and often impossible to separate formal devices from descriptive content, but Grünewald seems to have gone out of his way to give us, in the purely mathematical basis of the Crucifixion panel, the formal equivalents of emotional disturbance. A typically classic artist, tackling the same theme (Raphael's National Gallery Crucifixion, painted ten years earlier, for example) would not so much avoid such mathematical inventions as be incapable of imagining them. Where Raphael almost unconsciously eliminated the sense of pain by an emphasis on verticals and horizontals (based on the Cross itself) and absolute symmetry, Grünewald consciously suppresses them. The vertical of the Cross is hardly noticeable until it reaches the top of the panel; the horizontal is bowed. The only noticeable horizontal is the angry light in the sky above the horizon. Every emphatic element in the composition is diagonal—the arms of the Christ, the axis of the swooning Virgin and its parallel in the axis of St John who supports her, the echo in the thrown-back head of the Magdalen and the opposing thrust of her arms, the massive twisted feet of the Christ and St John the Baptist's upward pointing finger. These diagonals are certainly not prophetic of the grand, sweeping baroque diagonals of Rubens. They are stabbing, staccato diagonals invented for no other purpose than to disturb the eye, convincing proof—if proof were needed—that romantic art is based no less than classic on deliberate formal procedures. Again one could refer to Turner's ruthless diagonal that plunges down into the right-hand bottom corner of *Rain, Steam and Speed* and underlines the irresistible onrush of the express train. Symmetry, even had Grünewald desired it, is denied him by the necessity for keeping the body of Christ free from the division between the two halves of the panel, but even so there is no attempt to disguise the lack of symmetry. Grünewald has deliberately *used* the lack of balance forced upon him.

When we turn from torture to rapture (the Resurrection) and then to macabre fantasy (the two St Anthony panels) we discover again Grünewald's genius for inventing the very rhythms that will reinforce the mood.

In the Resurrection, Grünewald replaces the drama of line with a drama of light at a moment in the tradition of painting when the problem of light had hardly been considered. Indeed, only two prototypes occur to me, Piero's *Dream of Constantine* in Arezzo and Raphael's *Deliverance of St Peter* in the Vatican (1511), neither of which can have been known to Grünewald. But in the case of both the Italian artists one feels that an exceptional, self-imposed problem drove them to

Grünewald, Isenheim Altarpiece: Trees (detail)
Colmar Museum

make an exceptional study of the phenomenon of light, whereas in Grünewald's case the light is hardly a phenomenon at all. It is rather an imaginative *mode of seeing*, another instance of symbol disguised as description.

There is no need either to examine the subject-matter or the formal rhythms of the two *diableries*, 'St Anthony and St Paul' and 'St Anthony visited by Evil Spirits'. From the descriptive point of view Grünewald seems to have inherited the whole of Bosch's world of repellent fantasy without any of its whimsy, while the landscape and its flora belong to an uneasy nightmare that might have visited some fever-ridden explorer in the marshes of the Amazon. Dead and dying trees, hideously encumbered by growths of dripping moss, cut across the sky. Behind them rise impossible ranges of dream-mountains. Here is no avoidance of verticals, but again they are not used as a classic composer would use them, in order to suggest stability. In the form of the rocks they suggest inaccessibility: in the hanging weeds, darkness and decay. This is the true North European original of Tintoretto's two nocturnes in the Scuola di San Rocco. The difference between the two, though the ingredients are so similar, is extraordinary. Tintoretto's is the romanticism of moonlight and mystery that was to find its equivalent in the picturesque thrills of the Gothic revival. Grünewald's romanticism is infected by poison. The nostalgic fragrance of ruins is very different from the smell of corruption and decay.

We tend to think of Grünewald as the author of the great Crucifixion for the simple reason that we rarely see reproductions of either the radiant panels that lie behind it or the nightmare concealed behind them. Therefore we regard him as the master of symbols of suffering. But he is far more than that. In the Colmar altarpiece almost all the passionate Gothic dreams of heaven, hell, and earth find a final expression. Nothing could be more memorable and nothing could linger more uncomfortably in the memory.

All my three categories of romanticism—mystery, abnormality, and conflict—are to be found in Grünewald. His is the exact antithesis of the classic theory of art. Not one of those ingredients which we find so endearing in the art of the Italian Renaissance and High Renaissance—grace, suavity, discipline, restraint, the nobility and strength of man, the docility and friendliness of Nature—occur in his painting. None of the moods that medieval Christianity adumbrated—tension, asceticism, fear of the unknown, physical suffering in this world, fearful punishment or ineffable delight in the next—are absent from it. Far more than Dürer, who was cosmopolitan enough to have encountered, without properly assimilating, the genius of Italy, Grünewald summed up the feverish emotional excesses of a country in which romanticism was bound to flourish and had flourished in hundreds of tortured Crucifixions and ferocious martyrdoms or sentimental enthroned Madonnas

Tintoretto, St Mary of Egypt
Scuola di San Rocco, Venice

ever since its Christian inhabitants began to elaborate their own iconography. Much of the art produced by it was repulsive either in its brutality or its vulgarity, but all of it was romantic in that it shrank from nothing, avoided no excess within the range of the emotions that it wished to express.

But on the fringes of that excess, certain artists emerged in whom we recognize the less painful or embarrassing aspects of romanticism which we English—specialists in the more manageable kinds of romantic art—are apt to regard as normal. Cranach has already been mentioned as one of them. During the period we are concerned with in this chapter, one other must be referred to. I have already singled out Altdorfer as a type of artist whose romantic attitude to nature is hardly ever diluted by classic restraint on the one hand or by extrovert acceptance of the world of phenomena on the other. Altdorfer strikes us as being in a continual flutter of awed excitement at the world of forests and sunsets around him. Mankind, for Altdorfer, is dwarfed by them into insignificance.

It is by no accident that the romanticism of mystery so often finds its most powerful expression in landscape or in painting in which landscape predominates. Without the moonlit trees that hang above the saints in the two Tintoretto nocturnes, without the vista in Giorgione's *Tempestà* or the embowered backgrounds to Watteau's flirtations, there would be no possibility of expressing the excitement we always feel in everyday life in the presence of the grander or more exuberant aspects of Nature. With the exception of certain Chinese artists of the Sung period whose towering crags, fringed at the top by small fir-trees and cut off from the valley below by bands of horizontal cloud, hang threateningly above groups of small cottages and diminutive humans, no artist known to me has been so conscious of the 'humanity dwarfed by Nature' theme as Altdorfer. That claustrophobic tangle of immense trees through which St George attempts to force his way in the painting in the Munich Alte Pinakothek is far more sinister than the dragon that lies at his feet. The dense foliage thrusts itself upwards, as one looks at it, in a monstrous assemblage of Gothic rhythms. And in that other masterpiece of overstatement, the *Battle of Alexander*, all vegetation has been cleared away. The foreground is densely packed with an ant-like army of tiny humans while, in the distance, range upon range of spiky mountains recede to a remote horizon—a moon landscape savagely illuminated by a burst of light from an elliptical cavern in the clouds. This vision of a primeval world is an invention that could only have occurred in Germany. To Altdorfer it is a natural mode of

Elsheimer, Flight Into Egypt
Alte Pinakothek, Munich

self-expression, and one thinks that it could never penetrate across the Alps into Italy until one remembers a similar elliptical burst of light in the sky of Tintoretto's *St George and the Dragon* in the National Gallery in London. Yet the very similarity marks the difference between Nordic and Italian romanticism. The phenomena are the same, but the meanings are different. Altdorfer's sky is a metaphor of wrath, Tintoretto's, though no less startling, is somehow benign. Nature, in Italy, can be sublime, but rarely hostile.

The softening influence of Italy can be seen in Adam Elsheimer, who was born in Frankfurt, but early in his life (probably in his early twenties) migrated to Rome *via* Venice. Many artists from Germany and the Low Countries had made the journey before him, all with the same thought in mind, to acquire the kind of 'finishing-school' education that an artist felt he should have in the early sixteenth century. And almost all of them returned to their homes with a glossy Italian veneer, a set of superficially acquired idioms that almost prevented them from being serious artists at all. For the North European romantic tradition could only be disguised and therefore weakened by contact with Italian classicism. What Scorel, Matsys, Mabuse, Van Orley and their kind learned from their Italian journeys was little more than an artistic snobbery that drained away their natural energy and a copper-plate handwriting that disguised their true character. Classic and romantic modes of feeling are by no means mutually exclusive, but to superimpose one on the other can be fatal. Even Dürer, of all German artists the most sympathetic to classicism by virtue of his acute intelligence, had little to learn from his Venetian journeys that could enlarge his scope or his stature.

But Elsheimer, perhaps because he was lacking in the harsh assertiveness that characterized most of his predecessors, or perhaps because his migration to Rome was undertaken earlier in his life than theirs, did manage successfully to graft his own feeling for mystery on to a more genuinely balanced style and a more completely assimilated set of Italianisms. As Dürer was the first, Elsheimer was the last of his kind. One cannot feel that the balance he struck between romantic moods and classical forms produced memorable masterpieces, yet to strike a balance at all singles him out from all other North European *émigrés* to Italy and makes his work more significant as a signpost than as an achievement.

Elsheimer's mystery was a commonplace mystery based on the half-seen world of firelight or moonlight. The savagery of German art has evaporated in him and the sweetness has been diluted into something dangerously near to sentimentality—that pitfall that awaits the romantic who is deficient either in intensity of passion or discipline of form. But the formal discipline Elsheimer had absorbed after a lifetime in Rome saved him, and not only saved him but enabled him to sound a note that had never been sounded in art before, but was to be used frequently after him by more richly endowed artists than himself. Elsheimer's choice of moonlit or twilit themes is the superficial choice of the man who mistakes vagueness for mystery. But what raises him above the level of the sentimental moonlight-fancier is the gravity and dignity of his rhythms. There is, once one begins to look for it, a Germanic drama in his landscape, and nervous energy in the forms of the trees which points forward to the far greater energy of Rubens. And no Italian would have consented to fill the foreground, as Elsheimer did in *Noah's Offering* in Wiesbaden, with a group of corpses, even though no German who had not been submitted to Roman pressure would have disposed them so elegantly. One is not surprised that both Rubens and Rembrandt found Elsheimer good to steal from. His was the art of compromise in which realism based on conscientious observation and the romanticism that springs from a love of the unusual rather than the spectacular in nature were tamed and made acceptable to Italian eyes by a respectful study of the Caracci and Caravaggio. Rubens, that inspired eclectic, noted and understood Elsheimer's suave and polished drama. Rembrandt was impressed by his breadth and dignity.

Elsheimer was by no means the only successful product of a fusion between Rome and an alien temperament. He died in Rome in 1610. Ten years later Claude, who was born in Lorraine in 1600, was already painting in Rome. It is easy to say that Elsheimer was an Italianized German and Claude an Italianized Frenchman, as though that simplification somehow explained the difference between them. But it must be remembered that at the beginning of the seventeenth century Rome had become more than a magnet for artists (as Paris was to be in the late nineteenth). Rome was a centre from which radiated an attitude of mind. The Rome to which Poussin and Claude gravitated in the early seventeenth century was more potent as a civilizing influence than the Rome of twenty years earlier that had shaped Elsheimer's style. If one is attempting to separate what an artist derives, stylistically, from what is the natural expression of his temperament, there could be no better subjects for analysis than Claude and Poussin. Both painted with an unmistakable Roman accent. Both shared the classic artist's concern with balance, nobility, serenity: both indulged in grand generalizations, and neither ever permitted himself to put more trust in his observant eye than in his ordering mind. Yet as we compare them we are instantly aware of romantic overtones in Claude that are never to be found in Poussin, and of classic perfections in Poussin of which Claude was quite incapable.

The comparison, like that between Reynolds and Gainsborough, or between Turner and Constable, is one that no student of style can resist making, and perhaps everything worth saying on the subject has already been said. And yet, if romanticism is to be traced to its origin in a state of mind, there could hardly be a more rewarding subject for examination than Claude. Everything in his training, all the influences that surrounded him, seemed to drag him in a direction that he was unfitted to follow. Where Poussin was completely integrated with his artistic environment and, despite his French origin, was the noblest Roman of them all, Claude was continually at war with himself; yet the dichotomy, far from limiting his range, actually made him more expressive.

The clearest evidences of this dichotomy are provided by those drawings and sketches from Nature which invariably strike us as so 'modern' (by which we mean late nineteenth century) that they could not possibly be preparatory studies for the paintings, carefully manufactured to a theatrical formula, furnished with temples, silhouetted trees that no botanist could identify, and light-laden vistas. In the drawings the approach is quite different. They are carefully observed fragments in which accuracy of definition is often grafted on to dramatic (but never artificially dramatized) lighting. 'This is what interests me', on the one hand, and 'This is how I must please my public', on the other, hardly ever come together in the same work, yet what Claude did to please himself in the drawings manages somehow to alter, by a process of infection, the flavour of the paintings. Manufactured, as they could not fail to be in a generation and in a city obsessed by the conviction that art must be a superlative kind of manufacture, it still strikes us that their meaning for us lies in something that has nothing to do with manufacture but depends on a purely personal sentiment. Where his contemporary, Poussin, seems to have regarded Nature as raw material for picture-making—and raw material that required a good deal of reorganizing in order to make it satisfactory—Claude fell in love with certain aspects of Nature and fought hard to tell us so, even though such frankness concerning the affections was hardly considered good form in his day.

To be in love with Nature and to confess it openly is, of course, in itself romantic. Claude's sunsets and his skies that pour their light down on the middle distance (the foreground, of course, had to be sacrosanct, being devoted to 'incidents' or mythologies), his insistence that we can, if we wish, explore and enjoy the landscape he has created for us—these are the romantic elements in his art. A landscape by Poussin rarely produces this effect on us. The air in it is not breathable; faultlessly constructed though it is, it never occurs to us to plan a walking-tour in it. Its very formal perfection prevents us from regarding his world as habitable or enjoyable.

But Italian lyricism and German alternations between cruelty and rapture are not the only kinds of romanticism that must be noted in this account of the romanticism of mystery. One great artist in particular explored a romantic aspect of human experience that would have been equally unacceptable in his day in both countries. El Greco's contribution to the vocabulary of romantic art was unheralded. To watch its development from his early rather clumsy handling of Venetian mannerisms, through the even clumsier attempts to catch some of Michelangelo's muscular grandeur, to his final discovery in Toledo of new modes of expression that no Italian could have admired, is as thrilling an experience to watch as Turner's slow invasion of form by light. It is also a similar kind of transition. As with Turner, one can follow, stage by stage, the evolution of a new language, and in one or two well-known instances El Greco has left behind several versions, painted at widely separated intervals, of the same picture, so that we can actually note those shifts of emphasis, those eliminations of what he had acquired in Italy and introductions of what he invented in Spain.

The most revealing of these sets of milestones in his stylistic journey is to be found in the several versions of the *Purification of the Temple*. They range in date from just after 1570, when he was probably in Rome, though he had still not shaken off the influence of Venice, to about 1605, when he had been living in Toledo for more than twenty years. In the interval between the first and last the change is so complex and fundamental as to amount to a change of heart as well as of style, the most noticeable symptom of which (again, note the parallel with Turner) is a gradual disintegration of solid forms. What had once been flesh becomes flame, what had once moved solidly on the earth loses its weight, and not only its weight but its physical substance. In the earlier versions El Greco, like the Venetians whose vision he had absorbed, had been acutely conscious of the material world and especially of the rich variety of its textures. Flesh and velvet, marble and satin, are carefully differentiated. So are men and women. Here was a subject that solely concerned the world of men—traders and disciples—yet Venice with her special sense of feminine beauty persuaded El Greco not only to introduce three women into each of the earlier versions (the Cook Collection, *c.* 1570, and the Minneapolis Institute of Arts, *c.* 1575), but to emphasize their sex by the usual Venetian devices of exposed bosoms and falling drapery. The architectural setting is insistently Venetian—polished marble columns and pavements, an archway opening on to a piazza, through which one is conscious of the elaborate façade of an arcaded palace and a sky filled with the kind of clouds that would have appealed to Constable.

In the later versions (National Gallery, London, *c.* 1600, and the Church of the Sacraments at St Ginés, Madrid, *c.* 1605) women still appear at the sides, but they, like the men, are almost sexless. Velvet and satin are no longer differentiated, the marble columns are now a mere excuse for introducing a set of vertical stresses, and the piazza seen through the archway is ghostly. In the National Gallery version the patterned pavement has disappeared, and in the St Ginés version the architectural background has lost all its solidity and most of its space. With each stage in the development the traders and disciples progressively lose their individuality and humanity and take on the appearance of abstract lines of force; on the right the traders' limbs set up a sequence of toppling diagonals. In the centre the vertical figure of Christ, energetically twisted as he whirled the flail round his head, suggests a crimson flame.

During the last decade of his life (he died in 1614) the dematerialization of the physical world progresses to an extraordinary point. Flesh becomes lambent, drapery and cloud become indistinguishable, the law of gravity is replaced by a law of levitation. In the *Baptism* of 1608 (Hospital of St John the Baptist, Toledo) there is nothing in the whole crowded canvas that could offer a resistance to the sense of touch. Limbs and clouds have finally merged into each other, just as in the last works of Turner mountains and trees have been swallowed up by light and have lost their identity.

If the secret of the romanticism of mystery lies in the substitution of the imagined equivalent for the seen object, then El Greco and Turner pushed the method to its extreme. It was, of course, inevitable that early seventeenth-century Spain should be thinking in terms of theology and mid-nineteenth-century England in terms of pantheism, and that while El Greco was denying the solidity of man Turner should be denying the solidity of mountains. The difference lies in an attitude to religion. Temperamentally the resemblance is striking. Once, in the *View of Toledo* of 1609 (Metropolitan Museum, New York), El Greco attempted to effect the same miraculous transformation on a landscape that he had so often performed on religious themes: and on several occasions (for example, the Cincinnati *Crucifixion* of *c.* 1605) he used a landscape background as an integral part of his spiritual message. In the whole of graphic art there is nothing with which one can compare the *View of Toledo*. Yet when one tries to analyse the overpowering romanticism of El Greco's later paintings on Christian themes, the *View of Toledo* supplies suggestive evidence.

Every artist must build on foundations borrowed from other artists. And when El Greco found that, as time went on, the foundations provided by Michelangelo, Titian, and Tintoretto were becoming more and more useless to him, there was nothing he could do but revive the artistic memories of his youth and the Byzantine traditions that surrounded him in his native island of Crete.

Art historians have examined El Greco's work in detail, searching

El Greco, View of Toledo
Metropolitan Museum of Art, New York
Bequest of Mrs H. O. Havemeyer, 1929. The H. O. Havemeyer Collection

in it for Byzantine derivations. The search is a sensible one, but only an acute instinct for the true meaning of the word 'style' could make it rewarding. Occasionally, as in the *Mount Sinai* in Budapest, an early work, he actually used Byzantine imagery, and the *Dream of Philip II* looks like a Byzantine composition. But the strong Byzantine flavour of the *Toledo* does not depend on mannerisms or compositional tricks but on a mystical attitude of mind, on the same will to transform rather than to interpret that marks all his later painting. The city he has painted is, I am told, recognizably Toledo, just as the background of Giorgione's *Tempestà* is recognizably a corner of the Veneto. But both belong to the dream world—a world of lurid light and sinister skies. Giorgione's storm is a gentle one while El Greco's is terrifying, and terrifying in a Byzantine way. Even though the artist does not borrow the Byzantine conventions for mountains, trees, and palaces, yet there is the same effect of having painted with closed eyes and of being guided by an unusually intense vision based on feeling rather than memory.

El Greco furnishes a fitting climax to this chapter. The *Toledo* is probably the most remarkable example in existence of what I have been attempting to describe, namely the romantic temperament contriving to express itself just when one would least expect it. The love of mystery in periods when men were asking for and applauding clarity can be detected in almost every country in Europe (though one searches for it in vain on Flemish soil, where romanticism existed but took other forms), but no outbreak of it was more dramatic than that invented by El Greco at the very end of the period under review and in the very country that one would have expected to be least sympathetic to it. Perhaps this Cretan boy, after serving his apprenticeship in Italy, had a sudden moment of enlightenment and realized that Venice and Rome were softening the natural toughness of his fibre and that if he were to escape and become a free man he must journey, geographically, on to Madrid and, spiritually, back to Crete.

CHAPTER 6

The Romanticism of Mystery—The Nineteenth Century

Those gentle references to a nostalgic dream-world that first appear in Piero di Cosimo and Giorgione are certainly not the qualities that ushered in what we now agree to call the Romantic Age. Nostalgia played its part, but gentleness was not what appealed to the eighteenth-century devotees of the picturesque and especially the picturesque in Nature. The flash of lightning that occupies the centre of Giorgione's *Tempestà* contains no menance. The soldier and the girl are not only not alarmed by it: they are not even consciously aware of it.

That same flash of lightning, when it occurs in the last quarter of the eighteenth century, is no longer a dream. It is a threat. It is a symbol of a new relationship between Man and Nature which was to become commonplace enough in the early years of the following century, but which, when it was first experienced, seemed to deserve a new name. According to the intensity with which the hostility of Nature was stated, it could be either 'picturesque' or 'sublime'. In both cases the intention was the same. Its purpose was to point out that Man was sensitive and civilized, Nature unruly and untamed. What man had created Nature could destroy. But whereas the earlier half of the century had regarded such destruction as in every way undesirable and disgusting, the new romantic attitude began to find it impressive and, given the correct, the sensitive attitude to it, admirable. Ruins, once mere evidence of Nature's inconvenient habit of destroying Man's handiwork, now became eloquent symbols of the struggle between unspoiled beauty and the eroding hand of time. Struggle implied drama, and drama itself was a theme that deserved cultivating. Ruins could be, it was discovered, more eloquent than neat perfection, provided one looked at them in the correct way. And even there, Nature could help by adding her own mystery to the mystery of decay. 'If thou would'st visit Melrose *aright*, go visit her by the pale moonlight.'

Not only were ruins effective in themselves, but moonlight, for

Scott, could make them more so. But the operative word in Scott's lines is, surely, 'visit'. The spirit of Baedeker is creeping in. Melrose has changed from a once-flourishing but now useless Abbey to a place of pilgrimage to be 'visited', and visited *'aright'*. And the true object of the visit is to extract the maximum thrill from the experience.

The 'picturesque', by its very nature, preceded the 'sublime': since the 'sublime' was hardly more than an intensification of the picturesque. The thrill, as the movement developed, demanded stronger and stronger doses of the drama of Man versus Nature, until, at last, the appetite for horrific sublimity became jaded. And once that happens, as will be seen in the next chapter, romanticism ceases to be seriously concerned with mystery and transfers its attention to the abnormal: and in doing so tends to become decreasingly the expression of a sensitive mind and increasingly the description of a surprising scene or situation, until we reach the extremes of John Martin's melodrama, which, as will be seen, has doubtful claims to be called romanticism at all.

But when an age of reason is attempting to turn itself into an age of sensibility (and despite the clichés enshrined in the two phrases, that is not a misleading summing up of the situation at the time when the word 'romantic' first came into use) its very reasonableness forces it to analyse and codify. The 'picturesque' must be defined. Rules must be laid down and followed: signposts must be erected warning the artist against the vulgar errors that will ruin him as a practitioner of the picturesque. The 'sublime' itself must also be analysed and codified, and Burke's essay on the nature of the sublime is one of the most neatly categorized examples of aesthetic analysis that the English eighteenth century produced.

What Gilpin did in his written instructions for producing the picturesque is, perhaps, less intelligent, but equally precise. One imagines these authors, seated at their perfectly proportioned desks in their faultlessly and tastefully decorated rooms, reasonably inventing rules for producing exactly what was missing from their beautifully calculated environments—pleading for the introduction of roughness, of impulsiveness, of asymmetry, of power. If rules could produce suavity and perfection, then surely rules could equally produce the appeal of the rugged and the thrill of the powerful—in fact, of the unruly.

The movement was not only an English one, and in so far as its favourite theme was that of Nature versus Man, with ruined architecture as the symbol of the conflict between Man the builder and Time the destroyer, some of the most impressive products were almost bound to come from Italy, and especially from Rome, where ruins

Piranesi, Carceri
R.I.B.A. Library, London

abounded on a far more lavish scale than elsewhere in Europe. Gilpin had to seek them out or invent them, and his inventions often lacked conviction. He had to bolster them up with scenery and sunsets. But Piranesi, surrounded by a wealth of authentic specimens, had only to make subtle slight alterations of emphasis in order to produce the desired effect. In Rome man was at odds not so much with Nature as with his own half-forgotten past. What was left of Imperial Rome dwarfed all succeeding ages, and all Piranesi needed to do in order to make Man seem a puny animal was to underline the titanic grandeur of the Colosseum or the Baths of Caracalla, to exaggerate the symptoms of decay, the crumbling cornices, the vegetation springing from joints between huge blocks of stone, to create a general sense of oppressive height and weight and then (this was essential) to introduce absurdly small figures to give added scale, sometimes gazing up in awe, sometimes dizzily perched half-way up, peering downwards in vertiginous fear.

Having established his formula for this kind of drama, Piranesi then carried it farther by inventing a kind of architecture that even Rome could not supply. His fantasies on the theme of prisons open up a new vein of picturesque sublimity, in which man crawls helplessly up and down gigantic staircases, under overhanging vaults, among colossal sculptures and dark abysses that enclose him. No one has carried the terror of sheer bigness farther than he. The 'Carceri' etchings are the visual equivalents of the kind of literature that deals in shadowy dungeons and rattling chains and distant muffled cries of distress.

Again, as with Gilpin and Burke, it is not surprising that these frontal attacks on our emotions should come from a man who was in close touch with the kind of smooth, sophisticated seemliness in which the Adam brothers specialized. Piranesi was linked with Robert Adam by ties of friendship and admiration. He dedicated his great series of etchings to him. It was as though Berlioz had dedicated his *Symphonie Fantastique* to Mendelssohn.

Evidently this desire to be a little alarmed and overwhelmed in an age that had so successfully kept fear at arm's length and had specialized so deliberately in the smooth, the orderly, and the unemphatic, was something so new that the mechanism of alarm itself needed organizing.

But, in the end, this self-consciously cultivated attitude which regarded Nature merely as an effective foil to Man, and in particular to civilized Man, was bound to become unsatisfactory. It reduced Nature herself to a series of effective clichés and actually threatened to become a barrier to the more sympathetic and intimate study of landscape on which the later phases of romantic landscape were based and which was to reach its climax in Turner's maturity.

Turner himself, in his precocious youth, might easily have succumbed to it, for his first introduction to landscape painting was through the watercolours of J. R. Cozens, and had he not possessed an acutely observant eye and an even more acute artistic conscience he might have used Cozens as Piranesi used Roman ruins, as a basis for dramatic exaggerations. Instead of that he imposed on himself a strict topographer's discipline. One day, doubtless, he would travel to Italy and see for himself what Cozens had shown him at second-hand. Meanwhile England awaited his attention, and though of course it was the more picturesque aspects of England that caught his eye (and that would prove saleable when translated into watercolour drawings), once they had done so he set himself doggedly to describe the facts rather than underline the sentiment.

In examining Turner's progress from picturesque topography to the extreme of romantic mystery it will be useful to compare him briefly

Blake, Pity

Reproduced by courtesy of the Directors of the Tate Gallery, London

with William Blake, for though no two artists could be divided by a wider or deeper temperamental gap, both carried the romanticism of mystery, or mysticism, as far as it could be taken.

Blake's explosive comments on Sir Joshua Reynolds and his plea for 'minute articulation' as the proper language for the visual imagination: his protests against the 'blots and blurs' of the artist who made himself the victim of natural appearances—all this seems to be contradicted by Turner's minute articulation in his early non-imaginative attempts to describe natural appearances. And if Blake had lived long enough, he would have noted that the more completely Turner was able to release his visual imagination the more he indulged in what Blake had in mind when he used the words 'blots and blurs'. The two artists could never, despite the common factor of their romanticism, have understood each other.

Blake's method was that of the humanist. It was precisely that of Homer, whose images are equally minutely articulated. Homer's invariable description of dawn, 'rosy-fingered', is the description of a poet who can only describe by personifying. One can easily imagine Blake translating Homer into visual terms and drawing a rosy-fingered maiden when he *meant* dawn, just as he translated Shakespeare literally by drawing a naked, new-born babe when he *meant* pity, and the language of the Book of Job by drawing a chorus of angels when he *meant* the song of the morning stars.

All these mysterious meanings were equally within the range of the aged Turner, yet personification was the last method he would have thought of employing. For Turner was not a mystic but a pantheist. A mystic is one who reduces the world beyond the senses to human terms. A pantheist is one who loses his humanity by identifying himself with the forces of Nature and becoming the wave, the thunderstorm, the sunrise. Both translate the seen into the unseen by inventing a kind of visual metaphor, but neither artist would have understood the process by which the other arrived at his metaphors.

To Blake, 'blots and blurs', which he detested, would have been equally descriptive of the pictures Turner was to paint after his death and to the pictures Monet was to paint half a century later still. Blake and Holbein could be equally precise, Turner and Monet equally vague, yet Holbein and Monet are brothers when it comes to a patient exploration of the phenomenal world. Blake and Turner would have argued that the world of phenomena was, to them, no more than a starting-point on a journey. For Monet and Holbein the journey itself, had they understood its direction, would have seemed meaningless. For them, the problem of the unseen did not exist, the language of metaphor was useless.

But if Turner's later work was not, in Blake's sense, 'minutely articulated', it is certainly not because he was deliberately evolving a romanticism based on vagueness. He was groping for a set of 'equivalents' that happened to be, in their own right, mysterious.

The most cursory examination of Turner's gradual development from those early tinted topographical drawings, so consummately skilful in their handling of line, to the last opalescent films of colour in which line plays no part at all, makes it clear that what he was attempting throughout his life was not so much a gradual shift of emphasis from line to colour as a gradual relinquishing of the seen object in favour of the intensely felt experience. It was one of the most adventurous journeys ever undertaken by an artist, and only by moving slowly, step by groping step, throughout a long life of incessant experiment could he hope to succeed in making his final discoveries. They are so confident that we now have no difficulty in interpreting them—though they must have been quite inscrutable at the time—and so ultimate that no artist has ever found it possible to build on them or to carry Turner's method a stage farther. There are plenty of stories of Turner frantically attempting to get closer—physically closer—to Nature at moments when he felt passionately drawn to her. His insistence on being lashed to a mast in a storm at sea or on thrusting his head out of the window of an express train during a heavy shower. Partly, of course, these were attempts to stock a retentive visual memory with images of violent or momentary effects. But basically they were the efforts of a lover to come closer to his beloved, to identify himself with wind and wave and the cloud rack. Turner's attitude to Nature is remarkably close to that of the Psalms. 'These see the works of the Lord and his wonders in the deep, for he commandeth and raiseth the stormy wind which lifteth up the waves thereof. They mount up to the heaven, they go down again to the depths, they reel to and fro, and stagger like a drunken man and are at their wit's end.'

It is characteristic of the Psalmist's own romanticism that in his description one can hardly distinguish between the storm itself and his own experience of it. Is it the waves themselves or the man who observes them who staggers and is at his wit's end? The passage could easily be a description of one of Turner's storms in which one is equally in doubt as to whether it is Nature or Man, pantheistically identifying himself with Nature, who resembles a drunken man. What one does note is the mysterious process as Turner grew older, whereby the record of Nature's behaviour is gradually replaced by an equally eloquent record of Man's reaction to Nature. Therein lies the essence of an artist's progress towards the romantic. In Turner's *Shipwreck* of 1805 the waves are 'minutely articulated', even though it is their weight and power rather than their forms that remain in the memory: in his *Rough Sea* (National Gallery, London, Cat. No. 1980, once catalogued as *Storm off a Rocky Coast*) of *c.* 1840, articulation has almost disappeared, and we are given something that could not easily be called a 'record'. The waves, like the Psalmist's, are caught up into a rhythm in which they 'mount up to the heaven' and become indistinguishable from the piled-up cumulus clouds above them and the sunlit headland behind them. In the famous *Interior at Petworth* the violence that had once been a specific attribute of the sea becomes a general attribute of Nature herself, so that it is now the room that reels and staggers under the impact of the light that furiously invades it and the furniture that mounts up to the heavens.

Turner, Rough Sea

Reproduced by courtesy of the Directors of the Tate Gallery, London

Turner must stand as an example of the extreme limit that an artist can reach in the mystery of this orgasmic union between Man and the world he lives in. In his case we tend to mistrust such extremism, mistaking it for an obsession with the spectacular or the melodramatic. But it is unfair to him to think of him as a melodramatist. He is, on the contrary, prepared to accept and to glorify any mood that Nature is capable of offering to him. Like the Psalmist he can suddenly make 'the storm a calm', so that 'the waves thereof are still . . . so he bringeth them unto their desired haven'. It would be equally easy to compare the 'articulated' tranquillity of the *Frosty Morning* of 1813 with the *opalescent* tranquillity of *San Benedetto: looking towards Fusina* of 1843. In an intermediate masterpiece of tranquillity, the famous *Fighting Téméraire* of 1838, one sees an example of Turner's deliberate shift from description to 'equivalent'. The *Téméraire's* rigging is apparently faultlessly articulated, while, as the catalogue (1946) remarks, 'The construction of the tug is indefensible.' Yet Turner was, throughout his life, unusually knowledgeable about the construction of ships. In the same spirit of romantic defiance he placed the firebox of the express train in *Rain, Steam and Speed* (1844) between the buffers of the locomotive.

Blake lived, in fact, at a moment when the pantheistic vision of Turner had not yet become acceptable. Looking back at the growth of nineteenth-century romanticism, one can see how that growth was fostered by the great men who gave it its direction, in particular Wordsworth and Turner. Nothing could have altered their temperamental reactions to the world that so excited and stimulated them, yet the form in which they expressed their excitement was imposed on them by their period. It was lucky for them that they lived at a moment when the imposed form and the personal message fitted each other so admirably. Blake had no such good fortune. Whereas Turner achieved early and widespread popularity, Blake lived, for the most part, unadmired and misunderstood, for his was a period of conscientious neo-classicism. In France his exact contemporary was David, in England Flaxman. And while David rarely attempted to use the neo-classic vocabulary for anything but purely classical ends, and his follower, Ingres, mistook romantic subject-matter for the romantic attitude: and

Turner, Interior at Petworth
National Gallery, London

Turner, Rain, Steam and Speed
National Gallery, London

while Flaxman's nerveless purity of line merely succeeded in reducing the poetry of his chosen themes to inexpressive prose, Blake alone had the genius to use classic form for romantic purposes without seeming to contradict himself or to find himself in difficulties.

It took Turner a long lifetime to solve the problem of translating fact into sentiment by discovering the visual metaphor that would exactly convey sentiment. It was a problem that could only be solved by identifying himself more and more completely with the forces of Nature. In the end, it was, of course, still impossible to abandon fact entirely. Venice was still a city of campaniles and domes rising out of the water; the chain of the Alps was still a long structure with its own solid geological anatomy; and Norham Castle, a blue mass emerging from a bath of golden light, was still, just recognizably, Norham Castle. Pantheism must be linked with the observed world, but the observed world, for the pantheist, gradually becomes a series of grand generalizations. What, in earlier life, had been for Turner a description of a specific shipwreck or the conflagration of the Houses of Parliament became, in the end, a statement in lyrical terms about the power of wind and water or the consuming nature of flame. Turner worked his way, through the most rigorous discipline, to the concentrated essence of the sublime and the picturesque. He discovered by sheer unremitting study what Gilpin and Burke had treated as a kind of mathematical formula.

This was exactly what Ruskin succeeded in showing in those laborious but eloquent passages in *Modern Painters* that deal with the quintessential 'truth' of Turner's mystery. Ruskin was right. Anyone who has attempted to copy one of Turner's opalescent late water-colours will have discovered that they are not merely effective essays in the mysterious but that every faint gradation of tone is a translation of a corresponding gradation in Nature, seized and remembered twenty years earlier, digested and ultimately given lyric form. Ruskin, himself a romantic, took immense pains to prove that Turner was, at heart, a realist in order to explain his genius to the British public. The British public was in no mood for such explanations. They were avid for what lay on the surface of Turner's most effective paintings. Towering Alps, dreaming campaniles, doomed battleships towed down the Thames against the crimson glory of the dying day—all the easily understood paraphernalia of romanticism was there, and the appetite for them was exactly what Turner could satisfy. He became rich and successful—a purveyor of sentimental thrills. He could hardly fail to be elected a Royal Academician at twenty-seven and to have left a sizeable fortune behind at his death. What was vulgar in Turner (and there was much) ensured his success. What was the result of self-discipline and genius is only now beginning to be understood. He 'cashed in' on the romantic craze. He was the supreme example of the genius who appeared at the exact moment to make him fashionable, and, like all modish artists, he easily became unfashionable as soon as the pendulum of fashion began to swing back.

Turner had arrived at the culminating point of romantic mystery by self-discipline. Constable's equipment was simpler. It consisted almost entirely of love. The notion of evolving a pictorial language of metaphor would have been positively repellent to him. For him, the process of translating what he observed and loved into paint needed no help from metaphor. His power as an artist depended entirely on his capacity to observe and to love what had hardly been seen by human eye before him. Consequently his value for us is not that of using an existing language superbly but of forging a new language. Turner, the fashionable painter, had been welcomed into the Academy in his late twenties. Constable was forty-three when he was elected A.R.A. Full membership came ten years later—the usual time-lag for an innovator.

Constable's eye was his master and he, for all his love, was its devoted slave. Basically he belongs to the extrovert family. Nothing in his painting is transformed even when his vision is at its most intense. If Constable had treated Nature as Turner did or even as Rubens did, filling it with a mystery or an exuberance which lie beyond what the eye can see, he would have regarded himself as having betrayed the true purpose of painting. The muscular energy of Rubens's trees, the impression of rising sap and bursting energy, must have seemed to Constable an unnecessarily exaggerated display of temperament.

I have never been able to detect, even in the most impulsive or the most private of Constable's sketches, a trace of what I regard as romanticism. He is a rebel, but a rebel in a romantic period, protesting against romanticism itself, rejecting not only its language but its very purpose. When he said 'There is still room for a natural painter' and when he inscribed the time of day and the state of the weather on the back of his sketches he was protesting against the artificiality that had crept into landscape painting. He saw himself as what he, in fact, was—a rediscoverer of the visible world in general and the first discoverer of aspects of it that had escaped the eyes of all his predecessors. That he observed Nature in a state of excitement, and only hesitated to express that excitement when he was producing pictures for public exhibition, is not a sign of romantic vision. Excitement is the motive force for every artist, for Raphael and Velasquez no less than for Van Gogh. Constable's excitement was that of the man who has dared to discover truth and regards his discovery as an end in itself. It was no different in kind from that of the Impressionists, who were conscious of having done the same. It is not to be wondered at that Constable could speak to the Impressionists in a language that they could easily understand. Constable catches not the essence but the 'effect' of light, and however affectionately he may observe it he cannot sing. Nor would he have been at all dismayed at being told so. The man who could say 'There is still room for a natural painter' could hardly think of himself as expressing himself in song. Turner could not help doing so, and though Turner's romantic preoccupation with the forces of Nature led him to produce painterly effects that Monet could admire, there is little doubt that he admired them for the wrong reason.

The anti-romantic revolution inaugurated by Constable was not an isolated phenomenon. Inevitably a reaction set in at the moment when the romantic attitude to landscape was at its height. Constable's 'There is still room for a natural painter' was a protest against a habit of mind that had come to regard the art of painting as the art of impressing the mind by astonishing the eye. In his pursuit of the impressive in all its aspects Turner had found it necessary to travel incessantly across Europe in search of the best specimens he could find of mountain ranges and ancient cities. Constable could discover within a few miles of his East Anglian home enough subject-matter to supply him with a lifetime of work. Any enlargement of his field of research would merely have embarrassed him. One feels that when he turns his attention briefly to Salisbury Cathedral he is betraying a self-imposed trust, and, in doing so, slipping into picturesque or sentimental attitudes.

In France, a decade later, the same plea—'There is still room for a natural painter'—was uttered by Courbet, but in a more defiant and rhetorical tone of voice. And he, like Constable, belonged to his native village, in Franche Comté.

Unlike Constable, however, he found it necessary to indulge in defiant polemics. It was not enough for him to declare his love of the countryside at his door and leave the rest to his painter's instinct. When he declared that a painter's business was with the seen and not with the imagined he was, like so many French artists, putting theory before practice. And his theory of realism left out of account the fact that seeing is more than an optical process, especially where human situations are concerned. When he was looking at the meadows and woods and little limestone cliffs near Ornans, his eye was as honest though not as affectionate as Constable's, but the moment he introduced the human element romantic overtones at once appeared, and they almost invariably reveal the braggart, the country bumpkin, and the orator. In his monster studio allegory he and his model take the centre of the stage. He attacks his canvas with the gesture of a conductor about to guide an orchestra through the intricacies of the *Pastoral Symphony*, utterly confident of his own powers but doubtful as to what his players and his audience will make of him. There is more humility in the great *Funeral at Ornans*, but even here there is too obvious an emphasis on the rough dignity of the peasant and the callous professionalism of the priesthood. Velasquez would not have allowed himself such partisanship and Courbet's 'realism' would have been more honest if he had possessed more of Velasquez's detachment.

Detachment, however, in the second half of the nineteenth century was hardly to be expected. Landscape painting could just manage to achieve it because the old Man-versus-Nature theme had gradually exhausted itself, and the combined efforts of Constable, Courbet, the Barbizon painters and, finally, the Impressionists had at last discovered that Nature was neither amiable nor hostile but merely a complex of phenomena infinitely worth studying by a painter with a studiously objective eye.

But for the figure painter the overtones of romantic sentiment could less easily be banished. Man was too closely and too emotionally involved with his kind to achieve objectivity. In figure painting an

Courbet, The Painter in his Studio (detail)
Louvre, Paris

exhausted and effete romanticism lingered on in the academies, especially of France and England. It was the product of the literary mind of the romantic era and the extrovert eye of the realist revolution: and because of the contradiction between eye and mind it was practically worthless except as illustration to literary themes.

Only one group of painters, the Pre-Raphaelites in England, managed, by sheer intensity, and then only for less than a decade, to infuse into what they regarded as a realistic method a set of romantic intentions so vivid that they deserve a chapter to themselves.

CHAPTER 7

The Pre-Raphaelite Brotherhood

What the English Pre-Raphaelites did, in 1849, was something that had often been done in France, but it had never happened in England before. 'Brotherhood' is not a word that occurs easily in the history of British art: and to formulate an artistic creed before putting it into practice is not an English habit. None the less, the Pre-Raphaelites did formulate a creed and, in doing so, inaugurated an '-ism'.

The Pre-Raphaelites' ideal was, as it turned out, so antipathetic to the Latin and the Teutonic temperaments that their art has proved unexportable. The brotherhood was selfconsciously rebellious in a cause that was puzzling enough to their English contemporaries. To the rest of the continent of Europe it was either incomprehensible or so irrelevant to what were regarded as the central problems of art in the mid-nineteenth century as to seem not worth comprehending.

Much has been written about the formulation of the brotherhood. The three young men in their twenties who met to stimulate each other's latent enthusiasms and to discuss what was wrong with the art of their contemporaries were utterly different in temperament and, in general, dissimilar in their aims. What united them and gave them a common objective was their disgusts. Rossetti, the poet, son of an Italian political refugee, was an unskilful painter, but kept the enthusiasm of his friends at boiling-point. Millais, precocious, and in his earliest youth inflammable, was to paint the handful of pictures that burn, for us, with the clearest Pre-Raphaelite flame. Holman Hunt, dogged and persevering, became the self-appointed keeper of the group's artistic conscience. Madox Brown, older and already a painter, gravitated towards the brotherhood a year or two later, but, by an odd kind of osmosis, seemed to catch their spirit and grasp their intentions without having taken any part in the formulation of them.

These intentions were never stated with any precision. Any attempt to put them into words today, more than a century after their key pictures were painted, cannot fail to sound both vague and negative. Yet the results were both positive and precise. The British genius, in fact, worked through them in its usual way. They knew exactly what they wished to avoid, but never succeeded in stating logically what they wished to achieve. Yet their achievements, during the decade in which their creative powers were working freely, were utterly original and completely self-confident. What they achieved depended less on a programme or a creed than on a mysterious chemical process dependent on the heat of the crucible in which their art was produced.

The negative programme of Pre-Raphaelitism is clear enough. It is implicit in the title they chose for themselves. Raphael was, if not the arch-villain, at least the ultimate cause of a decline. He had betrayed the very purpose of art by putting beauty before truth. It was Raphael who had taken all character and meaning out of painting by insisting that countenances should be pleasing rather than expressive, gestures suave, meaning submerged by presentation, the world of observed phenomena replaced by a world of conventional formulae. This primrose path, it seemed to them, had been followed since Raphael's time until a point had been reached in which art had become nothing but false sentiment expressed in a language of conventional patterns.

It was necessary, therefore, for the young revolutionaries to do two things if art were to be restored to its pristine vigour and honesty. Firstly, it was essential to turn the clock back to a moment (they were not quite sure which moment) before Raphael had begun to undermine vigour and discard honesty—to rediscover, in fact, the true painter's language by seeing the world with fresh, innocent eyes, 'selecting nothing and rejecting nothing', as Ruskin was to put it in a much-quoted phrase. Secondly, the new language must be made to serve a a serious purpose—for it would be absurd to paint every vein on the ivy leaf if the result were to be nothing but the slavish imitation of a seen object. Nothing less than the restoration of a style that Raphael had destroyed and of the subject-matter that Raphael had treated as unimportant would do. It was a programme that asked for complete self-dedication and the strictest discipline and integrity. Millais, as it turned out, was to find it too exacting: tempted by his own facility as a painter and betrayed by his own lack of stamina, he gradually began to follow the very primrose path he had at first condemned. Holman Hunt continued to use the language, but lost the power to use it vividly. Rossetti soon discovered that a language that forbade selection and rejection was useless to a dreamer and a poet. Madox Brown alone continued to combine stamina with integrity. The first phase of a movement that began with such bright, untarnished resolves had lost its impetus within a decade. The products of that decade can now be seen as a telescoped version of the familiar progress from sharply focused innocence through sophistication to decay. It had happened in Florence between the first experiments of Fra Angelico and the last of Andrea del Sarto, and it had taken a century to happen. With the Pre-Raphaelites the same process occupied ten years. During that period keenness of eye, patience of craftsmanship and seriousness of purpose all dwindled; the self-imposed strain was too great. Yet a dozen masterpieces remained that, because they are unique, deserve a chapter in any survey of romanticism in painting.

The paradox of the Pre-Raphaelite purpose is that what they conceived to be a blow struck in favour of realism turned out to be, itself, romantic in intention. No Pre-Raphaelite could have said, with Constable, 'There is still room for a natural painter': no Pre-Raphaelite would have considered that Courbet's 'Paint only what you can see, not what you can imagine' was a programme worth announcing. Yet more than anything else they were determined to be natural: and though imagination was, for them, the grand highway to truth, they were determined to paint what they imagined as though it had been seen, and seen with a clarity that perhaps only Van Eyck and his followers had achieved in the past. Even Van Eyck, despite his infinite patience of hand and precision of eye, was not quite honest. Even he was the slave of certain conventions inherited from the medieval world. Flemish draperies, for example, fell into prearranged folds: gestures had not the odd spontaneity that was characteristic of real human beings acting under the stress of an imagined situation. Flemish primitives, in fact, had still, for all their meticulousness, not quite reached the truth. They lacked, in particular, a certain immediacy.

It is not easy for the mid-twentieth century to see 'primitive' art through the eyes of the mid-nineteenth. For us the word has almost ceased to have a meaning. But the model chosen—almost by accident—by the young Pre-Raphaelites was not Van Eyck but Gozzoli—the Gozzoli of the Campo Santo frescoes at Pisa; and even he reached the young men through the medium of mid-Victorian engravings. None the less they saw in him, at once, a certain freshness, even a certain *gaucherie*, an awkward animation that was not to be found in Van Eyck or Rogier van der Weyden. Here was no concession to traditional convention and, more important, no desire to substitute 'grace' for 'meaning' or sweetness for vigour.

In the earliest of the Pre-Raphaelite pictures, therefore, it is not difficult to find an almost deliberate search for the quaint or awkward gesture—provided it could be also a possible, meaningful gesture—and a Gothic stiffness, as though their purpose was to contradict rather than to ante-date Raphael.

To turn the clock back, to rebel against current traditions, especially if they led to a cloying sweetness—these are typically romantic atti-

Holman Hunt, Claudio and Isabella

Reproduced by courtesy of the Directors of the Tate Gallery, London

tudes, even though they were struck by self-confessed realists. But they were also defiant realists. The truth they insisted on presenting was always, at first, a truth that they knew would be startling and unacceptable. When Holman Hunt invented Claudio's nervous plucking at the manacle round his ankle as Isabella lays her tense, stiff fingers on his breast in her appeal to his honour, he selected not only the most eloquent but also the most ungraceful gestures his dramatic imagination could offer. The same eloquent *gaucherie* inspired Millais to emphasize the vicious tension of the leg and thigh with which Isabella's brother launches a fierce kick at the greyhound in *Lorenzo and Isabella*. Rossetti, taking his sister Christina as his model in his *Annunciation* (of 1849), makes her curl up awkwardly like a frightened, sulky schoolgirl on the dormitory bed. Millais's *Blind Girl* achieves a romantic intensity by the

Rossetti, Annunciation
Reproduced by courtesy of the Directors of the Tate Gallery, London

very fact that she behaves as a blind girl *would* behave, fingering a blade of grass to reassure herself of its material reality, lifting her face to the sun, while her little companion, who could so easily have wrecked the picture's honesty by being presented as a guardian angel, wears a tattered dress and has obviously borrowed her elder brother's boots.

These pervasive tensions—the result of close observation linked with a courageous Browningesque toughness—produce a cumulative effect that makes the words 'truth' or 'realism' inadequate. It was not the realistic Browning but the nostalgic Keats and Tennyson that inspired the early pictures. Later, for Rossetti, it was Dante.

The essence of Keats, and, for that matter, the essence of Tennyson's *Idylls of the King*, was the ardent pursuit of a dream, which is one at least of the essences of the romanticism of mystery. And the Pre-Raphaelites, in their effort to make nostalgia as vivid as they could, chose the language of what they conceived to be realism. Madox Brown's *Work*, in intention an allegory, is an accurate account of road-mending in Well Walk, Hampstead; seated at the table in Millais's *Lorenzo and Isabella* are Millais's own friends, painted with the firm control of a Holbein, but, unlike Holbein's characters, caught up in a drama that dictates their attitudes and expressions. The method—that of making their dream-world more real than the world they were compelled to live in—is exactly that of the Surrealists, but it was carried out with far stricter honesty. Surrealism, for all its superficial photographic verisimilitude, falls back on stage formulae for arresting the attention. The Pre-Raphaelites, by adding an almost breathless reverence to their basic nostalgia, and by identifying themselves, imaginatively, with the tensions in which their characters are invariably involved, made painterly formulae useless.

It was not until the first intense impulse had exhausted itself—or, to be more precise, had exhausted its originators—that the still intense but more conventional nostalgic romanticism of the later Rossetti and his new disciple Burne-Jones replaced the 'truth-at-any-cost' creed. Rossetti's long sequence of dreamy-eyed women, invented by an extraordinary feat of the creative imagination out of an amalgam of his wife, Elizabeth Siddal, William Morris's wife, Jane Burden, the Arthurian legends, Dante's *Vita Nuova*, in rhythmic attitudes reminiscent of thirteenth-century stained glass, and—most astonishing of all in view of the original Gozzoli inspiration—dressed in clothes borrowed from Palma Vecchio, achieved at last the climax of romantic nostalgia. Burne-Jones, less lush, more puritanical, but equally determined to be wistful, used a less complex amalgam. Medieval legend played the same escapist role in his choice of subjects, but it was Botticelli who provided him with his types of womanhood.

Truth in this second, late-flowering phase of Pre-Raphaelitism had ceased to be part of the method. Yet it had never been more than a method. As the creative crucible cooled, truth would no longer serve. It had begun by adding vigour to the inherent Pre-Raphaelite poetry. It ended by turning it into prose.

CHAPTER 8

The Romanticism of the Abnormal

'*Omne ignotum pro magnifico,*' wrote Tacitus in a moment of unusual insight. The unknown and the mysterious are related: they meet along a frontier that can easily be crossed, yet they are different in kind, for the mysterious may spring from the commonplace. Altdorfer's forests, Giorgione's flash of lightning, the wild sky that overhangs El Greco's Toledo, Claude's serene distances, are all references to normal human experience, even though they acquire a mysterious intensity because of the artist's response to them and because that response makes demands on him that involve new ways of making familiar statements. But the unknown, the abnormal, the unfamiliar, make a different set of demands. There is a fascination about the abnormal that need not call into being a new language or a new vocabulary: a plain statement will often suffice. In extreme cases —and the Surrealists have taken full advantage of this discovery—a conventionally photographic representation of abnormality will produce an authentic *frisson* more effectively than any heightening or distortion or excess in the manner of its expression.

In the romanticism of the abnormal, therefore, we are less likely to be confronted with unusual styles than with unusual subject-matter, and though the two may often be found together in the same work (in Grünewald's tortured landscapes, for example) the former need not be a vehicle for the latter.

I have suggested that the factor common to most romantic art is a rebellion against law, but what distinguishes the romantic pursuit of the abnormal is a desire to escape rather than to rebel. Obedience to law produces conformity, and conformity produces recognizable patterns of behaviour. The law of gravity, for example, produces a pattern based on downward thrusts: the classic artist's acceptance of that law produces an architecture in which columns are placed at mathematical intervals for the manifest purpose of resisting mathematically calculable downward thrusts. A Greek temple is a beautifully constructed device for distributing the weight of a roof, and a standing figure by Raphael is a representation of a human being who distributes his weight between two legs. In a Gothic building and in a standing figure by El Greco there is a refusal to acknowledge the patterns produced by these downward thrusts—a rebellion against the law of gravity. In both there is even a positive assertion of an *upward* thrust.

But the artist who sets out in search of the abnormal neither accepts nor defies law. He moves into an area of experience in which laws as he knows them do not operate. His journeys into such areas can be simple searches for the unfamiliar and the kind of experience for which he is starved in everyday life, like the crags in a landscape by Patenier which Patenier himself could never have seen with his physical eye: or they may lead him deep into the image-making recesses of his subconscious mind, in which he discovers those monsters, whimsical or ferocious, that inhabit the canvases of Bosch and occasionally invade the world of Pieter Breughel. They may be explorations of the supernatural or the apocalyptic, common enough in the art of the Middle Ages, which was hardly even conscious that there was anything abnormal in the supernatural. Such explorations automatically became rarer once the Renaissance had focused men's eyes on the material world. It was more difficult for Dürer to produce convincing imagery for his woodcuts for the great Apocalypse of 1498 than for the anonymous designer of the Angers tapestries of the same subject. Death and the threat of death as an end to the enjoyment of life—rather than as an open doorway between temporal life and the life everlasting—was a natural post-Renaissance subject. The Dance of Death provided a fruitful theme for woodcuts by Holbein and the Flemings. Indeed, Flemish artists of our own century like Baron Ensor have inherited the same preoccupation.

The escape of the European to foreign lands—the *chinoiseries* of Chippendale or Delacroix's preoccupation with odalisques, for example (though not those of Ingres, who used them merely as excuses for reviving the conventionally classical nude)—is one aspect of the romanticism of the abnormal. It culminated in Gauguin's escape, not in imagination but in physical fact, to Tahiti. Parallel to the escape to distant lands is the escape in time to more nostalgically acceptable eras. This is perhaps the commonest and most understandable kind of escapism, and one can almost invariably trace it to the natural discontent that human beings experience when they find themselves bound and disgusted by the conventions of their own civilization.

The classicism of the early Italian Renaissance, which rarely attempted to project itself into the past even when attempting narrative

Attrib. to Patenier, S. Jerome in a Rocky Landscape
National Gallery, London

that belonged to the past, or of the High Renaissance, which tended to substitute the timelessness of the nude for the costumes and behaviour of the contemporary world, felt no desire to escape from the present. Nor did the realism of the Dutch seventeenth century, which never tired of recording with the utmost faithfulness every detail of its own daily life. But the escapism of the romantic nineteenth century was an index of its own rebellion against itself. Almost any period in the past seemed to it more desirable than the present moment. The Greeks and

Romans of Leighton and Alma Tadema, the Moroccans of Delacroix, the medieval dreams of the Pre-Raphaelites, Rossetti's identification (after her death) of his wife with Dante's Beatrice, Burne-Jones's Botticellian maidens, were all excuses for an escape from the sordid materialism of the Industrial Revolution; the search for romantic beauty in the past became, in fact, so obsessive, in literature, in architecture and in painting and sculpture, that a frank reference to the present began to look like an act of defiance. The present itself, in order to become acceptable, had at least to pay homage to the past by its preference for ruins. The cult of the picturesque was merely another mode of escapism. *Not* to escape became, in fact, unforgivable. Courbet's *Funeral at Ornans*, even though filled with the vestments of priests and the national dresses of villagers, was regarded as an attempt to step out of the artist's proper sphere into the unpaintable present. And when Manet, in his *Déjeuner sur l'Herbe*, actually painted the present as though it were a continuation of the past, the result struck contemporary critics as a mischievous parody, an irreverent and almost obscene comment on the noble poetry of 1510 by a prosaic upstart of 1863.

The romanticism of the abnormal, therefore, covers a vast area of subject-matter that ranges from the supernatural, in all its forms, to the unattainable, and a vast range of moods from the horrific, through the whimsical, to the mildly nostalgic. It tends to be literary rather than emotional in its origins, and its impact depends on the nature of the subject rather than the way in which it is presented. Delacroix's *Sardanapalus* may owe its design and its colour harmonies to Rubens, but it is Byron's poetry that makes it memorable. Art that depends for its effect on literature is not necessarily bad art. The word 'literary' as applied to the visual arts was, until recently, almost always derogatory. Whistler and the 'Art for Art's sake' movement were largely responsible for the note of scorn that could usually be detected when the word was used at the beginning of the twentieth century. But if it meant no more than that the artist was referring, in visual terms, to ideas or even to moods already familiarized by literature, then the whole of mythological, religious, and historical painting would be under the same cloud. A *Bacchus and Ariadne* or a *Crucifixion*, even Madox Brown's *Goodbye to England*, would have to be condemned on the ground that in them the art of painting was invading the province of literature. Such a condemnation would obviously be as absurd as a condemnation of opera on the ground that it forced music to be descriptive. The influence of literature on the graphic and plastic arts has been enormous since the beginning of civilization, and it would be silly to assume that literary painting was necessarily romantic painting. Painting with a strong narrative or descriptive content, such as the almost diagrammatic illustrations of the days of creation and the story of Noah and the Flood in the atrium of St Mark's in Venice, came into being largely because an illiterate population needed either the spoken word or the pictorial image. To such a population art of this kind was no more than illustration made as clear and as comprehensible as possible. It is the opposite of romantic: it is, on the contrary, a branch of realism reduced to its simplest terms with all the visual irrelevances—light, volume, recession—pruned away.

And once the Renaissance had arrived, literature still dictated subject-matter. It is, indeed, precisely when literary sources seem to be missing or when we cannot easily detect them that the art of the Italian Renaissance strikes us as being romantic. The magic of the Venetian *poesia* depends—more, perhaps, than we think—on its absence of literary background. It appeals to us because it is *not* an illustration of a known text but a self-sufficient visual incantation. What I have called the romanticism of mystery is the least literary of all kinds of painting. It tells its own story and tells it in visual terms. If the aloofness of the soldier and the woman in the *Tempestà* proved to be a conscientious attempt on the part of Giorgione to tell the story of two deaf and blind persons who were unaware of each other's presence, half the picturesque magic would be drained away.

But the romanticism of the abnormal no longer depends on emotional overtones inherent in the painting itself, but on explicit and usually descriptive references to the unfamiliar. And it is precisely in that field of experience that literature makes a more powerful impact on us than painting. It is not by accident that the word 'romantic' was coined by literary and not by art critics. When Schlegel began to use the word and to search for concrete examples to explain what he meant by it, I doubt whether it occurred to him that such examples could be drawn from the visual arts. Possibly memories of wild landscapes by Gaspar Poussin or Salvator Rosa may have floated into his mind, but the art of writing would still have seemed to him far more suited to the evocation of such moods than the art of painting.

And, of course, he would have been right. He knew, as we know, that whereas visual 'beauty' rests largely in the eye of the beholder, visual 'interestingness' tends to be a product of the mind. Those romantic passions and agonies, those tragedies of unrequited love, those alarming irruptions of the macabre or the sinister or the supernatural into our daily lives, can more effectively find their expression in words than in form or colour, and the more alarming or impressive the effect aimed at the more unlikely the success of the artist who attempts it. 'Pity like a naked newborn babe' or the song of the morning stars are subjects just within the range of a William Blake—though how few serious artists would dare to translate such phrases into visual imagery—but 'crack Nature's moulds, all germins spill at once' could be tackled only by a specialist in romantic melodrama like John Martin.

The result is foredoomed to failure. Martin's cosmic catastrophes, his forked lightning splitting the heavens, his toppling mountains and bottomless abysses that swallow their screaming victims, are of the same order as the expensive effects aimed at by Cecil B. de Mille in the more colourful of his epic tragedies, and Martin certainly had an advantage over Cecil B. de Mille. Nothing that his visual imagination could conceive was impossible to portray, whereas Hollywood, for all its determination to astonish, can never quite conceal the fact that cameras and celluloid, canvas palaces and cardboard mountains, have intervened between the director and his vision. Martin could approach a good deal nearer to a full realization of his imagined world. Yet both the Victorian romantic painter and the Hollywood movie magnate are attempting the impossible. They are victims of an illusion. What can be imagined, they think, can be translated into tangible, visible fact: and that, in its turn, can be painted or photographed, with the result that what began with an emotion ends as a description. Metaphor, the romantic artist's only method of carrying conviction, has been abandoned. No equivalent of 'crack Nature's moulds' is allowed to appear.

Martin could only have appeared in a period in which the romantic thirst for melodrama had penetrated so deeply into the common consciousness that excess had ceased to be ridiculous. No light was too lurid, no Babylonian temple illuminated by torches too Gargantuan, to be acceptable to his admirers. Burke's *Enquiry into the Origin of our Ideas of the Sublime and the Beautiful* (1756) had already, in the second half of the eighteenth century, initiated not merely a consciousness of the difference between the suave and the sinister, but also a growing appetite for the more forbidden and sensational aspects of 'the sublime'. Once the taste for such drugs had been established, stronger and stronger doses became necessary, and during the second quarter of the nineteenth century, no dose, it seems, was strong enough to be fatal.

But Burke was a serious student of aesthetics. For him the effect of the sublime was produced by formal means—rough as opposed to smooth, angular as opposed to curved, strong contrasts as opposed to gentle gradations and so on. Burke was, in fact, an exceptionally per-

John Martin, The Deluge
Print Room, British Museum

ceptive student of the visual arts and thoroughly understood how emotion could find its equivalent in formal abstraction. But, side by side with the romantic swing from the formally beautiful to the formally sublime, a parallel path was being followed in literature. Inevitably the literary equivalents of 'the sublime' were less likely to appeal to the eye and more to the mind. The theme of pleasing horror, a taste for death and decay, a growing consciousness of the fascination of decadence in all its forms—such themes, adumbrated by Byron and developed by the whole of the romantic school of novelists and poets from Edgar Allan Poe and Victor Hugo to Baudelaire and Swinburne, could not fail to affect the minds of artists. Delacroix was a good enough painter to know that the Byronic mood is not to be captured in paint merely by 'illustrating' selected scenes from Byron's poetry. But to lesser artists whose visual imagination was too weak to evoke its own imagery illustration was the only form that their fervid romantic urges could understand. Martin not only painted as melodramatically as he could but also as realistically as he could.

It is in this sense that 'literary' painting—the straightforward description of scenes that are, in themselves, overdramatized—is a pitfall to the romantic artist, for he is no more than a creature with over-developed romantic appetites and an underdeveloped visual imagination. The combination of the two is destructive to the real purpose of art, but particularly so to Martin's, not because his themes were too melodramatic but because his powers as a realist were too feeble. He was an almost exact contemporary of Turner, for whom no mood however commonplace or however apocalyptic was impossible. One has only to imagine how Martin, deprived of his support from theatrical subject-matter, would at once find himself unable to produce anything arresting or admirable.

I have taken Martin as the extreme case of the spurious (and therefore the impotent) romantic. There were others less dependent on the *folie de grandeur* that was Martin's obsession, though they were equally victims of the itch to escape into the world of abnormality and especially the terrifying or the sinister. Gustave Doré's illustrations to Milton's *Paradise Lost* provide a typical example. Milton himself was wide enough in his range to need no support from melodrama, but Doré's pictorial imagination is released only when he is concerned with the forces of evil. His Adam and Eve are conventional life-class puppets in an elegant sylvan setting. It is only when he is following the fortunes of Satan and his rebel angels that his romantic obsessions rescue him from banality, or indeed that he even catches the inner spirit of Milton. Doré's Satan, plunging earthwards 'down from the elliptic' on bats' wings, through layers of cloud; or brooding, at the edge of a fearful precipice against a stormy sunset, among mountains of more than Himalayan grandeur; or massing his airborne troops over a rocky gorge filled with boiling clouds—these conceptions are full of the authentic romanticism which belongs to vision rather than to words.

It is true that by concentrating on the grandiosity of evil Doré confesses to his own limitations. But I suspect that this dilemma is by no means confined to the romantic artist. However admirable the forces of 'goodness' and their equivalent in the visual world, the shapes assumed by 'beauty' (in the rather specialized sense in which Burke used the word), there is no doubt that the forces of evil tend to be more interesting and arresting, both in art and in literature. Hogarth, who was certainly no romantic, found that stories of debauchery culminating in tragedy were more crowded with picturesque incident, and therefore more easily and effectively told, than stories of virtue and its rewards. The devil, it seems, has not only the best tunes but also the most varied shapes and a good many of the most impressive phrases. But what distinguishes the realists from the romantics in their attitudes

Gustave Doré, Illustration for *Paradise Lost*
British Museum

to the forces of evil is that the realist observes them objectively even though his object in doing so may be to preach a sermon or elaborate satire: whereas the romantic positively rejoices in them and, in using them as raw material for his art, intensifies them. Swinburne's rejection of the lilies and languors of virtue for the raptures and roses of vice, Baudelaire's less self-conscious because less rapturous songs on the same theme in *Les Fleurs du Mal*, are only two among hundreds of possible examples of the romantic inversion of moral or ethical values in the arts. Even Keats's 'La Belle Dame sans Merci' is the type of beauty linked with cruelty.

One thinks of the literary romanticism of the nineteenth century as being specifically concerned with sinister or exotic aspects of sex, and of regarding 'sin', in the analysis of which it specialized, as more obviously connected with sexual emotions than with other ethical values. And one of the oddest paradoxes connected with the arts is that the visual arts are almost incapable of reflecting or referring to such attitudes. For in spite of their power to describe outward appearances with such precision, painting and sculpture become powerless as soon as they attempt to explore those erotic emotions that literature can describe with such luxuriant, introspective detail.

I have already noted that nineteenth-century romanticism in landscape tends to be pantheistic, and that Man's attitude to his environment can be expressed in painting with surprising intensity by all kinds of visual metaphors and distortions without giving any offence. Martin's towering precipices, his rolling clouds, his flashes of forked lightning that destroy Brobdingnagian palaces, may strike us as overstatements—though when they were painted there was a more widespread appetite for the deliciously terrifying—but they are at least admissible attempts to portray awe and terror. But Man's attitude to mankind, and specially its erotic aspects, cannot find its equivalent in the visual arts, even though Man's admiration for the physical beauty of the human body has been one of the most persistent themes in their history.

In fact, it would be almost true to say that *because* the artist has been so tireless in his search for aspects of physical beauty, he has rendered himself powerless to record the intensity of physical love. A Titian, a Cranach, a Renoir, cannot treat the human body with the same reckless freedom with which Turner can treat a sunset or an Alpine valley. Each of them can say with truth, 'This is my personal extract from the beauty of the human body.' And each of the extracts may be memorable in that it is a symbol of homage to human physical beauty and may therefore inspire the beholder with physical desire. But it is not a symbol of love. The eye has played too large a part in its manufacture and the mind and the sexual emotions too little. It is well known that the artist, from the moment that he begins seriously to regard his model as an organization of interrelated volumes, contours and colour-harmonies (and as a specialist in formal relationships he has no choice but to do so), becomes incapable of regarding her as a stimulus to physical desire. In literature, which cannot, by its very nature, describe such purely formal qualities, the appeal to the eye is negligible. However painstakingly the writer may attempt such descriptions, he can never communicate to his reader the total aesthetic effect of what the artist sees, though he can easily refer his reader to the erotic stimulus aroused by it. In doing so, he is forced to distinguish between lechery and love, and the fact that he can do so with ease gives literature a fundamental advantage over painting. Love is almost the commonest theme in poetry, but there is no such thing as a 'love-painting'. However many references the visual arts may make to one of the most intense and widely experienced of human emotions, none of those references can be more than an illustration of a love-story or a communication by the artist of his admiration of a seen object. All the artist can do, in his attempt to invade this particular province of literature, is to hover perilously near to the precipice of pornography. Once he permits himself to do this, his control over the language of formal relationships, which is the only language in which a Titian has any advantage over a Shakespeare, is lost. He can report on phenomena, but he cannot link them with their appropriate emotions, and it is undeniable that pornographic phenomena in an emotional vacuum are at best embarrassing and at worst repellent. He is in exactly the same dilemma as the artist who attempts to introduce patriotic or political propaganda into painting. The artist who tries to paint the triumph of Marxism over Fascism by portraying the glad-eyed bronzed peasant gathering in the harvest or the triumphant march of a conquering army, can only arouse patriotic feeling in the spectator by means of his title. *Parade in Red Square* and *Parade in Unter den Linden* are visually indistinguishable, and they arouse precisely the same feelings of pride or anger according to who looks at them and reads the inscriptions beneath them. Physical suffering offers the same spectacle to the eye whether it occurs in Belsen or in Siberia. I remember, some fifteen years ago, when Russian official pressure on the artist was at its strongest, reading a Soviet directive to art critics which pointed out with considerable severity that a certain critic had failed to condemn a painting that depicted a field of ripe corn seen against an approaching thunderstorm. The painting, it was pointed out, was ideologically unsound because it revealed a pessimistic attitude to the Russian climate. Yet an alteration in the picture's title would presumably have appeased the authorities. 'Storm over Capitalist Cornfield' would surely have turned a pessimistic into a hopeful picture.

This digression on the theme of the limitations of the representational arts was inevitable, since it explains why certain important aspects of nineteenth-century romanticism, especially those we are accustomed to call 'decadent', have failed to find an expression in the visual arts. Two minor artists did succeed in conveying powerful hints of the special flavour of the time, Aubrey Beardsley in England and Gustave Moreau in France; both deserve a brief note at this point. Beardsley, at least, achieved the almost impossible. He tapped a vein of typically ninetyish romantic sentiment. In the illustrations to *Salome* Beardsley seized, with an extraordinary instinct for visual equivalents, on the morbid overtones of Wilde's little masterpiece—the sadistic fusion of death and desire, the passionless cruelty of Herodias, the innocent destructiveness of Salome, the horrified running commentary among the bystanders and the shower of decorative images addressed to the moon. Beardsley realized that this complex romantic machinery required something more emotive than mere illustration: he discovered the secret of translating the mood of the play into an arabesque of line that could represent Salome at one moment as a wistful Burne-Jones damsel gazing at Wilde's face in a full moon, at another leering through a headdress of peacocks' feathers or preening herself in a caricature of a Japanese kimono, or executing a stomach dance to music played by a grinning Nibelung dwarf, or dressed as a fashionable débutante while a masked pierrot powders her hair, gazing down like an adolescent Clytemnestra at Jokanaan's severed head, floating over a stagnant pool with the dripping head in her hands, and finally being laid reverently to rest in a large powder-box by a pierrot and a satyr. Beardsley runs through the whole fashionable repertoire of ninetyish moods, in which horror and frivolity are used as foils for each other.

It happens that Gustave Moreau, fascinated by the same undercurrents in the Salome drama, attempted in his more grandiose way to produce the same effect: and succeeded only in substituting for its decadent mystery a set of conventional overstatements. Moreau's failure can be partly attributed to his attempt to use the medium of oil paint where Beardsley had used pen and ink: for paint cannot respond so easily to the creative mind's extravagances. But it depends on something

Aubrey Beardsley, Illustration for *Salome* by Oscar Wilde

deeper than a choice of the wrong medium. It depends, I believe, on a French incapacity to grasp the essence of romanticism. Romantic clichés like '*Ton corps était un jardin plein de colombes et de lis d'argent*' or '*Ta bouche est comme une bande d'écarlate sur une tour d'ivoire*' defy the illustrator precisely because they are visual. Not only Moreau but the whole of the French romantic school is powerless to cope with them.

As soon as one begins to consider the attitude of French nineteenth-century critics to their own romantic movement, of which they were all acutely conscious but by no means unanimously proud, one becomes aware that in France the word 'romantic' had—and still has—a very different set of connotations from those that are generally accepted in England. In the critical writing of Baudelaire, the self-appointed champion of Delacroix, one senses a defensive note, as though he knew that rules had been broken and that those who had dared to break them (and, of course, Delacroix in particular) would need all the justification of which his eloquence was capable. Baudelaire saw himself as a rebel nobly arguing the case for rebellion against a body of opinion committed to the classicism of Raphael and Ingres. He begins his long essay on the Salon of 1846 with a spirited definition of romanticism in painting which leads into a lengthy description of the contribution of Delacroix to the movement.

What distinguishes the French from other nations is their consciousness of the meaning and importance of the word 'style'. It is essentially a professional attitude, and what seemed to Baudelaire to need defending was not so much an emotional attitude as a revolutionary style. Romanticism had invaded the sacred precincts of tradition by breaking through the 'minute articulation' of Ingres. 'Everything is in a state of perpetual vibration, which causes lines to tremble and fulfils the law of eternal and universal movement' . . . 'There is a flowering of mixed tones: trees, rocks and granite boulders gaze at themselves in the water and cast their reflections upon it: each transparent object picks up light and colour as it passes from nearby or afar.' These sentences from a long and eloquent passage on the function of colour in painting certainly describe what Baudelaire *saw* in Delacroix and was unable to discover in Ingres. But to us they seem more like a description of Turner and are certainly a remarkable prophecy of the use of colour by the Impressionists. Baudelaire, despite his exaggerated account of what Delacroix actually achieved, described the appearance of a painting and not the vision that prompted it. If he can write an elaborate description of a Delacroix in terms that could be equally applicable to a Turner or a Monet, he is manifestly more concerned with a painted surface than with its emotional content. When Ingres painted *Le Songe d'Ossian* (1813) as though he were seeing an elaborately moonlit theatrical tableau through transparent gauze, he was using every device known to French romanticism, including Celtic twilight as opposed to Greek clarity. But since Ingres had established himself as leader of the classicists no Baudelarian propaganda could persuade the French public that this was a romantic picture set in a classic mould. The two 'styles', it had been decided, were mutually exclusive, and no intermarriage of the two could be admitted. The most that could be said was that Ingres, in choosing so exotic a theme, had trespassed on the preserves of the opposition party.

Delacroix's painting reveals him as a revolutionary of major importance who appeared at the moment when revolution was certainly overdue. Yet so deeply rooted is tradition in French art that a certain academism seems to hold its best artists in check. Those who, like Poussin and Ingres, are wholehearted in their worship of the traditional show no signs of the inner struggle. What they are fitted to do they do with enviable perfection. Even those of them who are almost completely lacking in imaginative enthusiasm, like Vouet and le Sueur, are able to avoid failure by virtue of their scholarship. They are so completely professional in their approach to the process of producing a work of art that, however commonplace and pedestrian the vision, the form is faultless. It is only when professionalism just fails to serve an unusually vigorous or passionate mind that a conflict develops between the creative method and the creative emotion. With Delacroix more than with any other great painter the conflict becomes a brake on the smooth working of the creative machinery. No artist's style could have been more firmly based on close study of art: yet few artists can have been so anxious to express a range of feeling that the art of the past had not even wished to express. As a painter Delacroix was fully equipped, yet, paradoxically, his equipment very nearly prevented him from being himself.

The restless, romantic world into which Delacroix was born—the world which produced, in literature, Hugo and Baudelaire, Swinburne and Poe, which turned a spotlight on Byron and gave a new meaning to so much in Shakespeare that the previous century had missed—was bound to reflect itself in Delacroix's thought. In particular he was caught up in that haunting fusion of pain with beauty that pervades the literature of the time. There seems at first sight no connexion between Wilde's *Salome* and Byron's *Sardanapalus*, and even less between Beardsley and Delacroix, yet both authors and both artists are

Delacroix, Dante and Virgil
Louvre, Paris

fascinated by the *Liebestod* theme. The Massacre of Scios, the death of Sardanapalus, the tortured souls that writhe at the feet of Dante and Virgil, even the Death of Ophelia— all these preoccupations with the vulnerability both of the human body and the human soul—are expressed by Delacroix in the robust, exuberant pictorial language of Rubens. No wonder that, to English eyes, Delacroix seems to be fighting a battle with himself. His composition is based on traditional baroque principles: his themes demand the forging of a new language which he was incapable of inventing because he was too serious and too devoted a student of the past.

If we compare him with a lesser man—Odilon Redon, for example—who had neither the scholarship nor the intelligence of Delacroix, but who had the same preoccupation with the imagery of fantasy, it becomes evident that Redon was a true romantic, though a weak one, while Delacroix was a giant but romantic only in name. I have included him in this chapter on the 'abnormal' because his themes are those of the typical escapist. But his real claim to be called a romantic painter lies in his habitual obsession with the theme of suffering, and his real place in this book is in the chapter on 'conflict'.

Redon, on the other hand, deserves a brief paragraph as a visionary whose search for a convincing set of images of the world of dreams was always just thwarted by his lack of visual imagination. Typical of this frustrated search is the series of twenty-two lithographs founded on Flaubert's *Tentation de Saint-Antoine*. The theme should have been a rewarding one, for it takes him into the centre of the ghost-haunted area of the human mind. It is a theme that provided Bosch with all that we value him for. Bosch lived and breathed naturally in that area, and, indeed, is never quite convincing when he moves out of it. Redon gives us the impression that he forced himself to invent the creatures that disturbed the peace of the unfortunate saint, but, conscientiously though he urged himself to flights of fantasy, he could never succeed in making credible the images of horror that are essential to the theme. He takes his author *au pied de la lettre*. Like Moreau, he is an illustrator who hopes to find in Flaubert the forms that the true romantic-escapist invariably manages to discover in himself. When he explained his method—'*Toute mon originalité consiste dans le fait de faire vivre humainement des êtres invraisemblables selon les lois du vraisemblable, en mettant autant que possible la logique du visible au service de l'invisible*'—he gives himself away. It is not by such means that the tormenting dreams of a saint are made to 'live in human terms'. Flaubert needed no illustrator. His powerful verbal imagery could only be weakened by an attempt to back it up by 'the logic of the visible'.

It is by means of a very different kind of logic that Bosch creates his world. He is, of course, of all inhabitants of the country of the abnormal the most confident: one could go farther and say that he created it and that after him it could only be recreated by referring back to him. None of the later re-creators have approached him in their understanding of the inner processes of fantasy. The Max Ernsts, the Dalis, the Magrittes of our own century manifestly force themselves to invent images calculated to shock or surprise. To Bosch one would think such images came so easily that it is not they but the human visitors whom he allows into his kingdom that are surprising. In the great triptych in the museum at Lisbon, Bosch regards St Anthony in the way an inhabitant of the Island of Laputa might have regarded Gulliver on his arrival. The madness of the grotesque is the standard by which normality is to be judged and found wanting. And all the human visitors to Bosch's grotesque kingdom seem to have caught, by a process of contagion, some of the queerness of their environment.

Even St Anthony himself begins to share some of the uncouthness of his own dream.

This is the exact opposite of the Giorgionesque world whose inhabitants create their own dream-world. There is no possibility of describing the world of Bosch. To make the attempt would be to do for Bosch what Redon did for Flaubert—to lose the essential flavour by translating it into another medium. All one can say is that 'the logic of the visible' has been drained out of it. Not only is it inhabited by monsters (less disgusting and therefore less disturbing than those which 'tempt' Grünewald's St Anthony) who infest the air in the form of anthropomorphic fish or crawl about the earth, emerging from giant eggs or peering out from caves, with pigs' heads or bats' wings or bodies that turn themselves into earthenware vessels or limbs that terminate in dead branches of trees. It is their behaviour, partly obscene, partly mischievous, partly whimsical, that sets the tone, so that one is plunged into a playful ritual, based on the Black Mass, that takes place in a landscape and among buildings that behave as oddly as their inhabitants. There is no weight in Bosch's world. Forms are mean and spiky. Gestures are equally mean and spiky. Music is played, either through the elongated noses of witches or by skeletons on harps—and it, too, heard in the mind's ear, is mean and spiky. And in the distance the world is on fire. The flames of a burning city show red and scarlet against a black sky.

Naturally, all this is a fruitful ground for the iconographer. These creatures and these happenings are not merely products of an unusually riotous imagination. They are also symbols: and symbols have a 'meaning' that lies outside themselves. Much of it has been diligently explained and its sources traced—in the writings, for example, of Jan van Ruysbroek, who at the age of fifty became a hermit in a forest near Brussels, dictated mystical utterances crowded with symbolism and attempted to clarify meanings by means of analogies. Bosch's triptych contains a veritable dictionary of demonology, of symbolism concerned with the five senses, alchemy (originally contained in Arabic texts translated and introduced to Spain as early as the twelfth century) and eroticism. To be able to read symbolism of this kind is certainly useful, not only for the purpose of deciphering the literary significance of each detail in the painting but also as an index of the texture of Bosch's thought and that of his contemporaries. But 'meaning' to the iconographer is by no means the same as 'meaning' to the art critic or the art philosopher. And in an inquiry into romanticism it is the second kind of 'meaning' that counts.

The iconographer, for example, can explain the complex undercurrents of literary meaning contained in any representation of the Three Graces painted in Italy in the last decades of the fifteenth century. One can easily imagine that Raphael and Botticelli, both of whom painted their own versions of it, would have explained their intentions in precisely the same words. Yet their paintings, though they clearly embody those intentions, are quite different in effect. Style—the unconscious expression of a personality—intervening between intention and 'meaning' has modified 'meaning'. Botticelli's Graces are not Raphael's Graces for reasons that can hardly be put into words. Botticelli's litheness, his attenuated, swinging line, his nervous angular rhythms and their subtle modulations, are so different from Raphael's uncanny but static perfection and his more confident sense of balance that the all-over *patterns* of the two paintings are different. To say this is a platitude; but to add that *therefore* the Three Graces are different Graces is not quite so obvious. Three nervous, swiftly moving young women leave a fundamentally different mark on the memory from three majestically serene young women. Our memory image is not merely aesthetic: it is dramatic and psychological. The two trios may have precisely the same function, but our attitude to them cannot be —or can only vaguely be—governed by our knowledge of their function.

Iconography is a serious and a rewarding study and it has become more so during the last few decades, but what it reveals is not an attitude of mind or the essence of a personality, but a train of thought evolved and accepted not by one mind but by a *group* of minds.

The iconographical content of Bosch's *Temptation of St Anthony*, like that of Pieter Breughel's *Proverbs*, could be read and translated into words that would certainly help to explain the picture, but the romantic painter's central message is not one that can be read or translated. I have described Bosch's effect on the eye as 'mean and spiky', qualities not inherent in but imposed upon the monsters, the trees and the buildings he describes. If one were to search one's memory for those same qualities in the work of another painter, one would certainly discover another romantic, but not necessarily another symbolist. A fragment isolated from Bosch's *Temptation*—say the central group or the creatures that hover in the sky in the left-hand panel—would look, stylistically, remarkably like a fragment of a painting of the Venetian lagoon by Guardi. Both have the same love of attenuated, trailing shapes, sharp extremities, sagging robes, angular limbs, sudden small and wiry accents. It is by the constant repetition of these personal

Hieronymous Bosch, Temptation of St Anthony (detail)
National Museum, Lisbon

idioms that we learn to distinguish between Guardi and Canaletto, or between Bosch and Rubens. On the surface we know our artists by their addiction to the normal or the abnormal, but on a deeper level it is an addiction to *shapes* that matters, and a consequent set of purely muscular habits in the handling of the brush. The staccato accents in Guardi and their absence in Canaletto provide the key to two ways of looking at the same Venice. Topographically they have no quarrel with each other, yet the melody that means 'Venice' for both of them is played in the one case on plucked strings, in the other on woodwind. Bosch's melody, wildly different in shape from Guardi's, is also executed as a series of staccato passages.

It is the mysterious amalgamation of the two kinds of 'meaning'—the iconographical and the stylistic, usually reinforcing but occasionally weakening each other—that determines the total impact. But even so it is necessary to distinguish between the image as an invention and the image as a symbol. An anchor can be an anchor or it can, *in addition*, mean 'hope': a bagpipe had, for Bosch, obscene connotations; yet considered as abstract shapes there is nothing indicative of hope in the one nor of obscenity in the other. Such meanings are literary. They do not 'work' through the eye but through the mind, and the *word* 'anchor' would be just as operative as the *shape*. Yet the shape, as drawn by Bosch, would have its own aesthetic meaning. An anchor, or a fold of drapery, would both be equally spiky when painted by him: both would be equally suave when painted by Rubens.

'Considered as abstract shapes' is a phrase that cannot be avoided in any discussion of the relationship between form and content. It brings us face to face with the problem of abstract art. If one admits that the introduction of an anchor in a painting is, in itself, unimportant except as a recognizable description of a familiar object, and if one is also prepared to admit that the description of objects is not a major part of the artist's task, then the anchor is no more than one among a thousand combinations of straight and curved forms the artist could have invented. 'Anchor-ness' can be dispensed with. Spikiness and/or suaveness cannot. It follows that had Bosch and Rubens set themselves the exercise of painting an abstract picture, description would disappear:

Guardi, Sta Maria della Salute, Venice (detail)
National Gallery, London

spikiness and suaveness would remain. What, then, in terms of 'meaning' would have been lost?

The answer to me is clear, but to formulate it with any precision is difficult. The answer, if words could be found to express it, would explain the difference between the three broadly separable worlds that painting can call into being—romantic, classic, and realistic. Once we have admitted that a gondola by Canaletto and a gondola by Guardi belong, aesthetically, to different worlds, whereas a gondola by Guardi and a monster by Bosch are closely related, we realize at once that it is not the object depicted but the rhythm into which it is translated that settles the world to which it belongs. And once that rhythm has been established—if we can say, for example, that a wiry, staccato rhythm is the outward sign of both Bosch and Guardi—then that rhythm can exist in its own right, divorced from its allegiance to gondolas or monsters or any other recognizable object. It can, in fact, form the basis of a classic or a romantic statement. (It goes without saying that realism is incapable of such a divorce between the world of form and the world of phenomena.)

It follows that abstract romanticism (more modishly known as 'abstract expressionism', since the more recently coined word emphasizes the more exuberant side of romanticism) is recognizable by its insistence on rhythms that suggest the sudden, muscular response to experience. In its extremest forms, and especially in that variant on it now known as 'action painting', it concentrates almost entirely on such responses, or rather on the record of them left behind on the canvas by whatever media the artist may decide to use. Such records bear much the same relationship to the impulse that produces them as the line left behind on the paper by a recording barometer. One 'reads' them as supplying evidence of a temperament responding to a momentary stimulus, just as one reads the telltale line on the barometer as evidence of atmospheric changes. Classic abstraction cannot be read in this way. The difference between action paintings of Hartung and Matthieu and the classic abstractions of Ben Nicholson and Mondrian is the difference between a sudden specific excitement and a slow, brooding generalization.

But more detailed reference must be made in a later chapter to the special problems of abstract art. In this chapter, which deals with the artist's behaviour in the presence of the abnormal, there is no need to do more than note that the problem exists, It is clear, of course, that the romantic artist, whom we have loosely defined as a rebel or an escapist, must either react in a rebelliously personal way to the normal, or must deliberately escape from normality into a world of dreams or fantasy. In both cases he remains himself—a man whose reactions are more precious than his thoughts: and certainly a man who would regard the immediacy of those reactions as weakened and impoverished if he were to submit them to the slow, contemplative process of organizing them into an acceptable or traditional pattern. It is also clear that there is a close connexion between the rebel and the escapist. The artist who subtly turns a gondola into a dream is not, after all, so very different from the artist who disintegrates the normal world of people and reptiles, eggs and branches of trees, and rearranges them as monsters. Both are engaged on a task of translation that moulds the world nearer, not to *the* heart's desire, but to *their* heart's desire.

The difference between the two is fundamental. *The* heart's desire is, presumably, something that any group of people, at any given time, would agree upon as supremely desirable. The artists who pursue and achieve it may be mediocrities or geniuses—Flaxmans or Raphaels—but they are certain to be popular. They have made the supremely acceptable statement. They are smooth in an age that is hungry for smoothness or turbulent when there is a growing appetite for turbulence. It is even thinkable that, given a general demand for macabre fantasy, Bosch would have been no rebel at all but a popular conformist. And it is certainly true that in a romantic period like that which began at the end of the eighteenth century and continued until after the middle of the nineteenth, the rebellious romantic was hard put to it to produce something that would go beyond the common heart's desire of the period and be essentially the expression of *his* heart's desire. For that reason, in such periods, we note the gradual and rather sickening *accelerando* of romantic motives. The battlements of Strawberry Hill cease to be amusing: they move perceptibly across the frontier from the abnormal to the normal. Or, to be more accurate, the frontier moves imperceptibly across them and makes them unremarkable. It is at that moment that the tower of Fonthill must rocket upwards and assault the heavens in order to keep our interest in rebellion alive.

It is the fate of all rebels either to lose the battle and be mocked for their failure or to win it and become victims of the respectability that follows success. The result is, of course, a pendulum rhythm, in which the artist, driven to the extreme limits of what is possible within the framework of his own programme of rebellion, is forced to a halt. The pendulum pauses in a moment of temporary exhaustion and then begins to swing back.

In examining the progress of the pendulum between Schlegel's invention of the word 'romantic' and the moment when exhaustion occurred, one can see fairly clearly two stages—the first in which rebellion became gradually more frenetic until what had started with the eighteenth-century pursuit of the 'picturesque' at last exhausted itself, by way of Van Gogh, the Fauves and Munch, in the frenzy of Soutine. At that moment, in order to keep the pendulum swinging, the hectic response to the normal was replaced by the selfconscious pursuit of the abnormal. Surrealism was the result—and, as it turned out, the last shortlived attempt to keep the romantic movement alive.

I have already noted that Bosch invites the attention of the expert in iconography, but that even though we may not have the key to his symbolism his message as a romantic artist is still clear. But in the case of the twentieth-century surrealist, iconography carries the whole burden of the picture. The pictorial language used by the painter is no longer a personal expression of his vision. It is the language of the uninspired, painstaking journalist whose editor insists on limiting him to the sensational but who is incapable of commenting on it. The pictorial language of surrealism is the language of the hand-coloured picture-postcard. As the expression of vision it is without value, though it demands considerable technical skill. As the expression of an interest in dream symbolism it is interesting, though one suspects that its purpose is generally rather to be effective or sensational than to reveal the authentic imagery of the subconscious levels of experience. It deals in shock tactics by making the illogical as vivid as possible. In that its sole purpose is to produce photographically focused illustrations of a new kind of subject-matter—that of the dream-world—it is an entirely literary movement, and once the initial shock of recognizing a coloured photograph of the impossible has worn off, nothing is left. The human eye placed on a slice of ham, the feet that turn into a pair of boots, momentarily excite the mind through the medium of the eye, but they have no connexion with the world of fantasy that Bosch made his own. Words like 'staccato', which are necessary if one is to translate Bosch's flavour into words, are inappropriate in a description of surrealist painting. Its only claim to belong to the family of the romanticism of the abnormal is that its subject-matter is abnormal. In other respects we need hardly think of it as art at all. It is the attempt of the photographer to persuade us that he has returned from an unfamiliar world, as solid and tangible as the world in which we live—a world whose queerness was never part of an artist's insight, but which could yield up its simple secrets to us through the intervention of the camera.

Such an attempt is always bound to fail. One can imagine that some intrepid space-traveller may one day bring back to earth a photographic account of landscapes or events encountered on a flying visit to the surface of the moon or one of the more accessible planets. However interesting the results, as factual documents, they can do no more than mildly surprise us. They cannot be works of art, because they were not conceived in the imaginative mind of man. They came to him ready-made. In the same way, the world presented to us by the surrealist is not an imagined world. If we are to believe the Freudian theory of dreams, what our unconscious minds produce for us are ready-made symbols, and the picture the surrealist extracts from them is no more than a painstaking portrait of a symbol.

But that does not imply that an artist cannot use the material supplied to him from his own unconscious levels as a basis for art of an extraordinary and often profound kind. What has emerged as a new discovery by certain artists of our own century is an art that is fundamentally symbolic because the symbol itself is a visual metaphor invented by (perhaps one could say 'revealed to') the artist in his attempt to come to grips with his own vision.

Such an art is not easy to describe, and any attempt at description must inevitably be useless, since visual metaphor obeys laws of its own, unrelated to the laws that govern verbal metaphor. Only by referring to an artist who, from time to time, has used the metaphorical method with startling effect, can I make my meaning clear. I can think of no painter who has more vividly used metaphor as the very core of his art than the late Paul Nash.

To place his undeniably romantic art in the category of 'the abnormal' may seem to be straining the meaning of the word; for Nash could certainly not be accused of trying to produce a sensational effect by inventing monsters or by denying the logic of the world he painted. Yet some of his most memorable paintings depend on his power to give new meanings to the seen by referring us back to the unseen. Two instances will suffice to make this clear.

Totes Meer is Nash's attempt to express, by a purely descriptive method, his sense of the importance of the Battle of Britain. Everyone who realized what was happening at that moment in the Second World War when the contending forces were engaged in a struggle for dominion in the air as a step to a more complete domination will recognize the picture's message. No conflict could have been less

Paul Nash, Totes Meer

Reproduced by courtesy of the Directors of the Tate Gallery, London

paintable than the series of detached, single-combat incidents that, cumulatively, resulted in the unsuccessful attempt of an invading force to produce a temporary paralysis in the effectiveness of the defence.

Metaphor was obviously the only solution for any attempt to convey, pictorially, the meaning of the Battle of Britain. To paint the wreckage of destroyed enemy fighting planes was a preliminary necessity, and Paul Nash based his picture on a careful documentary study of torn and twisted metal machines. But the sense of conflict had to be added or the picture would be no more than a conscientious piece of reportage. What turned it into a work of art with a romantic message was Nash's decision to impose on the mass of wreckage the rhythm of breaking waves and to make, among the burned-out fuselages, discreet references to human skeletons.

This kind of metaphor is common enough in Nash's work. The inanimate object that becomes a personality, the clump of trees that develop groping fingers, are typical of him. But occasionally he carries the process a stage further by omitting the descriptive basis altogether and relying entirely on a metaphorical content. In a painting entitled *The Soul Visiting the Mansions of the Dead*, whose origin was an illustration to Sir Thomas Browne's *Urne Buriall*, the problem of finding a visual equivalent to convey the sense of a journey through infinite space has been solved by erecting a scaffolding of planks and metal tubing through which the searching eye of the beholder is compelled to travel as it examines the picture's surface. The effect is hypnotic, and the rather trivial symbol (a bird-aeroplane enclosed in a circle) of the human soul as it diminishes, in perspective, down these corridors of scaffolding is hardly needed. The scaffolding metaphor, which must, of course, have had its origin in an actual seen construction, is sufficent and convincing.

I have introduced this parenthetical note on Paul Nash because it provides an instance of the subtle use made by artists of our own time of the abnormal. The shattered aeroplane that becomes a crushed dinosaur or a breaking wave can be charged with a richer meaning than the composite monsters of Bosch or the accepted symbolism of specialists in the macabre or the fantastic.

CHAPTER 9

Conflict

Opposing forces, equally balanced, produce an equilibrium that may, superficially, resemble the tranquil equilibrium that classic art invariably attempts to discover. That final classic discovery, in a world governed by tensions, can, of course, never be made. The universe can only achieve stability by virtue of thrust and counterthrust, of centripetal and centrifugal forces eternally cancelling each other out, of never-ending processes of birth leading to death, growth to decay, exuberances balanced by disciplines. And if all art is the expression of human experience, then all art is ultimately concerned with a description of conflict: therefore all art is basically romantic. If it were possible to cancel out the tensions which govern the pattern of our lives, art would disappear. It would have no *raison d'être*. The Last Judgments in the tympanums of Romanesque cathedrals would be meaningless if the conflict between good and evil were not a major part of Christian consciousness. Equally the formal exercises of Mondrian would be boring and unnecessary if the conflict between vertical and horizontal, the antiphony between black and white, red and blue, broad and narrow, were not major elements in our aesthetic consciousness.

Yet, if all art is essentially a romantic phenomenon, not all artists are equally concerned to underline or even to describe these eternal tensions. They may be unavoidable, yet the classic artist would like to avoid them: he invents all manner of devices to persuade us either that he ignores them, or that somewhere, hidden amongst his secret desires, is a world in which they do not exist, while the romantic artist seizes on them avidly, forces us to watch him as he removes the veil, reveals them at work and asks us to share his understanding of them—his admiration of their complexities, his delight in the power or his terror at the danger he is so anxious to exhibit to us. The sculptor of a Last Judgment, we feel, has no aim but to make the conflict plain. Mondrian, on the other hand, would resolve the conflict. Yet if he were to succeed his occupation would be gone.

Not conflict, then, but the exposure of conflict, is the romantic's intention. It could be argued that my other romantic categories are included within it. For mystery is the sign of tensions unresolved that leave behind them an unanswered question. And abnormality is a sign that the conflict is still undecided, the resolution beyond guessing at, and wonderment more potent than satisfaction.

But however closely interlocked the categories I have enumerated, it is necessary, for the purpose of analysis, to separate them, if only for the sake of making the analytical process manageable. In heading this chapter 'Conflict' I am aware that in each of the previous chapters tensions of various kinds have been involved. Yet tension was not the central theme. What we are here concerned with is a type of artist whose mind is, by nature, focused on the interplay of opposing forces, and whose central theme is the conflict between them and the ultimate, precarious balance achieved.

The Greek theory of art, with its emphasis on the imitation, as far as the visual arts were concerned, of visible phenomena, with an overwhelming emphasis on the human body, and its search, within that framework, for a limited range of 'ideals', was almost committed to the avoidance of such tensions: when the artist was forced to acknowledge their existence—as in such subjects as Medea slaying her children—he found himself in a dilemma that could not easily be solved: it was Plotinus with his startling substitution of 'inspiration' for imitation who first stated the alternative possibility that art was concerned with the invisible and could not, therefore, make imitation its primary aim. It was from that moment that conflict became a theme to be faced rather than avoided. The physical lost its importance and became not an end but a means. Venus and Apollo as examples of female and male bodily perfection, lost their meaning, since 'meaning' itself had taken on a new set of connotations. 'Meaning', from the moment when Christianity took over from Paganism the burden of dictating iconography, transferred its attention, not from the seen to the unseen, but from the seen to an interplay between the seen and the unseen. Consequently, the seen lost its power over the mind and became a symbol.

Symbolism increases its potency when it reduces its vocabulary to a minimum. The beauty of Venus does not cease to operate as a factor in human life when it becomes a symbol, but it is no longer to be described as a thing seen: it can only be alluded to as a thing understood. Above all, it must be sharply differentiated from the equally potent beauty of 'goodness', which, in its turn, must be equally sharply differentiated from the ugliness of evil—a problem which could never have presented itself to a Greek artist, since evil had never been a vivid concept to the Greek mind. Misfortune—the passive acceptance of imposed suffering—was certainly a part of daily life: but the notion that misfortune was punishment for evil intention hardly occurs in Greek literature and can never be suggested in Greek art, since 'intention' is beyond the power of the eye to see and the hand to express. Intention, on the other hand, becomes so strong a motive in the art of the Middle Ages that the power of the eye to observe and the hand to imitate was allowed to decay until symbolism at last became the very core of pictorial and sculptural language, and the sense of conflict between body and soul weakened until that equilibrium which has been postulated as the result of a balance between forces lost its importance. The result, in theory, should be an excess of romanticism as I have defined it; yet in practice romanticism itself had been overlaid by an excess of symbolism.

None the less the language of medieval art, by virtue of that excess of symbolism, has come to be regarded too much as an impersonal device for holding a minimum of expressive and a maximum of iconographical content. So strong are the accepted conventions, at any moment in the development from early Romanesque to late Gothic carving, for the fall of drapery or the repertory of gesture, that we are apt to lose sight of the individuality of the artist or the occasionally observant eye asserting itself behind the insistent stylistic pattern.

Behind the majesty of the great tympanum at Vézelay and even more so behind the less ambitious carvings over the west door of St Lazare at Autun, one can detect a very personal tone of voice. The 'meaning' at Autun is by no means dependent on the use of a set of Romanesque stylistic clichés. And the sculptor himself must have been aware that he was being quite consciously what would today be called an 'expressionist', a close observer of the physical attitudes and gestures that imply prayer or suffering or (to a less extent) triumph. It is just at this point, when Romanesque art has developed its own set of idioms, and certain artists—many of whose names are unknown—have begun to combine those idioms with personal discoveries of their own, drawn directly from life itself, that we can guess at a set of possibilities that were, in fact, never developed. The romanticism of conflict, as I have defined it, can be detected in the tympanum and in certain of the capitals of St Lazare at Autun, and the sculptor, knowing, surely, that what he had done was no conventional or academic job, signed his name, Giselbertus, at precisely the point in that crowded organization of carved forms where the figures become most agitated, most expressive, most closely observed and yet—the usual paradox of romanticism—most distorted. The seated Christ in the centre, for all its majesty, is a traditional figure: but the group of Apostles on the left, the St Michael weighing souls on his right, or the thrusting downwards of the damned by devils are exceptional.

Throughout the Middle Ages nothing so balanced in its use of physical symbols for spiritual states occurs. With the advent of the Gothic formulae in the thirteenth century the tension disappears. A sweetness of rhythm takes its place in France and an excess of realism in Germany. The Madonna of Rheims is weak, the statues of Naumberg unimaginative, as compared with the best of Giselbertus's carving in the mid-twelfth century at Autun.

Autun and Vézelay are exceptional. The romanticism of conflict can only begin to be fully eloquent for us at a point late in the Renaissance, when, after a century of endeavour during which the artist had once more begun to use his observant eye, the balance has been restored: physical beauty has become once more an accepted value, but it has also become, as it were, a vessel to contain hidden meanings which the Greeks had ignored and which the medieval world had reduced to a set of wonderful hieroglyphics.

One sees that romantic eloquence emerging in Donatello's agitated bronze reliefs in Padua and Rome, and in those extraordinary free-standing statues in which the human body has at last asserted itself as an organization observed with furious intensity and with no thought of idealization. The 'Zuccone' is both a rather harassed old gentleman and a symbol of human wisdom: the Mary Magdalen is a study of haggard weariness but also a metaphor of a shipwrecked human soul. Even more striking because less obvious, the young David, naked but for an elegant sun hat, would have been the exact equivalent of a Greek Hermes but for the jaunty swagger that turns him into a symbol of youth starting out with careless confidence on the journey of life—the essence of the handsome, intelligent undergraduate. No classic artist could suggest these double meanings.

But the climax of the art of conflict between double meanings arrives with Michelangelo. The recumbent figures of the sacristy of San Lorenzo, uneasy in their relaxed perfection, the seated figures of the Medici princes above them, symbols of thought on the one hand and energy on the other, are too familiar to need description as examples of the balance between body and mind. Even more specific as expressions of mood interpreted by gesture are the Prophets and Sibyls of the Sistine Chapel ceiling. Each one of them is not merely a superb

Donatello, Entombment of Christ (detail)
From Tabernacle, St Peter's, Rome

invention in terms of bodily rhythm but also a precise statement of some inner urge. One is apt to be a little misled by their power into regarding them merely as specimens of Michelangelesque rhetoric. But they are more than that, as one can easily see by comparing them with their equivalents by Michelangelo's bewitched followers, who could easily echo his rhetoric but could never understand, much less imitate, his precision. And it is to be noted that, for once, he achieved this explicitness of mood without resorting to the nude. The blanket-like draperies that cover them compel him to express his meanings largely by the turn of a head, the gesture of an arm or the swing of a seated body on its pelvis.

To pursue in detail the theme of Michelangelo as the arch-romantic of conflict would be useless. Little that is new can be said of him. He is the supreme example of an artist who has solved problems of extreme difficulty with such assurance that no one could miss his intentions or fail to acknowledge his complete success in carrying them out. He is the easiest of all great artists to understand, and for that reason there is no need to dwell on his particular brand of romanticism. What makes him all the more extraordinary is that he so rarely tackled the problem of a dramatic situation, a conflict between one human being and another. His most explicitly stated tensions are those between man's body and the inner life that makes it a functional rather than a beautiful machine.

It was, of course, essentially a sculptor's rather than a painter's problem to discover the equilibrium of conflict in a single figure. Grouped figures in dramatic relation to each other are rare in free-standing sculpture. One thinks of *Niobe's Daughters*, the *Laocoön* or Rodin's *Burghers of Calais*, and none of them is particularly successful. From what remains of the pediment sculptures of the Parthenon we can feel fairly confident that the figures could have been no more impressive by virtue of their mutual relationships than they are in isolation. Such relationships are as contrary to the nature of sculpture itself as they are natural to that of painting. For that reason one might have expected Michelangelo, offered the full spread, as a painter, of the Sistine Chapel ceiling, to welcome the opportunity to fill the great space with groups dramatically involved with each other, and, at the very least, spatially related to their environment. Yet, even here, Michelangelo persists in pursuing the theme of the single self-contained figure in which the whole meaning depends on the fact that the activity of the soul finds its equivalent in the action of the body. The least satisfactory of the ceiling panels are those which are most densely populated. The story of the Flood is—dare one say it?—a failure. As to an environment, whether for descriptive or for spatial reasons, Michelangelo refused, almost to the point of eccentricity, to supply one. Adam was presumably created in a garden. In the Sistine Chapel he finds himself on a slab of rock. The tree round which the serpent winds itself in order to offer the fruit to Eve is no more than a stark column rooted in the arid earth, Michelangelo adds it, reluctantly, as a stage property, unfortunately necessary to his narrative.

Michelangelo died in 1564. In the late fifties he carved two groups that seem to contradict much of what I have said about him. In the Pietà of the Duomo in Florence the four figures are as closely interlocked from a formal point of view and as intimately related to each other in a dramatic sense as in any free-standing sculpture known to me. Yet the two women who support, on either side, the crumpled and sagging body of the dead Christ are little more than conventional

Giselbertus, Tympanum, Autun (detail)

supporters to a coat of arms, though the shrouded head of Nicodemus that towers above the Christ and looks down on him is far more than an heraldic crest. Without it, the tension between his protective tenderness and the angular, Z-shaped body of Christ would be lost. As shapes, both figures are complete expressions of an inner meaning; the function

Michelangelo, Pietà
Rondanini Palace, Rome

of the two Marys on the other hand is almost entirely formal. They add bulk and little else to the main mass, which would otherwise have been painfully weak and linear in construction.

In the Rondanini Pietà, Michelangelo's last work, physical substance disappears. The conscientious and brilliant young student of anatomy who had conceived the Pietà in St Peter's between fifty and sixty years earlier has played no part in the design of these two wraith-like creatures.

They have no weight. We are back, at the end, in the Romanesque world of symbolism. One could almost expect to discover their counterparts in the tympanum of Autun.

This final renunciation of the human body and especially of its expressive energy was like the almost unheard cry of a dying man. No one heeded it or even noticed that the most eloquent of all devotees of physical nobility had, as it were, renounced his faith on his deathbed. Had they done so the disaster that followed might have been avoided. A new and a more profoundly expressive asceticism than that of the mid-twelfth century might have been developed in the latter part of the sixteenth century. But the sublime drama of Michelangelo's middle period proved irresistible. The Sistine Chapel ceiling and the five figures in the new sacristy of San Lorenzo in Florence became a dictionary that was used almost exclusively for half a century in Northern Italy, and the artists who used it utterly misunderstood its purpose. In doing so, they developed a style that was never founded on an inner vision, and for that style the word 'mannerism' had to be invented. Raphael, whose genius had always been at the mercy of outside influences, and who, up to the last year or two of his short life, had been strengthened by them, was the first artist to suffer. For a short time he managed to 'use' Michelangelo, and there are passages in his *Incendio* fresco in the Vatican to prove that he used him to good purpose. Then he succumbed, painted his last picture, the *Transfiguration*, and in doing so announced his own downfall and led the way to that of the next generation. He showed them that theatrical effectiveness *could be used as a substitute for dramatic meaning*.

Michelangelo had discovered that the human body was capable, by the subtlest inflexions of gesture and rhythm, of expressing an infinity of human moods, but the mannerists were almost incapable of thinking in terms of human moods. For them gestures and rhythms were ends in themselves. For them the human body—preferably nude or wearing skin-tight clothing whose only purpose was to change the colour of the figure—was merely a wonderfully flexible machine for enlarging the artist's repertory of attitudes.

No art that depends on the use of such a repertory can be seriously romantic, even though, superficially, it copies a romantic formula. What produced the writhing rhetoric of the Tuscan mannerist painters was a set of pressures from outside. Not the desire to communicate but to surprise or impress was the basis of their style. In enlarging the repertory of attitudes they seriously diminished the repertory of 'meanings' and in doing so ran counter to the very spirit of romanticism. All the outward signs of conflict are visible in their work, but they can never persuade us that tension, in any serious sense, is the cause of it. Sir Kenneth Clark points out the connexion between the angular rhythms set up by the legs of the dead Christ in the Florentine Duomo and those of Venus in Bronzino's *Allegory* in the National Gallery. The resemblance is close, but the motive is different. Michelangelo invented the zigzag form by identifying himself with a lifeless body lowered on to the earth: Bronzino was incapable of identifying himself with anything but Michelangelesque devices, which he then used without at all understanding what made them inevitable. In his picture they have no meaning. They are compositional tricks.

What the mannerists did communicate in the best of their work was both obvious and inevitable. Being mainly concerned with the nude, one aspect of it—inescapable even to fanatical admirers of Michelangelo—its erotic connotations, forced itself on them. Calculating though they were in their elegant distortion of it, it still retained for them its primary stimulus. The enormous range that Michelangelo could command is reduced by them to a single element, seductiveness. The pin-up girl and the superman are multiplied to supply the cast of their agitated dramas.

It would, of course, be absurd to deny that erotic emotions are a legitimate motive for romantic art. It has been noted already that the visual arts cannot distinguish between love and lechery, and that therefore there can be no such thing as a 'love-painting' in the sense that we speak of a 'love-poem'. But there are refinements of erotic sensibility that can easily supply the motive power for masterpieces. Correggio knew their secret well enough. So did Cranach, and so, among the mannerists themselves, did the painters of the school of Fontainebleau. But in each case that translation of emotion into what I have called visual metaphor—those caressing veils of light that are typical of Correggio, those slightly mischievous exaggerations used by Cranach, the 'chic' of the Fontainebleau paintings—saves the situation.

It is not prudery but a serious aspect of aesthetics that creates the situation and makes it reasonable to speak of 'saving' it. A work of art is, in essence, an expression of emotion whose validity depends on our pleasure in contemplating it. In that respect it enables us to share the state of mind of its creator, thereby enlarging our own emotional experience. But contemplation and action are mutually exclusive, and the 'situation' created by a type of art that is *primarily* erotic is one in which an attempt is made to combine the two, thereby making both less potent.

The Greek 'mimetic' theory of art produced masterpieces that we can contemplate without the embarrassment of this double demand on our responses, but it evidently created a good deal of confusion among Greek aestheticians. The legend of Pygmalion reveals a state of mind in which contemplation and action become so confused with each other that the word 'art' itself almost ceases to have a meaning. That an artist should create an expression of his attitude to the physical beauty of the human body and then wish to transform it from an object to be contemplated to a creature that can share with him his own life of action is to us both unthinkable and unforgivable. It is not merely a question of turning marble into flesh. It is a question of moving into another dimension; of translating art into nature.

It seems absurd to charge mannerism with pursuing the Greek fallacy, for our first impression of a mannerist work of art is never that it is too 'realistic', too 'close to nature': we almost always see it, on the contrary, as something unusually artificial. Yet because its artificiality robs it of every meaning except one that can hardly be contemplated, it becomes suspect as art and certainly unclassifiable as romantic.

The end of the century that saw mannerism emerge, flourish briefly and expire because it had exhausted the thin soil in which it grew, was marked by an artist who can only be called mannerist by those who are anxious to discover a category for a man who can hardly be classified under any accepted heading.

El Greco has already been described [1] as an artist who escaped from Italy because he wished to escape from materialism. In Venice, Titian and Veronese had frankly exulted in the solidity of flesh and the texture of satin, and El Greco, in his youth, had half-heartedly attempted to see the world through their eyes; in Rome, Michelangelo had been the supreme poet of physical virility, and the young El Greco, half bewitched by him, had caught some of his mannerisms but could never share the faith in humanity that made him convincing. Under the spell of Italy, El Greco did become an uneasy mannerist and, had he not made his escape to Spain before it was too late, he might have remained a mannerist all his life, ending up as an eccentric and exaggerated Parmigianino, who borrowed stylistic tricks from the Venice and Rome of his day.

When he did escape it was not as an exile but as a released prisoner. Spain did for him what Provence was to do for Van Gogh. I have suggested that what marked him as a romantic in his later years was the

[1] See p. 104 f.

quality of mystery, the refusal to be specific about the nature of flesh and satin, the hardness of polished marble and the softness of clouds. Clouds and drapery become, in his last years, indistinguishable. His world is made of a substance that is weightless and offers no resistance to the touch; that exists only because every artist must at least pretend to be describing a tangible world, otherwise he cannot paint at all.

Mystery is certainly, in the superficial sense, the keynote of these last pictures. Yet in a deeper sense they belong to the romanticism of conflict. If Michelangelo's recumbent figures in the New Sacristy of San Lorenzo are symbols of the conflict between body and soul, El Greco's vertical figures are expressions of the conflict between the earthbound and the volatile. The forms appropriate to what we know to be solid adopt the rhythm and behaviour of flames: consequently his favourite system of composition is based on a set of flickering, ascending verticals, and the paradox of this interchange between flesh and flame can only be interpreted in terms of conflict.

El Greco escaped from the seductions of Italian materialism at the end of the sixteenth century and had already developed his semi-mystical protest against it by the first decade of the seventeenth. It was during that same decade that the young Rubens crossed the Alps, fell a willing and enthusiastic victim to the same materialism and out of it forged the basic structure of the new Baroque language. Knowing as we do how quickly and how confidently he forged it, giving it a new energy and a new dynamism, we might be misled into thinking that he, too, had romanticized it. The restless, sumptuous diagonals that begin to appear almost immediately after he made his first contacts with Venice, Mantua, and Rome might be mistaken for symbols of conflict. But they are not. They are expressions of a natural energy. In Rubens there are none of the unresolved tensions that proclaim the romantic preoccupation with opposing forces. Where the bodies of Michelangelo's supermen always seem to be driven into expressive gestures by their inner thoughts or emotional moods, the figures, however contorted or energetic, in a painting by Rubens are expressions of the painter's own vitality. What I have called conflict is not the result of physical energy meeting physical resistance—the struggle of Laocoön with snakes or Herakles with a lion. There is plenty of that kind of struggle in Rubens and it provides him with plenty of excuses, as it did for the sculptor of the Laocoön group, for impressively energetic poses. But that is not the conflict which the romantic takes as his theme.

Rubens was too healthy a materialist to understand the kind of conflict between opposites that we find in Michelangelo and El Greco. For all his complexity and enthusiasm he is one of the least romantic of great artists. In him there are no visual metaphors, no double meanings, no overtones or mysteries, above all no exploration of the unseen or attempts to discover visual equivalents for the unseen. Even in the most apocalyptic of his paintings he is earth-bound. His Madonnas are hardly distinguishable from his portraits of his wife: his cherubs are his own offspring. Half-way between the realist's grateful acceptance of the earth's opulence and the classicist's determination to avoid whatever is ignoble or unhealthy, he stands, a gigantic eclectic, on the exact borderline between the two.

And yet the Baroque movement was far from incapable of mystery and conflict. 'Earth-bound' is never the word that occurs to us in the presence of those extraordinary buildings which, by virtue of their lighting rather than their form, seem to deny masonry its weight and marble its density. Baroque architecture has its own romanticism—the romanticism of paradox, utterly different from the athletic romanticism of Gothic building.

For Gothic never denies its own weight. On the contrary it even boasts of it. The immense clustered piers of York or Amiens never pretend that they are not designed to support equally immense weights, but they also give the impression, which no classic building can give, that they transmit an upward thrust which spreads outwards along the ribs of the vaulting and continues its vertical movement till it emerges on the skyline in pinnacles and pointed *flèches*. That same upward thrust, carried along the leaping lines of flying buttresses, makes of a Gothic cathedral an organic whole. The thrust and counterthrust is something we are intended to feel. The equilibrium is never in doubt, but it is the equilibrium of gravity which never works, as it does in classic building, at right-angles to the earth's surface but diagonally. It is not the static steadiness of a capital H, but the dynamic steadiness of a capital A in which everything depends on the apex, where two diagonals meet and achieve balance by leaning towards each other.

Baroque architecture, on the other hand, develops no such tensions. Its romanticism is equally based on conflict, but on a theatrical conflict. Gravity is not, as in Gothic, converted into power. It is denied altogether. Stone and marble forsake their own natures and become malleable in the hands of the great Baroque architects, twisting and fluttering capriciously so that the eye is defeated in its attempt to discover a basic logic behind the construction of their buildings. Walls merge imperceptibly into sculpture, sculpture into painting. Space and light contradict each other, and both are used, as they are on the stage, to create an illusion.

If this book were concerned with architecture, it would be worth while to trace the dramatic romanticism of Baroque building, especially in Germany and Austria, where illusionism was carried to fantastic lengths. Just as the theatre designers discovered how to turn canvas and plaster into the semblance of stone, so the builders of churches and palaces built cloudscapes out of solid masonry.

But in painting and sculpture, though illusionism was still pervasive and the artists who, throughout the seventeenth century (but mainly towards its end), enabled the architects to achieve their dizziest effects of space and lightness were masters of the art of large-scale *trompe l'oeil*, the very size of the spaces they were asked to cover obliged them to work on strictly classic principles of design. When we look upwards into (and 'into' rather than 'at' is the word we can hardly avoid using) the great fresco by Gaulli that surmounts the nave of the Gesù in Rome (1674–9), or the even more overpowering virtuosity of Andrea Pozzo's ceiling of the church of San Ignazio, which actually continues, in paint, the upward perspective of the church itself before we are allowed to emerge, through the final cornice, into the sky, we experience the authentic, vertiginous thrill that we associate with so much romantic art. Yet, in Gaulli's case, the effect is completely dependent on planning of the most elaborate and intelligent kind: and in the case of Pozzo, despite the *trompe l'oeil* architecture which ought to provide a firm basis to the design, the first effect is of confusion—a lack of control, a failure to provide a focal point. Such an effect is not the result of a romantic intention. It is rather a sign of Pozzo's failure to apply the principles of classicism in a case where only the strictest adherence to them could succeed.

Romanticism, and especially the romanticism of conflict which is the concern of this chapter, will not 'work' on this superhuman scale. When painting and sculpture are so closely integrated that the eye is deliberately baffled when it attempts to discover the dividing line between the two, organization becomes compulsory. And organization, by its very nature, defeats the basic intentions of the truly romantic artist. To paint, at the request of Jesuit patrons, the kind of vision that the militant Counter-Reformation had in mind when it built these Baroque masterpieces, is by no means the same as being a visionary.

In order to discover the true proto-romantic of the seventeenth century we must look among the carvers of single statues or self-contained groups and the painters of easel-pictures, in which the artist is free to work out his own programme instead of contributing to a dictated effect imposed on him, at several removes, from above; or, to put it more simply, what is romantic in the Baroque style is not the temperament of the individual artist but the intention of his employer —the Church itself, exerting its full powers in an all-out emotional attack on the spirit of the Reformation.

But among the artists who were not involved in this mass attack, there are definite signs of a romantic attitude. And, as had already happened in the case of Giorgione in Italy and Altdorfer in Germany, the outward signs of that attitude are to be found in an unexpected emphasis on the moods, and especially the threatening moods, of Nature and the resultant belittling of Man. The best known of such artists is Salvator Rosa, who may be said to have invented something bigger—at least, more influential—than himself, namely the range of moods that run in a crescendo from the picturesque to the sublime.

The words were not invented till a century after Salvator Rosa had painted what they were to stand for. It was not till the eighteenth century that what Salvator Rosa had done by instinct began to satisfy a growing and rather self-conscious appetite. Sir Joshua Reynolds praised him for his 'power of inspiring sentiments of grandeur and sublimity'. Reynolds did, in fact, come near to defining one aspect of romanticism itself when (in his Fifth Discourse) after complaining that Salvator Rosa 'though void of all grace, elegance and simplicity . . . yet has that sort of dignity which belongs to savage and uncultivated nature', he adds: 'Everything is of a piece: rocks, trees, sky, even to his handling, have the same rude and wild character which animates his figures.' Horace Walpole put it more succinctly when, describing his crossing of the Alps, he wrote 'torrents, wolves, rumblings—Salvator Rosa'. But Reynolds's discovery was that 'handling' had something to do with the effect of what was handled. It was in much the same spirit that he praised Gainsborough (in what amounted to an eloquent obituary) for his fluttering lightness and then, remembering his duties as the upholder of the classic tradition, warned his students not to imitate him.

Reynolds's tribute to Gainsborough is a significant one. When the Fourteenth Discourse was delivered, in 1788, the spirit of romanticism was already stirring, though the word had not yet attached itself to the visual arts and it would certainly not have occurred to Reynolds to apply it to Gainsborough, though we now see Gainsborough as a painter whose romantic temperament was always trying to assert itself despite the obstacles it encountered.

Salvator Rosa, St John the Baptist in the Wilderness
Glasgow Museums and Art Galleries

The formidable nature of those obstacles can be realized as we read through Reynolds's Discourses. They are the eloquent utterances of a man who was thoroughly in tune with the spirit of his own generation, though he was never quite a big enough man to insist on putting his own theories into practice, and never quite sensitive enough to realize that in his later years that spirit was changing. The Discourses were delivered at intervals over a period of twenty-one years—between 1769 and 1790—and the basic tone of them never varies. He was always the pious upholder of the great tradition of elevated painting even though he realized that his powers as a painter were not equal to his theories. There is something a little pathetic in the final paragraphs of his last Discourse—a solemn eulogy of Michelangelo. 'It will not, I hope, be thought presumptuous in me to appear in the train, I cannot say of his imitators, but of his admirers. I have taken another course, one more suited to my abilities and to the taste of the times in which I live. . . .' And he adds: 'I feel a self-congratulation in knowing myself capable of such sensations as he intended to excite . . . and I should desire that the last words which I should pronounce in this Academy and from this place might be the name of—Michael Angelo.'

In literal fact, they were his last official words. And they were words of unusual humility from a man to whom humility did not come easily. They were, perhaps, also the last words of the classic eighteenth century, the century that was convinced that to love art at its loftiest was more important than to experience intensely what life had to offer.

Reynolds looked back. Gainsborough looked forward; and if Reynolds had been as sensitive about what Gainsborough was doing as, ten years later, Schlegel had been about what Goethe was doing, he too might have toyed with the word 'interesting' and wondered whether perhaps it was not destined to oust 'the beautiful'. Ten years later Reynolds himself would perhaps have realized what was happening. Not only would he have been less condescending about Gainsborough, but he would also have taken a different view of Michelangelo himself. For while Reynolds was still alive, Blake and Fuseli were both making Michelangelesque drawings that proved that what they saw in Michelangelo was certainly not what Reynolds saw in him. To Fuseli, Michelangelo was surely more 'interesting' than 'elevated'.

To Gainsborough he was probably neither, for, as Reynolds frequently and rather patronizingly pointed out, he was no scholar, and the 'grand style', which for Reynolds was a thing to be aimed at even if he could not achieve it, was something he was hardly even conscious of ignoring. The two men were, in fact, forced by the society in which they lived to perform the same feats of formal portraiture unwillingly. Yet their unwillingness sprang from opposite temperaments. Gainsborough's innate romanticism could be seen in his earliest work—to which, oddly enough, Reynolds never referred in his obituary Discourse. Three paintings—all of them double portraits—done in the years between 1749 and 1755 (see *Mr and Mrs Andrews*) show him as a completely original artist with none of the light-handed flutter for which Reynolds praises him and against which he warns his students. What is remarkable in them all is that almost certainly without any possibility of influence he hit on that same device of the romantic that we have already seen in Giorgione, Altdorfer, and Watteau—the device of reducing the size of the figures in order that Nature may contain them, and of thrusting them into a corner in order to allow the eye to bypass them and explore the distant landscape without interruption. In each of the three the picture could be divided exactly into two halves down the centre, and the figures would still remain intact in the one half, leaving the other half an uninhabited landscape.

Such an acceptance of the duties of a portrait-painter combined with

Gainsborough, Mr and Mrs Andrews
National Gallery, London

a refusal to obey the conventions of portrait-painting would have seemed both eccentric and purposeless to Reynolds. In Gainsborough's case it was an act of romantic rebellion which he himself could not maintain. In the end the sitter's vanity brought him back into the centre of the canvas, and Gainsborough's romanticism had to find another means of asserting itself, and, more important, of replenishing its own easily exhausted powers.

We know well enough the light-handed flutter that marks the later Gainsborough and makes him seem to become more romantic as he gets older. But in point of fact that flutter is not evidence of romanticism but of charm. Gainsborough was capable at almost any moment in his career of producing a masterpiece that would pass all the tests of romanticism. But the percentage of those masterpieces is comparatively small, and for a good reason. They could only be achieved when an electric spark of mutual understanding passed between himself and his sitter. It was only then that his natural charm became intenser and that his responses became more urgent. It was in such moments that the fluttering brush-stroke provided him with the ideal method for the expression of urgency.

Sir Joshua would have been quite incapable of the sketches Gainsborough produced, in an inspired moment, of his two daughters, or of

The Morning Walk. At once we realize that Gainsborough had to be half in love with his sitter before the 'flutter' could be of any use to him. And certainly what captured Gainsborough was not a pretty face or a fashionable pose. The young newly-weds in *The Morning Walk* are hardly good-looking; their characters are commonplace and their features are irradiated by nothing but a flood of healthy contentment. It is on that all-pervading wave of mild happiness that the pair are carried onward through the park, and Gainsborough is carried with them. Sir Joshua could not have achieved such an effect of self-identification. Being more concerned with his picture than with his sitter, he could neither fail so dismally when he was bored nor rise to such heights when he was excited.

To Sir Joshua both the charm and the 'flutter'—since he himself was capable of neither—were marks of the amateur. Being a hard-working professional with a formula based on a study of tradition, Gainsborough's method of caressing his canvas into life was bound to provoke Sir Joshua into a kind of jealousy—the jealousy that professionals always feel when an amateur scores an easy success. And yet when Gainsborough died, praise was wrung out of him. To succeed without having laboured to earn success was not a negligible achievement. To be sure, students must not be encouraged to emulate such short cuts. Gainsborough's reliance on intuition as a substitute for scholarship, Gainsborough's habit of using his impulsive responses to provide a creative head of steam, deserved praise but was not to be imitated. It must have seemed to him that an enthusiastic amateur—a freak among painters—had scored a momentary success. It did not occur to him that Gainsborough was the herald of a romantic movement that was to rely, before the century was ended, more and more on enthusiasm, less and less on science. Without knowing it Gainsborough had started a revolution. The portrait-painters of the future were to look back to him rather than to Reynolds as a model.

Gainsborough's romanticism, to which charm and affection contribute in various proportions, is captivating but never powerful. If we are looking for the kind of conflict in which body and soul are at variance with one another and in which the artist himself, like some excitable, quick, temporal judge, stands by to make his own personal comment, we find it in its most uncompromising form in Goya. Gainsborough's comment had alternated between gentle enthusiasm and boredom. Goya, as a portrait-painter, can range from the vitriolic to the passionate. And when he abandoned portrait-painting for allegory or statements about human cruelty and suffering, what he has to say can be charged with a fury of hatred, mockery or indignant compassion whose only parallel is in the painting of Grünewald.

What differentiates the two artists is that Goya, despite the violence of his emotional messages, takes up his position far nearer to the

Goya, Saturn
Prado, Madrid

frontiers of realism than any of the German apostles of overstatement. For Grünewald, distortions of a hysterical kind were necessary in order to raise conflict to its highest power. Goya had no need to use such distortions. His hatreds are cold; they find their outlet in disgust rather than anger; his mockery is sardonic rather than macabre. When he describes, as he does in the series of etchings called 'The

Disasters of the War', the merciless cruelties of the victor toward the vanquished, fury against the torturer is balanced by compassion for the tortured.

If it were not for Goya's genius for pictorial metaphor in some of his more extravagant prints in the series of 'Caprichos', one would hardly know whether to describe him as a realist whose passions were too easily aroused or a romantic whose passions could only be made tolerable by translating them into realistic language. Occasionally, as in one or two of the more extreme of the war etchings, he refuses to soften the edges of horror, and once—in the *Saturn*, part of the frescoed wall-painting in his house, the Quinta del Sordo—he must have decided that on a wall that belonged to his own private environment he could dispense with all inhibitions. This image of the mad, bearded god devouring his own children comes near to the frontier of what the eye and mind can tolerate. It is as though the deaf painter in his final retirement had locked himself up in his own house and given full rein to the horrors that obsessed him. In some of the 'Disasters of the War', he wrote, as Jan van Eyck wrote on the wall of his Arnolfini portrait 'I was here'—'I saw this'. It is an attempt to convince us that he is not overstating his case. But in the *Saturn* he has no need to connect himself with the image. Not 'I saw this' but 'This always happens' should be the title.

It is easy enough to prove an artist romantic by selecting the most extreme examples of his art. But the same underlying emphatic reaction can be seen in all of his portraits. They are vivid rather than profound, and that is natural, for they are all records of sudden intimacies and responses. One imagines Rembrandt's greatest portraits painted in silence. Not so Goya's. Dr Peral is making a sudden sneering answer to a challenge from Goya; Dona Isabel Porcel preens herself in response to an extravagant compliment. This is not the snapshot vision of Impressionism, the snapshot of unpremeditated gesture. What Goya achieved, as no other artist, is a snapshot of a character—the revealing momentary expression, the outward sign of a state of mind.

CHAPTER 10

Romanticism in the Twentieth Century —Picasso

The reader will find the following sentence on page 29: 'If the essence of romanticism . . . is a refusal to look for absolutes of law and harmony in the outer, material world and an attempt to discover, empirically, any means that will serve to symbolize the inner, spiritual life, it follows that romanticism in any of the arts is always characterized by experiment—attempts to discover new formal devices whose only requirement is that they shall be appropriate to the mood to be expressed.'

There is no doubt that the period from about 1907 to the present day has seen the birth of more experimental devices that any other half-century in the history of the visual arts. And of the artists responsible for the sequence of such experiments I propose to consider two who seem to me to have experimented more decisively than any other in the twentieth century—Picasso, whose inventiveness in the use of form, and Paul Klee, whose researches into the possibility of meaningful imagery, have so remarkably enriched the pictorial language of romanticism.

The distinction between form (the stylization of a given object) and imagery (the invention of a new category of object) can never be a precise one. It would be an exaggeration to say that Picasso tends to distort familiar shapes while Klee creates shapes that are unfamiliar, yet it would be true to say that what I have called 'the mood to be expressed'—equally important to both artists—depends mainly, for Picasso, on his ability to create a new formal language and for Klee, on his fanciful and irresponsible imagination which can light-heartedly, and often with a touch of humour, create a world peopled with creatures formally unrelated to ourselves.

Both methods are intrinsically romantic. Klee's is the romanticism of the abnormal, Picasso's is the romanticism of conflict. Both artists differ from their predecessors in that the 'mood' is dependent on their

Picasso, Guernica
Collection, The Museum of Modern Art, New York

pictorial language rather than on their choice of subject-matter. When, for example, Picasso decided to express, with all the exasperated indignation of which he was capable, his attitude to the bombing of Guernica during the Spanish Civil War, it was inevitable that his picture should include recognizable references to death and physical suffering, yet it was not on those references that the power of his picture mainly depended—as it certainly did for Delacroix when he painted the *Massacre of Scios*—but on the pure vocabulary of form which, after a good deal of trial and error, he invented for the purpose.

That kind of inventiveness is ultimately based on a hard-won discovery, a twentieth-century discovery, that form and content, never separable, are related to each other in a way that had not been consciously realized in any previous century.

Form, we may say, is that aspect of a work of art which is perceived by the eye of the beholder or impressed on the ear of the listener. As such it has recognizable harmony, rhythm, pattern and colour. But as soon as form is communicated to the mind of the beholder or listener it begins to convey a set of meanings, and those meanings can be conveniently called content. Seen as form, *Guernica* consists of a series of curves and angles and of areas of low-toned colour. If we can imagine a man, blind from birth, suddenly granted the gift of sight and presented, as the first object offered to his inexperienced eye, with Picasso's picture, its form would be all that he could see. No passage in the picture would 'mean' bull, fallen warrior, or agonized horse, since he had never seen a man nor an animal. It is possible that he might grasp the underlying mathematics of the design—its broken symmetry or the contrast of pattern between empty and crowded areas—and that a certain satisfaction somehow related to mathematics would result. Too little is known about the relation between a blind man's aesthetic and that of a man accustomed to visual experience to say how deep or how real that satisfaction would be. But, for all but the man whose eyesight was backed by no visual experience at all, the picture would quickly resolve itself into an organization of meaningful images, and with that resolution, content would begin to emerge out of form. 'In *Guernica*,' we must then say, 'we are presented with images of a bull, a horse, a fallen warrior, an arm holding a lamp, a woman holding a child.' Or, to use the language of everyday speech, '*Guernica* is "about" these phenomena.'

As we contemplate the picture we begin to realize that we are not being offered information about the appearance of the objects and personages, but that, in some strange way that must be accounted for, the imagery is charged with emotion. The horse is agonized, the bull noble but angry, the warrior defeated, the lamp encouraging. And this happens partly because we can refer back to our previous knowledge of agonized horses and stricken warriors. We recognize that the artist has selected and isolated whatever, in the shape of a horse, will 'mean' an *agonized* horse. Yet that could have been done by a photographer who would take the trouble to inflict pain on a horse or slay a warrior and then take a photograph of the result.

The photograph would, of course, still convey descriptive visual information, but this time it would be descriptive information of a more precise kind. And it is evident from a comparison between the *Massacre of Scios* and *Guernica* that Delacroix has given us more precise information about the appearance of suffering persons or persons inflicting suffering on others than Picasso. Delacroix, to put it in its simplest terms, has been more photographic, and his success in conveying emotion has been more dependent on what was depicted (content) than on the manner of depiction (form).

None the less the words 'more' and 'less' are indicative of degree and not of kind. We feel quite sure that had Ingres tackled a subject whose power to convey emotions of pity and indignation was its principal object he would have been less successful than Delacroix, and that the reason for his failure would not have been his inability to describe in paint the appearances of suffering or of cruel persons, but his failure to discover the appropriate form. One begins, therefore, to suspect that there must be a hidden correspondence between form and content and that within the limitations of the stylistic traditions or conventions of the period in which the artist lived, certain families of form will refuse to express certain kinds of content; that the smooth untroubled surfaces of Ingres cannot convey the savagery implied in Goya's painting of Saturn devouring his children: and that however completely Ingres could have imagined the man-eating monster his painting would have failed to convey the innate ferocity of the idea—the 'literary' idea, to employ a useful but inexact word—behind it.

The very fact that in describing Ingres's form one cannot avoid using such words as 'untroubled' makes it plain that a correspondence exists between form and the emotion it attempts to convey. A line or a surface cannot in itself be troubled or untroubled, though it can be rough or smooth. To describe a surface as 'smooth and untroubled' is to pass from a fact to a metaphor. And we feel instinctively that an untroubled surface will not express—will not 'mean'—a troubled content.

But we also know that the limitations of the stylistic traditions or conventions of the period in which the artist lived exert an unavoidable steady pressure on his form, and therefore, in view of the correspondence noted in the previous paragraph, that same pressure must affect his content. Ingres and Delacroix, by virtue of their inevitable adherence to a 'descriptive' style of painting, are closer to each other than either is to Picasso, despite the difference between their temperaments.

I said just now that form resolves itself into content, in the spectator's mind, *partly* because it can refer back to a previous knowledge of warriors and horses, and even though Picasso's form in *Guernica* refers less descriptively to such knowledge it is still quite easily read as imagery. But 'partly' implies that our description of the form-content relationship is still incomplete. In what sense could it be said—if it can be said at all—that form can resolve itself into content without any help from such references to previous knowledge?

Non-figurative art has attempted for half a century to abandon such references, but no non-figurative artist would admit that in doing so he had abandoned content, even though he would probably maintain that he was pursuing a different kind of content. Picasso's semi-heraldic image of a bull refers us back to our knowledge of a seen bull. But does Ben Nicholson's painting of a square or a circle refer us back to our knowledge of seen squares and circles? And if it does what is its 'content'? If we regard it as a description of a square or a circle it adds nothing to our existing knowledge of squares and circles. The artist has selected or intensified nothing out of our experience of squareness. He would probably maintain that what he had presented us with in his work of art 'is' a square or a circle and not a representation of a geometrical figure.

This really does mean that the content of non-figurative art is different in kind from that of a figurative art—or rather that it is of only one kind whereas that of figurative art has a double appeal. It refers back, as already stated, to forms already seen and remembered, but it has also been suggested above that a man blind from birth and confronted, at the moment when his sight was restored to him, with a work of representational art would not see it as a representation, but would certainly accept it as a formal organization and might derive a certain satisfaction from 'the underlying mathematics' of the design.

The same underlying mathematics is, of course, available to us all in every work of visual art, and if the work of art contains no representational elements—as in a building, a piece of furniture or a non-figurative painting—it is the only ingredient in it that is available. The 'satisfaction' I have postulated that comes from the contemplation of that ingredient is undeniable. And that satisfaction must be regarded as the result of recognizing its 'content'. Would it be true, then, to say that 'content' is of two kinds, one operating through the enjoyment of purely mathematical (or harmonious) relationships, the other arousing emotion by virtue of its appeal to our visual experience?

Plato, in an oft-quoted passage in which he says that beauty is to be found in geometrical figures, certainly recognizes the satisfaction provided by mathematical relationships. And Plato would certainly not have denied that beauty was also discoverable in a well-proportioned human body—and *therefore*, presumably, in a marble or bronze replica of that body. But what now concerns me is the problem of whether these two kinds of beauty are related. Is it, for example, partly by virtue of their innate mathematics that the shapes that compose the *Guernica* panel succeed in communicating an emotion of suffering and grief?

If, as has already been suggested, an 'untroubled' line of surface is inappropriate for communicating trouble, one would suspect that there is such a correspondence, and that therefore the critic, attempting to estimate the success or otherwise with which Delacroix had communicated suffering in the *Massacre of Scios*, would be better advised to say 'Note the acute angle of the shoulder' than 'Note the tear-drop in the eye.' And even so, the critic must be on his guard to distinguish, if such a distinction can be reasonably made, between the acute angle that invariably indicates pain in real life and the acute angle that the artist has invented as the visual, mathematical equivalent of pain.

'If such a distinction can be reasonably made' is certainly a necessary saving clause in attempting to solve such a problem. For there seems good reason to suppose that the connexion between mathematics and human emotion has its ultimate roots in human experience. Vertical lines suggest not only stability but also energy: they repeat the natural line of the tree-trunk that seeks the most direct way towards the light. A tower, we say, 'rises', knowing well enough that it does not rise, but that we, by the process known as empathy, lift our eyes and our heads upward as we follow the line from its base to its summit. Horizontal lines suggest even greater stability, for we demand for our comfort a level surface to walk on: but they suggest less energy, for the horizontal is the line ultimately achieved by whatever, from the fallen warrior to the line of the sea's horizon, has given up the struggle or has no need to raise itself upward and no longer resists the law of gravity.

A glossary of such correspondences could easily be compiled. The most imperturbable of all geometric forms, because the most difficult to overbalance, would be the pyramid, whose weight decreases as it ascends: the most unstable the inverted pyramid for the opposite reason. Diagonals—the line of the tree or the warrior during their fall —*must* involve and therefore suggest movement. And we know that nothing but an opposing diagonal will arrest their movement, and that once the opposing diagonal has arrived the movement will be arrested, since an immovable pyramid has come into being.

Curvature of various kinds can be added to our glossary until we are at last furnished with a vocabulary that will serve well enough for the most elementary human requirements. We can use it to say 'serene', 'active', 'unstable', but not 'sensuous'. Not until we have added recognizable imagery to it can we say 'fear', still less can we say '*Guernica*'. But once we have produced the woman, the warrior, the horse and the bull that will enable us to say '*Guernica*' we can then return to our glossary, and by using all the extracts from it that will serve our purpose we can immeasurably increase the romantic or emotional impact of our statement 'about' *Guernica*.

Perhaps this brief excursion into the fundamental relationship between form and content should have occurred earlier in a book whose main purpose is to inquire not only into the nature of romantic content but also into the methods it employs to communicate that content. What has just been said about a mathematical basis which could be analysed into a glossary has, of course, always been true of all the arts. The problem of discovering a form that will give content its maximum force was a problem to the sculptor of the Parthenon pediments, to Giotto and to Rembrandt just as it was for Klee and Picasso. But it was never a problem that was tackled self-consciously or intellectually by them. The glossary of correspondence was never envisaged until the twentieth century. It would have been unthinkable for Rembrandt to say that an untroubled line could never depict a troubled mood or situation. And even had he or any pre-twentieth-century artist had the courage to make such a statement he would never have been logical enough to face its consequences and abandon his own descriptive style (however personal it might have been) in favour of a series of formal devices invented for the occasion.

Once the decision to do so had been made—and the sacrifice involved in doing so must always be considerable—the descriptive method of painting loses its importance: form becomes its own master; or rather it becomes the aggressively dictatorial servant of content, and the 'descriptive' method slinks away unmourned and becomes unnecessary.

This is a new situation and it calls for a new assessment. Hence the intrusion of this argument in a chapter confined to the twentieth century rather than as an introduction to a book. It was in 1907 that form as the 'aggressively dictatorial' servant of content made its first appearance. Therefore it is the situation of 1907 that must be analysed here, even though it is an old situation. In the twentieth century it was heightened until it is now almost unrecognizable. One could almost say that the observant eye had almost ceased to play a part in the creation of form.

The change-over, as is well known, happened suddenly. Up to the year 1906 Picasso's romanticism had followed the normal course of isolating and intensifying the emotive object or personage. During the 'blue period' he had been obsessed by pathos and expressed it in paintings of emaciated creatures, deliberately elongated and made cadaverous. The method was still that of Delacroix—the method of selecting a model and of emphasizing or exaggerating whatever in the model would increase the emotional impact he had already decided upon. In 1907, with the *Demoiselles d'Avignon*, so often hailed by critics as the 'beginning of modern art' (though it seems to me, despite its courageous experimentation, a far from satisfactory work of art), the descriptive method is abandoned. The new glossary of mathematical form makes its arrival in its rudimentary stages, operating for the first time as a weapon for the expression of content. It would, of course, have been more than any human being, however inventive or audacious, could have achieved, to produce a completely organized new language of formal equivalents at such short notice.

During the 'pink period' that followed, pathos ceased to be an obsession, the elongations and emaciations were toned down, the clouds of colour became gentler, the subject-matter changed to a mood of amiable, carefree life with the vagabondage of circus folk as the chief interest. The romanticism of pathos was being replaced by the more conventional romanticism of the *vie de bohème*. The observation of 'life' became closer, the descriptive method became more conventional. It looked as though another brilliant and precocious specialist in sentiments were diligently perfecting his own variation on a traditional style, perhaps a warmer-hearted, more human Degas with the same Ingres-like gift of expressive line. Then, suddenly, tradition was abandoned.

It is surprising that in a major work, and without a longish period of trial and error to prepare for it, the new formal language should be as coherent as it is.

No language, whether verbal or visual, can ever be invented *ab initio*. However familiar it may seem at its first appearance, it must have been developed out of something already seen and already digested. It is tempting to think of the formal rhythms that appear for the first time in the *Demoiselles d'Avignon* as being based on African sculpture. But apart from the heads of the two women on the right, which stylistically contradict the rest of the painting, it is impossible to discover African idioms anywhere. The schematic treatment of the blue and brown curtains behind the women reminds one of one of El Greco's skies—themselves among the most remarkable examples of stylistic invention in the art of the past. The incisive angular forms of the five nude women probably trace their origin to Iberian sculpture. But the refusal to model by shadow, the attempt to suggest volume by lines superimposed on the flat areas of flesh colour and the almost total negation of space, could come from any school of pre-Renaissance painting—in Picasso's case it would probably be Catalan.

But what is most remarkable is the rhythmic unity of the picture. The angular pattern of the figures overflows across the whole canvas and holds together the 'negative' shapes left by the gaps between them. In these gaps the treatment of the folds of the curtains, their linear character and the density of the pattern made by them, binds the picture together into a formal, compact unity. It is this replacement of descriptive painting by rhythmic invention that is the startling innovation. The new type of form that Picasso has invented can be used equally well for a woman, a folded curtain or a bunch of flowers. It is in this respect that the traditions of the past, which had operated without a break from the thirteenth century up to 1907, were jettisoned and that a new conception of form—form unfettered by any obligation to be faithful to appearance—took their place.

The effect even on Picasso's most sympathetic and intelligent friends —certainly on Braque, Matisse, and Apollinaire—was shattering. It was inevitable that it should be so, for a work of art in a language so unfamiliar and strange does not carry its glossary with it. Only by constant repetition of new forms in varying contexts can we begin to guess at new meanings. It is by the same kind of repetition that the child learns its own language, and if Braque and Matisse could not fathom the meanings of the new '*Demoiselles d'Avignon*' language, it is not likely—indeed it would be impossible—for less sensitive or less accomplished linguists to do so.

But exactly thirty years later, when *Guernica* came to be painted, Picasso had not only perfected his own gift of linguistic formal invention, but he had established the fact that his paintings could not be read until we had accepted him as a language inventor. During that period of thirty years he had offered us so many different kinds of syntax and vocabulary that we had accustomed ourselves to the new method of reading. The cubist system of formal invention was sufficiently suggestive of our knowledge of the form of crystals that we were able to make use of that knowledge in reading a cubist painting. The sensuous curvature expressed in fierce but flowing black line and the clear primary colouring of 1932 was sufficiently reminiscent of the flowing lead lines and the vivid colouring of Gothic stained glass to give us a starting-point in the task of deciphering a new kind of content. It turned out to be a new way of emphasizing the indolent sensuousness of the female body. As content, that aspect of human experience is familiar, but, apart from certain erotic carvings on Indian temples, no previous artist had succeeded in discovering a formal language that could isolate and intensify it with such unmistakable impact.

Presumably, in the year 1932, Picasso's own experience of *volupté* demanded the invention of a new set of formal and chromatic rhythms. But it is quite certain that in 1937, when he came to design *Guernica*, those same rhythms would have been quite useless to express the *Guernica* content. They would, in fact, have destroyed its very essence.

This, surely, is the core of the romantic method, and it is the surest index of Picasso's romanticism that he has carried it to such lengths.

The genesis of the *Guernica* panel (11 feet high and 25 feet wide) is worth a brief note. During the two years that preceded it Picasso's emotional preoccupations had been largely centred on the Spanish Civil War. Consequently his stylistic invention had developed in the direction of indignation at cruelty and injustice. During those years and especially in the latter months of that period he had been experimenting with shapes of unusual angularity and ferocity—or, to be strictly precise, angularity which became in his hands the equivalent of ferocity.

But this stylistic development, as happened so often in his formal development, was often almost independent of the descriptive or narrative content. Portraits of Dora Maar and Madame Eluard painted in 1937 show the same set of angular conventions but contain no implications of anger. It is as though the formal vocabulary he had been evolving to fit a dominant mood had overflowed into paintings that had no connexion with the mood.

But parallel with these ferocious paintings and interspersed with them was another series of works left over, as it were, from the voluptuous 'Gothic' series of 1932, but far more poetic in their imagery. They vary in mood between suave pathos and tenderness, and in content they are among his most memorable essays in a private mythology dominated by the Minotaur. This extraordinary creature, sometimes a symbol of brute strength, sometimes of Caliban-like bewilderment, sometimes triumphant, sometimes subdued and even slain by beauty, is developed in a series of drawings and etchings that culminated in one of the most pregnant and memorable of all his works, the *Minotauromachie* of 1935.

That etching contains the germ of a great deal that was to reappear in a simpler, savager form in *Guernica*. The bull, the frightened horse, the vulnerable woman, the child holding a symbol of hope in an outstretched hand. A familiar melody has been reorchestrated. From richly elaborated *andante* it has become a stark *allegro furioso*. *Guernica* combines the symbolic imagery with the fierce angularity of the years that preceded its appearance.

But also—as was inevitable in the case of so large a picture—its planning is purely classic. If proof were needed that romantic content need not be contradicted by a classically deliberate basic plan, *Guernica* supplies it. Mathematically speaking, the picture is based on a firm central pyramid strengthened on either side by groups whose dominant rhythms are vertical. And the verticals are carried across by further references to verticals within the pyramid itself. The accompanying

Picasso, Guernica Diagram
Collection, The Museum of Modern Art, New York

diagram will make the basic architecture of the panel plain. It is that of a Greek pediment flanked by columns, and despite the almost hysterically expressive separate ingredients it contains, nothing could be structurally firmer than this overall plan.

The pyramid rises, in two shallow curves, to a strongly marked centre line. Within its framework is packed most of the violence and suffering. On the left, the group of the bull and the woman mourning over her dead child makes a compact group, tapering upward: on the right the woman with arms outstretched, falling downward through a burning house, balances the bull, in a shape that tapers downward. Nearer to the centre line are two more supporting shapes. On the left the horse-image and the sun-image, on the right the head and the arm that thrusts itself across the point of the pyramid and holds a lamp that adds another vertical.

This is the kind of basic architecture that a Raphael or a Poussin could easily have invented. That Picasso should have used it as a steadying framework is no sign of genius. Any good artist with a feeling for the laws of composition could have arrived at a similar solution to the problem of planning a large horizontal surface. It is not until we begin to read the picture in terms of the invented glossary of form and the not very obscure language of accepted symbolism that the picture begins to count as a masterpiece. And it seems clear that Picasso, in designing it, was determined that it should be read entirely in terms of its linear construction and the alternating masses of light and dark areas, since he ultimately decided to eliminate colour and make his final statement in grisaille, even though he was quite capable of fusing form-content with colour-content in order to double the emotional impact of the final product. He did, in fact, paint, in the same year, a head of a weeping woman, clearly connected with the mood and imagery of *Guernica*, in which the colour, acid and brilliant, is both appropriate and insistent.

The picture contains a good deal of symbolism, and here again is a painter's device that makes no demands on genius, for symbolism is fundamentally imagery that is valid for the spectator only by virtue of having an accepted meaning. It is, in fact, visually no more than a short cut—a device that overflows into the domain of literature, but happens to use a formal instead of a verbal medium. To represent hope by an anchor and justice by a blindfolded woman requires neither talent nor ingenuity. Its presence in a work of visual art is no indication of a romantic urge to increase the impact of emotional content. *Guernica* could conceivably have dispensed with the bull, the horse, the lamp and the formalized sun with rays radiating outward from an electric bulb. Even the broken sword in the hand of the fallen warrior is merely an easy way of indicating that he has been engaged in some form of combat with an anonymous adversary.

Once the literary content of the symbol has been accepted as adding something, however little, to the message, its function has been fulfilled. Beyond that it can only add a note of obscurity. And this Picasso has succeeded in doing, for his symbols have a life of their own which lifts them out of the category of 'accepted' imagery and gives them a range of meaning that is normally beyond the range of the familiar stereotypes of literary symbols. The bull is another reincarnation of the mysterious Minotaur, with all its patience, its pathos and its nobility: the horse is the most arresting item of imagery in the picture's surface, partly because of its central position, partly because it has become the crowning statement of anguish. Packed with 'meaning' though they are, the meanings conveyed by these two creatures is not simple or precise. Equally dubious is the almond-shaped form with the electric bulb in its centre that seems to mean the sun—but is it, in its turn, a symbol of hope? Or does it contain a hint of claustrophobia—the only source of light in a crowded, violated underground shelter?

But the secret of *Guernica*'s romantic impact is found neither in its classic, architectural symmetry nor in its symbolism, but in the innate character of the forms themselves. If one regards them as wilful departures from descriptive idealism, they are distorted with the kind of intelligent recklessness of which only Picasso knew the secret, and which even he could use to its fullest effect only at certain moments when passionate emotion and formal intentiveness were working in perfect harmony with each other.

The eye is riveted immediately on certain details in which the formal invention is working at white heat. The outstretched empty hand of the warrior on the left—its fingers clumsily grasping the air, its palm crossed by a cat's cradle of brutal lines—is balanced by the foot and ankle of the woman who rushes in from the right. These two fragments—architecturally important because they mark the limits of the pyramid's base—are emotionally arresting because they establish the kind of linear tension that pervades the picture.

It would be possible, though it would be tedious, to analyse these formal tensions in detail. Some of them have a childlike obviousness, others sink in slowly and convey their meaning gradually to the mind behind the eye. Some are mere rudimentary simplifications of something that had to be included for clarity's sake but added nothing to the content: others, which occur at the most vital points of intersection, are evidently the result of a long process of trial and error, where the lines gather themselves together into knotted complexities. In particular, the horse's head, more ruthlessly 'distorted' than any other piece of imagery, has been arrived at after a longish sequence of experimental drawings—attempts, as it were, to see the inside of the open mouth, to isolate the teeth, to turn the thrust-out tongue into an important dagger, to reduce the eyes to tiny circles, as though they were sightless in death.

The whole of the process by which the imagery of *Guernica* came into being tends to disturb those of us who have absorbed, in our childhood, the theory that illusionism, though not the whole of art, is a major part of it. We call it, for convenience, a process of *distortion*, implying that the artist, if he wished, could pin his faith on a faithful rendering of appearances, but that, finding this faithful rendering failed to deliver the message he had in mind, deliberately *distorted* those appearances in order to make them expressive. If that is how we account for examples as extreme as *Guernica* (as well as for less extreme examples that recur by the thousand throughout the art of the world) we cannot help being disturbed, for we are continually comparing, in our mind's eye, the appearance of a bull or a man with Picasso's description of a bull or a man and trying to account for the difference between the two. According to the theory of distortion an artist continually departs from what he sees in order to express more clearly what he feels.

I do not believe that we can ever come to grips with the meaning of any work of romantic art if we think of the artist as a man tethered to the world of appearances, but continually straining to lengthen the tether in order to extend his range of expressiveness. To speak of *distortions*, whether they occur in *Guernica* or in the Pietà of Avignon, is surely to misunderstand the creative process and to think of the artist as somehow taking his stand at a certain distance (a distance always chosen by himself) from the world of phenomena, and doing his best, at the fixed distance, to express himself: Velasquez, if that is the image in our mind, has adopted an unusually short tether; the unknown Avignon Pietà painter a longer one, and Picasso a longer one still.

In his *Metamorphosis of the Gods* Malraux speaks of a Truth that exists 'beyond the above appearance' and suggest that the great artist subordinates 'what is seen to that which *is*' even though in doing so he may (not *must*, otherwise non-figurative art could never have come into being) make recognizable references to what is seen. This is not an easy notion to grasp, but I believe it must be accepted in all art, though it is only in the case of extremists like the Picasso of 1937 that the difficulty becomes acute.

Once the difference between lengthening the tether to 'what is seen' and shortening the tether to 'that which is' has been grasped, the pictorial language of a *Guernica* becomes comparatively easy to read. We are concerned not with departing from what is *seen*, but with approaching more closely to that which *is*. The invented images of grief, cruelty or hope are no longer pictorial imitations of the gestures and facial expressions of grieving or cruel or optimistic persons. They are translations into line and colour of grief itself made 'readable' by minimal references to women or warriors. In such references the artist need no longer pay even lip-service to human anatomy, or to space and light. The arm holding a lamp need make no reference to bone and muscle, but it must make clear the act of thrusting: the head behind the thrusting arm need not possess a body, but it must suggest urgency and perhaps an open mouth to suggest a warning cry. The lamp, on the other hand, must be a recognizable lamp with a recognizable flame, otherwise it will 'mean' nothing but a set of curves with a vertical axis. The vertical axis would have been explicit enough to 'mean' steadiness: but steadiness is not enough. 'Lampness' must be added, and all the artist can do is to glance back at the seen world and hastily borrow a lamp from it.

When we look at *Guernica*, therefore, we are not looking at a wilful though expressive set of distortions, but at a direct translation of 'that which is' into visible terms, and we must judge its success by the excellence of the translation and not by the persuasiveness of the distortion.

Clearly the demands on the creative imagination are more severe in the latter case, and not many artists have managed to meet them with so few backward glances at the seen world and so few borrowings. And among those few not many have felt the need so often and so imperatively to found a new formal vocabulary to meet the demands of a new set of emotional impulses. It is in that respect that Picasso differs from his great predecessors.

A Giovanni Bellini or a Turner may spend a lifetime slowly developing the means to an end which had always been in view. Between Bellini's *Agony in the Garden*, which borrows its formal vocabulary from Mantegna, and his *Feast of the Gods*, which uses a vocabulary invented by himself, is a long and steady progress during which he slowly moved towards a style which we can only describe as more suited to his temperament. But Picasso's temperament has none of that steadiness. He can alternate with alarming rapidity between tenderness and anger, between an obsession with the natural and a grasping for the supernatural, and with each alternation he has to lay aside the old pattern of form and invent a new one. That each one of these patterns has had its origin in something already seen—perhaps a drawing or a Greek vase, perhaps an Iberian or a Nigerian sculpture—is only natural. What is unusual is his willingness to find a new stimulant whenever he found himself in the grip of a new mood.

The consequence, as far as his 'style' is concerned, is that he is quite incapable of development. For him there is no 'end that has always been in view'. During the paintings of *volupté* of 1932 it would have been impossible to predict the passion of 1937. His life as an artist has not been a steady advance in a known direction, but a series of lightning raids in unforeseen directions and on unforeseen objectives, so that his power is never cumulative. He is, of course, capable of building on past successes and returning unexpectedly to old battlegrounds, as though he had left something behind in an earlier raid that had to be retrieved. But such returns are not typical. They occur frequently, but only, one feels, in order to give his creative imagination a holiday from the strain to which it had been submitted.

It is useless and also insensitive to ask where, in this sequence of violent changes and experiments, are we to find 'the true Picasso'. Behind each one of them is an easily detectable flavour, not quite the equivalent of a personal handwriting, but certainly the result of a set of personal gifts or preferences. He is, for example, a brilliant draughtsman, but not more than an adequate painter. One cannot praise him for his *'matière'* as one can praise Bonnard or Manet. It is the organization and tension of his line that bears the main burden of each of his major statements. During the two crowded months between the first conception of *Guernica* (news of the bombing reached Paris on 29 April 1937) and its completion and its placing in the Spanish pavilion in the International Exhibition, his friend Dora Maar photographed it at each stage. And during that period it underwent a good deal of revision. But from the beginning, when the basic pyramid and the basic symmetry were established, to the last brush-stroke all the adjustments were linear. And it is significant that, though the disposition of light and dark areas played an important part, colour, either descriptive or emotional, was never allowed to contribute. *Guernica*, like so many of his most forceful paintings, is, in essence, a drawing. And it is well known that a personality can express itself more forcefully and unmistakably in line than in any other medium, whether it be a hurried scribble or a painstaking statement and whether its author is Mantegna, Tiepolo, or Ingres. Picasso, for all the romanticism of his content, in which 'beauty' was invariably, as with all romantics, sacrificed to 'meaning', is in essence a classic draughtsman. The design underlying the romantic detail is always as solidly constructed as in a Raphael, a Poussin, or an Ingres.

Too much has been written about the stylistic adventures of Picasso in his search for formal conventions to express the 'Truth that exists beyond and above appearance'. Those adventures have been labelled by his biographers, as though a label could define a discovery. Since the impact of such inventions cannot, except in the vaguest sense, be described in words, no useful purpose would be served by enumerating them. If an artist's announcements in visual terms about the large family of truths that have always obsessed Picasso could be translated back into words, he himself would have been better employed as a writer, for what an artist has to say is itself a translation. To produce a translation of a translation would only be useful to those who cannot read the language of form, and for such people the language of form can never speak vividly.

They can only approach that language by thinking of it as a branch of illusionism. To them the pity and terror conveyed by the *Massacre of Scios* and *Guernica* must, in the end, depend on the skill and accuracy with which the artist has described the appearance of persons inflicting cruelty or suffering pain. And since Delacroix has manifestly succeeded in doing this and Picasso has not even attempted to do so, no amount of persuasive argument about the difference between what is *seen* and what *is* will convince those to whom illusionism is a normal procedure that it can be dispensed with.

To dispense with it to such an extent—to substitute an equivalent for a description—is a twentieth-century experiment. It is not a necessary one, though it can produce results denied to the illusionist painter. Those results can be seen in all medieval art, but not in the art that appeared in Europe at the beginning of the fifteenth century and ended with the decay of Impressionism at the end of the nineteenth.

Naturally, even the devotees of illusionism are not so foolish as to equate illusionism with photographic accuracy. They recognize that between Titian and Rubens there is a fundamental difference of approach to life itself and that what Titian has to say about the meaning, *to him*, of the human body, is not the same as what Rubens has to say. They are well aware that what makes both artists precious to us is precisely that difference. What unites them is the fact that both of them observe, and observe with enthusiasm, the same object—the trunk of a tree or the naked body of Venus. What gives them their value is that in describing those objects their enthusiasms have been stimulated by different aspects of them, and their statements in pigment have therefore a different set of emphases.

To be blind to such emphases is exceptional, and whoever attempts to describe them has a comparatively easy task, for what he is really doing is comparing two descriptions, both of them heightened by strong personal emotion, with an imagined reality—an actual tree or an actual human body. They prefer the description to the reality, for it carries with it a highly charged comment, which the object described does not. This sensitivity to the comment is what all of us, in various degrees, possess. It makes our approach to the Titian version or the Rubens version of a tree or a woman comparatively easy.

But when we are faced with the languages Picasso has invented, the problem is different. The Picasso tree or the Picasso woman is not a comment on an observed object but a caricature of a new object. It may be that we have to call it for clarity's sake 'tree' or 'woman'. But it is different in kind from the Titian-Rubens tree or woman. Only in the remotest sense is it based on what is seen. Therefore, it cannot be a comment. It is a separate creation—a metaphor in visual terms. Perhaps, after all, to call it a symbol would be the least misleading way of describing it.

Perhaps the cleavage I have tried to describe between the method (but not, of course, the intention behind the method) of the Titian-Rubens faction and the Picasso-Klee faction (Klee must be dealt with in the next chapter) could best be expressed by saying that that age-old intermediary between the artist and what he produces—the artist's model whether it be a tree or a woman—has disappeared. We look at Titian's Prado *Venus* or at Rubens's *Judgment of Paris* and we know that the goddesses with which those masterpieces are concerned could not have made their way on to canvas without the co-operation of real women. Titian and Rubens had devoted their lives to the close study of models and to the technical procedures that would enable them to produce an illusionist account of their appearances, just as Picasso had done before 1906. It was not that either Titian or Rubens thought that the art of painting consisted in the production of such illusionist accounts, but that they took it for granted that without a model there could be no question of isolating and intensifying that aspect of the human body that passionately interested them. For to isolate and intensify implies a concrete object as a starting-point for the journey of creation, however long and tortuous the journey may be and however radically the resultant work of art may differ from the model.

That the model herself had been invented in Periclean Athens is unimportant, though both Titian and Rubens must have been unconsciously influenced by Greek sculpture when they contemplated their posed models. But that was not necessary. Gauguin had taken what he thought was a revolutionary step when he left Europe behind and journeyed to Tahiti.

The step was *not* revolutionary. Gauguin had merely changed one model for another. The Tahitian girls in his paintings were still the starting-points for a journey.

But that Picasso's human images are not evolved from models hardly needs sayings. What does need saying is that the method of using a model as a starting-point always involves the artist in a reference, however disguised, to a seen object: and that a seen object exists not only in space but in time, and must therefore carry with it the sense not only of a specific but also a *momentary* appearance, and in doing so the figures in the painting can never be timeless symbols. They can, in fact, never be goddesses.

By the Picassian method the timelessness of the symbol is assured. There never were any models for the *Guernica* panel. 'This happened to those people at that moment' is an inconceivable thought in the presence of such a work. The images are formal embodiments of an abstract emotion: and emotion itself is only worth expressing because it is not anchored to a moment in time.

CHAPTER II

Romanticism in the Twentieth Century —Paul Klee

Picasso drives forcefully towards his objective and ruthlessly clears all obstructions, especially the obstruction of illusionism, out of his path on his journey to it. Klee is incapable of ruthlessness and almost incapable of anything that could be called 'driving'. His method is almost the exact opposite of Picasso's. The only obstruction he will admit is the natural behaviour of whatever medium he uses, and that he almost miraculously turns to advantage, by using it as a guide, allowing it to impose its will on him and arriving unexpectedly at a destination that he himself had only half envisaged. His art is almost dependent on the opportunist use he makes of the medium.

The method, far more than that of Picasso, is at the very root of romanticism. It is the apotheosis of what is known as 'doodling'. He himself has described certain drawings as 'an expressive' movement of the hand that holds the recording pencil, 'in which the hand is the tool of a remote will'. Will Grohmann has acutely compared him [1] to a seismograph that almost automatically records the psychic effects of musical vibrations. Such an artist would have been no more than a drifter playing games with the tools of his trade had he not also been a poet, a musician, a philosopher, and a profound thinker, who had discovered that by means of his art he could, as it were, tap the contents of his own subconscious mind on any level. Rilke, who was not entirely happy about Klee's refusal to 'describe' his subject-matter, sensibly accounted for his art as a 'short-circuiting behind the back of nature and even of the imagination'.

In order to accomplish this he had first to become a craftsman. 'Almost automatically' are the operative words in Grohmann's description of Klee's creative processes. The 'remote will' Klee speaks of as being served by his hand would have been powerless to control the hand had there not been a co-operation between the two so complete

[1] *Paul Klee,* by Will Grohmann (Lund Humphries).

as to be almost mystical. And that co-operation could only be achieved by craftsmanship so highly developed that what Grohmann calls the seismograph's needle could record the slightest psychic disturbances with uncanny precision.

Being a philosopher, Klee found it possible to explain in words the exact relationship between the disturbance and the tremulous record of it produced by the needle. In doing so—in a set of rough notes for a lecture—he has come nearer to describing the creative process than any other writer known to me. In the notes for a lecture delivered in 1924[1] he centres his remarks on 'that part of the creative process which mainly takes place on the unconscious level'. Having referred briefly to the conventional distinction between form and content, he adds: 'To achieve some sort of balance between the two appeals to me.' This, too, is conventional. What follows is not.

> Let me use a simile: the artist . . . is like a Tree. He receives the sap that flows through him and through his eye.
>
> His work is like the crown of the tree, spreading in time and space for all to see.
>
> Now nobody would expect the crown of a tree to have exactly the same shape as the roots. Clearly . . . the fact that they belong to different realms must of necessity produce important differences of structure. Why, then, do people deny the artist's right (which is not so much a right as a necessity) to depart from the appearance of his models . . .? After all, in his capacity as the trunk he only gathers and transmits what comes to him from below. He is neither a master nor a servant but a mediator.'

This tremendously condensed statement contains a profound truth that had never been stated quite so clearly before. That the nourishment the artist receives from the roots that attach him to 'life' (the life of the senses) belongs to a different category from the use he makes of it in his work of art is so manifestly true, once it has been stated in such simple words, that one wonders why, for six centuries, artists had been at such pains to close the gap between them. The trunk of the tree in which those mysterious correspondences are born was, for Klee, far too complex an instrument to waste its powers in trying to turn correspondences into resemblances.

There had, of course, been romantic artists in the past who were dimly aware that they were seismographs rather than copyists (and in almost every case their progress throughout their lives had been away from the copy in the direction of the sensitive needle-point): but none of them had acknowledged to themselves that the artist's main concern

[1] Grohmann, p. 365.

was to perfect the sensitivity of the needle and to keep the channel between experience and the visual statement of it free from the obstruction that invariably besets the illusionist artist.

The obstruction—the need to allow a description of visible fact to intervene between himself and the statement of his chosen theme—was not one that Paul Klee found difficult to circumvent after his thirtieth year (1912). For him the creation of images drawn from or based on the seen world came easily, but his use of such images was very different from that of Picasso. In his hands they became diagrams or hieroglyphics, inexpressive in their own right but full of meaning in the contexts he provided for them. They are the kind of diagrams that children invent, forms that 'stand for' a moon, a cluster of stars or a pine-tree, as simple as the vocabulary Blake used in the *Songs of Innocence*, but also as pregnant with meaning when gathered together and used as ingredients in the crucible of his poetic imagination.

'Poetic imagination' is a phrase that the critic uses too thoughtlessly whenever he is confronted with a work of visual art that seems to contain more meaning than 'meets the eye'. Titian paints a more or less illusionist Venus lying on a couch. Her body, slightly distorted in order to pay homage to the Venetian feminine ideal of the mid-sixteenth century, departs, we feel sure, from the appearance of the model Titian used only by very slight differences of emphasis; and those differences we recognize at once as evidence that Venice is speaking to us through the mouth of Titian. And what is true of Titian's treatment of his model is equally true of everything in his picture; the same kind of differences of emphasis have also determined the folds of the curtain behind the goddess, the sheet on which she lies, the way in which Titian has envisaged the corner of the room and the glimpse of sky behind the column. All this adds up to something recognizably Titianesque, and we know that had Rubens or Velasquez been given the main outlines of the same composition and told to develop them into a painting the results would have been equally recognizable expressions of the Rubens or the Velasquez view of women, curtains, and interiors.

All three pictures would depart by a mere hairbreadth from what would result if a skilful and patient colour photographer were to select his model, construct his environment and still-life accessories and photograph the result. Yet we know well enough that those hairbreadth differences amount to something we are in the habit of calling 'personal vision' and that when the addition sum seems to us particularly interesting or evocative we attribute it to the artist's 'poetic imagination'.

The phrase is a rough-and-ready attempt to recognize, without defining it, the distinction between comment and description: and it is useful enough as a pointer for a critic who wishes to establish the essential difference between what the artist's eye accepts from the visible world of phenomena and what reorganization or extract from that grand total he decides to pass on to us in his work of art.

But what Paul Klee passes on to us can seldom be described as a reorganization of or an extract from visual experience. For him the substance drawn upward from the roots of the tree by the stem has undergone such a radical series of transformations by the time it is presented to us in the guise of flowers or foliage that an entirely new critical approach is necessary before we can grasp the essence of his creative mechanism.

One cannot think of Klee's imagery, as one can of Titian's or even of Picasso's, as a reorganization of appearances—slight in Titian's case, violent in Picasso's, but decisive in both. Titian's *Venus* is a descriptive statement about *a* woman translated by a series of subtle shifts of emphasis into an image of Venetian womanhood. In short, an artist has extracted from a visual total only that part of the total that is Venetian.

Picasso's woman thrusting out an arm that holds a lighted lamp is also an extract from a visual total, though in Picasso's case less has been extracted and the extract itself has been intensified and exaggerated. If the word 'Venetian' explains Titian's woman, the words 'urgent' and 'thrusting' explain Picasso's. And since 'thrusting' and 'urgency' describe something less specific than 'Venetian', Picasso's extract can afford to be incomplete. Only an arm and a head are needed to tell the story and transmit the emotion. We can, therefore, easily accept and understand Picasso's extract. It may omit more than Titian's and what it does not omit may be more radically distorted, but it does not differ in kind.

But I have grave doubts whether Klee's imagery, once his creative method had been established, could be thought of as an 'extract' in any reasonable sense of the word. When Grohmann describes him as a seismograph he is thinking of a different kind of creative process from Picasso's. A seismograph translates a tremor on the earth's surface into a line drawn on a sheet of paper. The line is in no sense an *extract* from the tremor: it is a translation of it into a different medium, and there would be no reason for such a translation if the result—the line—were not more vivid, more easily apprehended, than the cause—the tremor.

One could say that the seismograph's record is both a symbol and a metaphor of the event, and one values it for its precision. The earthquake is formless and confused, and for that reason its significance is not easily grasped: the metaphorical line that describes its progress is of a miraculous clarity, though in order to determine its relationship to what it describes is not easy.

Throughout the whole of Paul Klee's considerable output since about 1920 that relationship has to be studied and understood. Each of his paintings and drawings is a readable symbol of an emotional event —as the symbol contained in Turner's *Rain, Steam and Speed* clarifies the event of a sudden squall as an express train crossed a bridge over the Thames. But Klee's symbols are more closely related to the event than Turner's. They are capable of infinite variations between mathematical precision and vague adumbration. Each of them seems to require a new stylistic formula, and one can only come to grips with Klee's creative method by selecting and examining a few specimens in order to discover what personal creative method could account for results so superficially different from each other. One suspects that, for Klee, each of the events had, as it were, its own texture and that the texture had to find its exact equivalent in the final work of art.

Such a procedure could be defined as a double romanticism, in which all personal tricks, all the artist's habits of vision, have been abandoned and replaced by something that is far more closely interwoven with the nature of the subject-matter itself.

This is wholly unlike the usual romantic method in which the artist's personality is his most recognizable asset. Wagnerian sequences of harmony betray Wagner, whether his theme is tenderness or cruelty. The opalescent surfaces in a late Turner painting are the same whether he is describing a sunset over a Venetian lagoon or a flurry of rain in the Thames valley. But Klee spreads no such stylistic veneer over the subject, and it is for that reason that he demands from us a rather different critical approach.

What actually happens in the trunk of Klee's imaginary tree, that turns an experience into a drawing, resembles nothing that we can trace in the creative processes of any other artist. When Rilke describes Klee's process as a 'short-circuiting behind the back of nature, and even of the imagination' he certainly succeeds in illuminating the process although he hardly explains it. If it is explicable at all in the normal language of art criticism, the explanation can only be based on a detailed examination of a handful of selected drawings.

As is well known, every drawing by Klee is inscribed in his own handwriting with a title and it soon becomes evident that title and drawing are related to each other in an unusually intimate way. When Titian entitles his picture *Danae* or Picasso *Guernica* or Turner *Rain, Steam and Speed* we know that we have been given rough directional signposts to guide our eyes and minds in the direction of a theme with which we are already familiar. We know the story of Danae: the title merely suggests that we should look for a shower of gold and notice what Titian made of it. 'Guernica' is a word that carries with it connotations that have already aroused our indignation and pity: when we look at Picasso's picture we are already half tuned in to it. We examine it for symbols of cruelty and despair: we are prepared for narrative and we know that we must look for narrative heightened and condensed by an artist capable of feeling and expressing indignation to an exceptionally intense degree.

Klee's titles are not of this kind. They are not signposts: they are named situations. The drawing itself is the signpost: the title is no more than a hint about the drawing's origin. And almost invariably we find that it refers not to a known event but to an imaginary situation. And by noting what kind of situation interests Klee and seems to him appropriate for his own method of translation and visual terms, we are enabled to guess at the kind of man he was—though not, of course, at the kind of artist he was.

Bearing Grohmann's seismograph metaphor in mind, one has only to draw up a list of typical titles in order to guess at what kind of psychological tremor started the delicate needle moving. One notes, for example, that an etching of 1903, made before Klee's method of translation had been perfected, is called *Two Men Meet, each Supposing the Other to be of Higher Rank*. It describes a situation that would only interest a student of the Comedy of Manners. At that early date Klee was only capable of illustrating it as though he were a Dürer with an unusually highly developed sense of humour. It is a purely descriptive essay whose humour depends on the same kind of slight exaggeration of emphasis that a Titian would use in order to express the meaning of the word 'Venetian', or Turner the words 'rain' and 'speed'.

Later, brief titles like *Family Outing, Laced into a Group, Apparatus for Delicate Acrobatics* and *The Twittering Machine*, or titles with a more insistent meaning like *A Sailor Feels the End is Near* or *Downward*, reveal a man perpetually aware of the infinite variety of human experience and also aware of his own capacity for seeing each experience as a mixture of fantasy and seriousness. Such titles must have been invented by what Klee would have called the roots of the creative tree, which, in his own words, 'copes with this bewildering world—

reasonably well'. That double quality of coping—of 'bringing some order into the stream of impressions'—and of being bewildered by it is evident in everything he produced, but in the process of making this ordered bewilderment visible there was never anything hesitant. What seems miraculous is the confidence with which he could use what I have called the glossary of visual equivalents. The immense range of his stylistic devices makes even Picasso's formal vocabulary seem impoverished.

'Art does not render the visible but makes visible,' he says. 'We used to represent things visible on earth. . . . Now we reveal the reality of visible things and thereby express the belief that visible reality is merely an isolated phenomenon latently outnumbered by other realities.' It is an easy phrase to write, and one that would arouse suspicions that whoever wrote it had formulated a creed that no human being could put into practice. But Klee, by some intuitive process for which 'short-circuiting' seems an adequate if mysterious explanation, did put it triumphantly into practice. The family outing includes realities that lie far beyond the visible, and yet they are 'made visible'—the glossary of equivalents never seems to fail him.

The Family Outing[1] (1930) is drawn mainly with a ruler, like an architect's blue-print. The lines, severe and unbroken, lean gently forward to suggest a progress from left and right. The whole design is built up of triangles and rhomboids with the exception of three black dots (which one is compelled to interpret as eyes: they belong to the creatures that lead the little procession and which are not only manifestly dogs, but dogs of a recognizable breed and behaviour, despite their purely geometrical forms). Behind them the father moves easily forward. In form he seems to be somewhere between an adjustable music-stand and an organization of folded newspapers. He is followed by the mother, who carries an infant in the crook of her right arm and leads a child with her left. That anything so close to a diagram of a proposition in Euclid could contain so many and such complex correspondences with human character and behaviour is a mystery. Yet one no more doubts Klee's capacity to describe in Euclidian language the realities that 'outnumber visual realities' than one doubts the power of Debussy to construct a web of sound that will describe the afternoon of a faun. One suspects that there is a closer correspondence between form and sound in Klee than in any other artist, and when one remembers that at the outset of his career Klee did, in fact, choose between music and

[1] Grohmann, p. 274.

Paul Klee, Family Outing
Kunstmuseum, Bern

art as a career, the form-sound correspondence begins to have a meaning that it never quite achieved in any earlier artist.

In this drawing, as in so many of Klee's drawings, the descriptive references to human anatomy or to natural phenomena have been reduced to a minimum. Apart from the dots that 'stand for' eyes and a sequence of L-shaped signs at its base that equally 'stand for' legs on the march and suggest by their angle the exact speed of the procession, the drawing refuses to use the descriptive method; yet the essence of a large, imperturbable father, an overburdened and harassed mother and two eager, panting dogs has been made abundantly clear.

Another drawing of the same year (1930) [1] entitled *Laced into a Group*, uses an utterly different linear method. The line is of spider's-web delicacy, but it is limp and boneless, as though a length of black cotton had been carelessly thrown down on to a sheet of paper and had become so entangled with the notion of a group of people inseparable from one another that only a few dots, indicative of eyes, and lines that suggest noses and mouths were needed to complete the illusion of the fantasy suggested by the title.

[1] Grohmann, p. 275.

Paul Klee, Laced Into a Group
Kunstmuseum, Bern

Here, since there is no dominant sloping rhythm to suggest movement or progress, as in the *Family* drawing, the central meaning of the drawing is quite different. Or, as Klee would have put it, the foliage that emerges from the selfsame stem is of a different botanical species.

Again this mysterious web of line has been given a minimum of human reference by the addition of six of the L-shaped leg-and-foot signs to indicate that no more than three creatures are concerned. But because the length of black cotton that supplies the linear character to the drawing is limp and directionless, the three creatures we are persuaded to believe in are themselves limp and directionless. They are furnished with a set of hieroglyphics which 'mean' legs, but they do not stand upright. Nor is there a base for them to stand on. They are as flabby as worms, and their bodies have no axis. Two of them seem to lean helplessly in opposite directions, and a third moves towards them as though confused by their interpenetration.

After completing the drawing Klee must have felt the need to clarify his own method of inscribing the continuous, meandering line. At intervals throughout its course he has added small directional arrows, as though to make sure that one's eye followed its progress in the same direction as the pen that drew it.

One could easily go on examining drawing after drawing in this way and noting this curious marriage in each one of them, between subject-matter and the infinitely variable glossary of form that serves the subject-matter, and noting also that the 'content' involved in each subject has been enriched and reinforced by the 'content' implied by the form.

In the *Family* a group of adults, children, and dogs has become married with stiff, folded paper. In the *Laced into a Group* drawing, the marriage is between a human situation of people entangled with each other and the behaviour of a yard of black cotton. One turns the page to find another drawing of the same year, entitled *Dancing Master*, whose subject-matter is the muscular tension of a ballet-dancer whose arms act in energetic movement and whose legs are about to execute an acrobatic leap. Yet the formal design is surely based on a set of overlapping architect's set-squares.

The impact on the spectator's eye of such works of art is immensely powerful. The situation is invariably an 'idea' that can only be communicated when it has discovered a formal equivalent. But Klee's formal equivalents have the odd effect of having been picked out of the inexhaustible variety of visual experience and then used as vehicles for communication. This surprising marriage between an idea and an apparently unrelated memory of a thing seen is the essence of Klee's creative machinery. For that reason I have called it a 'double' romanticism. Where other romantics translate an emotion into a visual language that is always recognizably their own and gives to whatever they produce a common stylistic factor that is unmistakably Titianesque, or Turneresque, or Picassoesque, there is no such personal handwriting in what Klee produced. He invented no language, because he invented—or rather discovered, as he searched through the visible world—a thousand languages. It would certainly not have occurred to Picasso to accept dictation from a length of cotton at one moment and a collection of set-squares at another, or to substitute what seems to be a pair of crumpled gloves (in a drawing called *Goodbye to You*[1] of 1927), for a set of features, and yet achieve a facial expression of agonized despair.

And yet, though it can be truly said that Klee invented no language or used no personal tricks of handwriting, there is no difficulty in identifying him in any of his paintings or drawings. What makes him identifiable is precisely his habit of welding together these irreconcilables, thereby enabling himself to tackle the problem of expressing one

[1] See Grohmann, p. 251.

level of reality in terms of another. When he claims that he does not 'render the visible', but that he 'makes visible', he is describing a creative mechanism that belongs exclusively to him and which could never be mistaken for anyone else's. One could call it the use of double metaphor, and that in its turn is the sign of a fantasist—a man who light-heartedly inhabits two worlds at once.

In doing so Klee reveals his own personality far more clearly than if he had been 'rendering the visible'. In 'making visible' a family outing or a ballet-dancer in action or a tragic parting between two people, it was always himself that he made visible. And the self he revealed almost always had a hypnotic charm. His was the fantasy of a man perpetually in a condition of quiet delight. It is that quality and not a set of stylistic habits that makes his work so easily recognizable, and also so fundamentally romantic.

We are apt to think of the romantic temperament as one that works almost blindly, by trial and error, and of the romantic artist as one who gropes intuitively towards his destination. And in one sense one could attach him to the family of intuitive gropers and accept his own explanation of his creative process as one that 'mainly takes place on the unconscious level'. Yet perhaps more than any other romantic artist he was not only acutely conscious of the pattern of his creative method, but as a teacher of students at the Bauhaus he worked out with detailed precision each logical step in the training of an artist on every level from purely technical equipment through the observation of natural phenomena to the imaginative use of such phenomena in planning and executing the finished work. And as he left behind copious written notes that sum up his practical methods and his pedagogic approach to art, it is possible to follow the workings of his acute analytical mind. Having done so one begins to realize that what at first glance looks like series of inspired doodles is the result of a planned practical philosophy.

The *Pedagogical Sketchbook* (published by the Bauhaus in 1925) is by no means his only exposition of his method and the philosophy behind it, but it is the most complete and condensed account of how a basic training of the strictest and most disciplined kind can enable an artist to release his own pictorial or symbolical imagination. The exuberant fantasy is the final product of a discipline that could be compared with the self-imposed discipline of a virtuoso pianist whose muscular control enables him to execute the most difficult passages with apparent ease: with the difference, of course, that what Klee was aiming at was creation and not interpretation.

To describe his methods in detail would be tedious and inappropriate here. But it is worth mentioning that a detailed description of the elements of pictorial language—with diagrams showing proportion, symmetry, balance, and the nature of linear dynamics—forms one half of it. In the other he examines the possibilities of training the eye by confronting it with the physical nature of various materials—paper, steel, glass, wood-shavings, textiles. Such confrontations acted as a double spur, firstly to the imagination, secondly to the possibilities of pure craftsmanship. What could be 'made of' (both physically and imaginatively) such materials by using them without betraying or mishandling them? Every physical, tangible object in the world possesses its own expressive possibilities. Klee's students as well as himself trained themselves to be hypersensitive to those possibilities.

That hypersensitivity had, as its ultimate goal, the development of a capacity for 'amazement'. That anything so surprising and delightful as a sheet of paper or a ball of string was available to the artist as raw material for his creative will was something that had to be taught, and taught by an elaborate method. It was as though Klee had discovered that the aesthetic responses could be refined and developed in a kind of gymnasium of his own invention.

There is surely a moral to be drawn from this brief account of Klee's highly personal form of romanticism. It is tempting to assume that certain artists have a natural gift for what Rilke called 'short-circuiting behind the back of nature', and that Klee possessed the gift to an uncanny degree, so that the imagery that was created so copiously in his thousands of smaller paintings and drawings came to him almost as naturally as breathing.

But as soon as one looks more closely at those evocative drawings and paintings, so remote from the seen world and yet so tightly packed with oblique references to it, and as soon as one knows with what methodical care Klee constructed the machinery for that 'short-circuiting behind the back of nature', it becomes evident that Klee's romanticism is anything but a natural gift. He took infinite pains to clear all obstructions away from the path that led from the craftsman's hand to the 'remote will' that guided it.

Conclusion

I have attempted in the preceding chapters to examine samples of romantic visual art in the hope that a definition of the romantic attitude of mind might eventually emerge. I am conscious of having failed to produce such a definition: I have equally failed to describe with precision any common factor that would give a recognizable unity to all the expressions of action—and especially the kind of action that results in a work of art—that we think of as romantic in origin.

One assumed that since it had been necessary to invent the word and then use it freely and frequently in a large number of different contexts, it might be possible, by examining those contexts, to discover what common ground in all of them would help us to understand the nature of romanticism itself.

For two reasons any formula that might be useful is bound to be elusive. In the first place it is obvious that expressions of the romantic attitude in human behaviour and in art vary so much in their degrees of intensity that we must be prepared to meet them in places where they are so diluted as to be hardly detectable or so exaggerated as to be almost absurd.

And secondly, they vary not only in degree but also in kind. If we think of a romantic work of art as one in which the artist has told us more about the nature of his emotional reactions to experience than about the experience itself, it follows that there must be as many kinds of romanticism as there are kinds of reaction. We may agree that Giselbert's tympanum over the west door of Autun Cathedral and Turner's *Rain, Steam and Speed* are both works of romantic art. But what formula would help us to detect the common quality that makes them so?

To say that both are vivid expressions of a heightened state of mind is to say no more than that they are unashamedly personal, and if we find them both unusually satisfying that is because whatever is both passionate and personal is valuable in proportion to the value of the personality of the artist responsible for it. Even though we regard the Romanesque sculptor as a man caught up in the passionate gestures of his generation and the Victorian painter as a product of an exaggeratedly romantic period, and even though we conclude that the attitude of a period can only find its full expression in the stylistic tradition of the period, it is still the genius or the sensitivity of the artist that counts. There is an abundance of Romanesque sculpture that is made up of Romanesque clichés and that would be devoid of interest if the clichés themselves were not somehow stimulating and exciting to us. And there is a great deal of Victorian romantic landscape that is merely romantic by contagion. It is not a record of a personal response to nature, but the result of an acquired habit of underlining whatever has been accepted by its Victorian contemporaries as dramatic or effective.

Giselbert and Turner were *not* romantic by contagion. They were merely fortunate in living at moments when the emotional climate they enjoyed found them supremely acceptable, and when the stylistic traditions they inherited were exactly what they needed. They possessed the passion and the personality without which true romanticism cannot exist, but they were also products of an age that made the appropriate demands on them. That gives them common ground, but it does not define them as romantic artists. In order to regard them as members of the same family it will be necessary to set them beside their counterparts in other families.

The Autun tympanum must be compared with a metope from the Parthenon, Turner's painting with a landscape by Poussin on the one hand and one by Courbet on the other—types of the classic and the realist approaches—chosen because they, too, are free from the charge of being realist or classic by contagion.

There is no need to repeat what has already been said about the temperaments of our three families. They are alike in that they are all dependent on the thing seen: they are unlike in the use made of the thing seen. No artist can take a single step on the creative journey unless he starts with a well-stocked visual memory which has already half-crystallized itself into a set of visual images. What distinguishes the romantic artist from his fellow lies in the relationship between the image and the visual memory. For the romantic vision invariably insists that symbols of the unseen or the unseeable should become fused with memories of the seen.

The word 'symbol' at once poses a problem which the classic artist is rarely and the realist never required to solve. 'Symbols of the unseen or the unseeable' is a phrase the romantic artist can hardly avoid using as soon as he begins to explain his intentions. Like all painters, without experience of what has been supplied to him by his eye he can do nothing. But to make a realist's record or a classicist's generalization is not a part of his programme. What he wishes to communicate is something that is largely a state of mind generated by the thing seen, but in order to make that communication he finds it almost obligatory to refer quite specifically to the thing seen.

This involves him in a difficult situation. The sculptor of a Romanesque Last Judgment is primarily concerned with the communication of a sense of awe engendered by an 'event' (he must inevitably have envisaged it as an event) of great solemnity and also of great complexity. To depict the machinery for administering justice involves him in a task that can only be carried out by means of descriptive narrative: but to portray the workings of Divine justice makes a different set of demands on him. Fear of what is inescapable, either in the presence of God in the medieval world, or of Nature in the pantheistic Victorian world, is one of the strongest incentives to romanticism, and since fear of Divine justice and awe at the onset of a thunderstorm are not in any sense things seen, symbols must be invented—visual equivalents not only engendered by emotions but also calculated to arouse the same emotions in the beholder.

To produce a recognizable description of angels blowing trumpets, human souls being weighed in balances, groups of the blessed enjoying felicity and groups of the damned undergoing punishment, would be the normal task of any artist who had undertaken the subject. But to raise all this from the realm of description to the realm of apocalyptic vision involves not the addition of symbolism but the translation of the whole conception into symbolic terms. And each symbol must be based on human visual experience. The Divine Judge himself can only be depicted in terms of human anatomy, but human anatomy so distorted that not for a moment could it be thought that a human being had consented to act the part of the Deity.

Symbolism is therefore visual metaphor, with a twofold function. Like all metaphor its purpose is to make the unfamiliar vivid and meaningful not by comparing it with the familiar but by insisting that it is an exceptional example of the familiar. No romantic artist can dispense with it. The flash of lightning in Giorgione's *Tempestà* is a symbol of wonder, the Crown of Thorns in Grünewald's *Crucifixion* is a symbol of physical suffering. The thrusting arm holding the lamp in Picasso's *Guernica* is a symbol of hope. True, Klee's extraordinary symbolic repertory is derived from a different principle, in which metaphor becomes metamorphosis and human beings may find themselves made meaningful by turning them into sheets of newspaper or lengths of cotton or recollections of set-squares. But the essence of romantic symbolism is that it contrives to relate the unseen emotion with the seen form, and that the seen form only becomes an expressive symbol when it can be translated back by the beholder into the unseen.

The realist and the classic artists are both equally unwilling to regard the unseen and the unseeable as part of their subject-matter. When Velasquez undertakes to paint a Bacchus, his god is made in man's image and so can never indicate man's relationship to his gods. And when Ingres paints a *baigneuse* he improves her contours not by discovering in her the symbol of a goddess but by using a pair of compasses in order to connect her more closely with the Platonic mathematical ideal.

The romantic artist, on the other hand, equally dependent for his unseen gods and goddesses on his memories of seen men and women, and equally unable to ignore those memories, uses them as a basis on which to graft a symbol, and in doing so ceases to regard them as made in man's image or even as generalizations based on man's image. Cranach's Venuses have no connection with the odalisques of Ingres. They are diagrams of women who have become so entangled with overtones of eroticism that we can no longer think of them as 'distorted'. The descriptive element—which, of course, must be their basis even for Paul Klee, otherwise we should not recognize them as women—has been so closely integrated with the symbolic element that we can easily accept them for what Cranach intended, namely as expressions of his reactions to women, and Cranach's reactions can only be interpreted in terms of eroticism.

To compare Cranach's reactions with those of, say, Velasquez in the *Rokeby Venus* on the one hand or by Ingres in a nude on the other was the first step towards elucidating the meaning of the word 'symbol'. None the less it is a confusing approach, since the human body is so intimately related to human experience, and so much of that experience is visual, that to disentangle visual description from visual symbolism is more difficult in the case of figure-painting than in any other branch of the visual arts. One could almost say that to paint or carve the human figure is, by its very nature, a romantic activity, and because the human reaction to the human body is in itself romantic, as the subject-matter of art becomes less closely related to normal human experience, it becomes progressively easier to distinguish between description and symbol. The typical subject-matter of the romantic artist is the supernatural or the remote or the inhuman. The typical symbols of romanticism are, for that reason, religious or nostalgic or they refer to the more impressive aspects of man's environment. We recognize them at once, into whatever category they fall, for all of them are symptoms of wonder or bewilderment which we find it easy to share provided we are ourselves capable of experiencing wonder or bewilderment and provided we can recognize the description behind the symbol.

The wonderment, for example, contained in that symbolic diagonal in *Rain, Steam and Speed* is not difficult to read. It 'means' the relentless, unswerving progress of a machine cutting its way through the confused flurry of a storm. But potent though it is, it would not be intelligible as a symbol if it were not also recognizable as a description of a railway-track on a bridge over a river. The realist might have described it in greater detail and with a good deal more respect for it as a sample of bridge-building, and in doing so would have sacrificed its relentlessness. The classic artist would probably have rejected it as being too uncouth to be useful as an ingredient in a composition that must, at all costs, be 'beautiful'.

What the romantic artist invariably does, in his attempt to make us aware of his state of mind, is to reduce the percentage of description to a minimum and allow the symbol to carry the main share of the burden. But he does so at his peril, for that very attempt to jettison visual description must, if carried too far, weaken the impact of the symbol. A diagonal that refuses to make any reference to a railway-track loses its power to convey relentlessness.

It is at this point in every discussion about the romantic artist's 'obligation to reality' that one must face the implications brought about by twentieth-century experiments in non-representational art. There can be no question as to the artist's right to throw overboard all his traditional habits of observing the phenomenal world and of describing at least certain aspects of its appearance. If he feels that description, even of the most elementary or diagrammatic kind, will cramp his powers of self-expression, then he must abandon description altogether as a useless and irrelevant form of artistic activity. And there are plenty of instances of artists who have defiantly ignored or deliberately avoided every reference to the optical experience that comes to them from the phenomenal world.

As early as 1910 Kandinsky had found it possible to make the complete break with everything that could be thought of as the fruits of 'observation' or 'looking'. And years later, Mondrian had limited his vocabulary of self-expression to the use of vertical and horizontal lines and a narrow range of primary colours.

Conscious that some apologia was needed for taking such a decisive step, both artists wrote volubly about their reasons for doing so. Both felt the need of an elaborate intellectual justification of the aesthetic adventure on which they had embarked. And if we, in our attempts to see the artist's visual language as a fusion of the descriptive with the symbolic, decide that no other kind of visual language is possible, we must, in fairness, listen to their explanations. They have deliberately abandoned description as part of their programme. In their written polemics they have given us their reasons for doing so. Are we to assume that they have fallen back on pure symbolism as their only means of self-expression? Surely not. For we have just decided that a symbol can only be intelligible if it is a metaphor. And a metaphor is meaningless unless it is a translation. Turner's diagonal cannot be a symbol in a vacuum. It can only be meaningful in relation to a specific length of railway-line and a specific headlong journey along it. The line inscribed by the seismograph is only meaningful in relation to a specific earth-tremor, of which it is a translation.

If, therefore, the organization of form and colour created by the non-figurative artist is to be thought of as a symbol, what specific experience, seen or unseen or unseeable, does it elucidate? What, to put it briefly, is it a symbol *of*? The question, asked after half a century of assiduous experiment in abstract art, may sound a trifle naïve. Or it may turn out to be an irrelevant question. But if we are to envisage the romantic temperament as capable of expressing itself in abstract terms it must surely be asked.

Mondrian's puritanical reduction of all problems of visual expression to the tensions produced by verticals and horizontals need not concern us. His solution of such problems is that of the classic artist, whose only purpose is to seek perfection and if, in doing so, he reduces his statements to a set of faultless mathematical diagrams, it is evident that the romantic attitude of mind is antipathetic to him. But Kandinsky had no such purpose. The work he began to produce after 1910, and which continued with little stylistic change up to 1916, under such titles as *Improvisation* or *Painting with Two Red Spots* or *Composition*, strikes one, at first sight, as turbulent and undisciplined. It is, in fact, nothing of the sort. It is the result of a strenuous endeavour to work out the grammar of a purely formal language freed from any obligation to refer to the world of phenomena. But being, as he himself admits, easily swept away by the violence of his own emotional responses, the formal language he needed had to be as flexible as possible, and its vocabulary as extensive as possible.

Consequently, Kandinsky's writings, and especially his long essay *Point and Line to Plane*,[1] are mainly concerned with the pure architecture

[1] Published by the Bauhaus in 1926.

—or 'composition', as he would prefer to call it—of visual language. For, inevitably, the artist who refuses to use the ready-made vocabulary of forms supplied to him, through his eye, by the world outside him, is compelled to invent his own vocabulary of form and colour from within as his only means of expression. And as soon as the phrase 'means of expression' becomes (as it inevitably must or there can be no *raison d'être* for art) the core of his argument, the question at once arises 'Of expressing *what?*' and the answer can only be 'Of expressing human experience.' And to the artist who refuses to make any reference to experience of specific, observed facts and his reactions to them there is no alternative but to find a visual expression of a generalized state of mind, which comes—as Kandinsky rather repetitiously points out—'from within'.

Such states of mind are familiar enough to us all, and there is no lack of words to serve as rough indications of their nature. Words like 'warm', 'cold', 'lethargic', 'dynamic', 'rigid', 'yielding' and so on are challenges to the artist, whatever his medium, to discover equivalents in terms of the medium. What distinguishes the visual artist, whose appeal must be to the beholder's eye in purely static terms, from other kinds of artist is merely the fact that until 1910 it had never occurred to him that a set of visual equivalents could possibly find expression without any support from references or descriptions derived from the phenomenal world.

It was not that any particular virtue lay in the use of references or descriptions, but that, once recognized, they release a flood of associations. When a Rubens paints a *Rape of the Sabine Women* his value to us does not depend on his revealing to us the appearance of an incident in Roman history but in presenting us with an easy 'lead in' to an expression of all that is implied by the word 'violence'. What a Kandinsky, as opposed to a Rubens, attempts to do is to make 'violence' visible without reference to Roman soldiers, Sabine women, or indeed any recognizable material object whatever.

Obviously the sacrifice involved in doing so is considerable. It is the rejection of all appeal to association. The thoughts and memories that come to us so easily once we have noted the forms of energetic males and struggling females are denied to us, and for that reason the 'architecture of violence', which Rubens can, and does, use just as freely and inventively as Kandinsky, becomes less readable.

On the other hand, as a compensation for the sacrifice of association, the non-objective artist enjoys a freedom hitherto undreamed of. Skies no longer need to be blue, or rather, once there is no reference to sky,

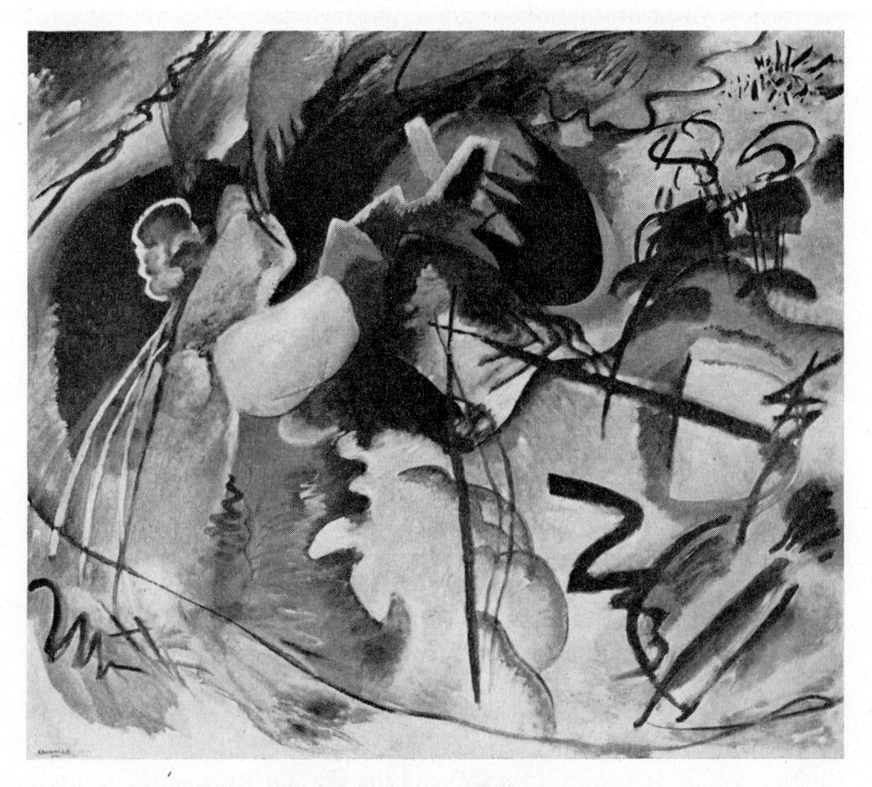

Vasily Kandinsky, Painting with White Form No. 166, 1913
The Solomon R. Guggenheim Museum, New York

there need be no use of blue, and if the artist decides that blue is not a reasonable equivalent for violence, his release from a hampering obligation to the colour of the sky cannot fail to increase his expressive power.

It is this acceptance of sacrifice and freedom, the former robbing him of power, the latter enormously increasing it, that involves the abstract artist in the invention of a new formal language, and it is the grammar of that language that Kandinsky is at pains to establish in his essay.

Now, it was almost inevitable that a visual artist anxious to justify and explain his rejection of the *seen* world and, with it, of the specific reference, should look round him for an art that could equally dispense with it. And, of course, the art of music was bound to occur to him as one whose most profound emotional impacts could be made without reference to the *heard* world. And it is not surprising to find Kandinsky attempting, in the first few pages of his essay, to construct a purely visual pattern that would correspond to the opening bars of Beethoven's Fifth Symphony.

If Kandinsky's translation of Beethoven's sound-pattern into a visual pattern had succeeded in conveying to the spectator any of the emotional impact of those shattering opening bars, he would have made one of the most important discoveries ever made in the technique of self-expression. On the face of it his translation is faultless. Each note is represented by a dot whose size corresponds to the force of the note. The spaces between the dots correspond to the time-intervals between the notes and the drop of a major third between the third and the fourth note. In theory Kandinsky has succeeded in translating the language understood by means of the ear into an equivalent that would equally affect the eye. In practice he had done nothing of the kind, and for a simple reason, namely that intervals of time and pitch, on which the very meaning of music depends, can have no visual equivalents. A space interval of two inches between two dots is not the equivalent of the descent of a major third. If it could contain any such meaning it would be a far less precise means of expression than the purely visual aspect of Beethoven's score, which does at least indicate the *direction* as well as the speed of the time-sequence of music. There is no innate mechanism in the eye which compels us to *read* a visual language from left to right as we read the musical score of the printed page.

To put it shortly, Kandinsky omitted to take into consideration the fact that the eye can only grasp visual relationships simultaneously, and that the grammar of any visual language which he explores in great detail is not a grammar of sequences but of instantaneous relationships. One does not, for example, 'read' the human body by following its progress from the head downward to the feet. If one were presented with the first four notes of Beethoven's Fifth Symphony in the reverse order, beginning with a *fortissimo* pause and ending with three short stabs, the effect would not only be meaningless. Its proper meaning would be contradicted. To write 'End the is this' instead of 'This is the end' is meaningless, and to write the four words on top of one another is to contradict the purpose of language.

It would be unjust to Kandinsky to suggest that the whole of his visual grammar is based on this fallacy. The bulk of his theoretical writing is concerned with the effect on the eye of points, lines, and surfaces, their distribution, their interrelationships and juxtapositions, the interplay between vertical and horizontal, between straight and curved. But in order to convey to the reader any sense of the 'meaning' of these relationships, he is compelled to regard them as metaphors or symbols by a set of purely arbitrary attempts to equate them with other kinds of sensory stimulus. Horizontals are 'cold' as well as 'flat' (i.e. 'the supporting plane on which the human being stands or moves'): verticals convey 'warmth' (as well as 'height'): diagonals are 'a union of coldness and warmth'.

This attempt to construct a dictionary of correspondences between two kinds of sensory stimulus would be helpful—it could indeed form a basis for a language of abstract art—if we could agree that Kandinsky's correspondences had any roots either in logic or intuition. Evidently, to him, verticals *are* warm and horizontals cold, and therefore for him it is possible to compose a purely visual symphony as meaningful (though not necessarily as forceful) as a musical symphony. But unless one can share his convictions about the 'meanings' of line, point and surface, the abstract painting based on these convictions can be nothing more than decorative. And yet, the non-figurative artist's plea is almost always that he is engaged in expressing a reality that underlies 'mere' appearance, and that to refer to the specific object in a painting is to bind oneself in unnecessary fetters.

This is an ambitious programme, and the one thing we can be sure of is that to express 'reality' is by no means the same as to decorate a surface. 'Reality', as opposed to 'appearance', is not a word I find I can use with any confidence in any argument that concerns the content of what an artist attempts to express in his work of art. As a philosophic concept without which no Platonic thinker can construct a framework for his thought the word is not only useful: it is necessary. But as a word to describe what a non-figurative artist has set himself to express it seems to me meaningless.

Kandinsky and, after him, a host of abstract artists, insists that what he has to say in the visual language he so minutely describes 'comes from within'. But if the phrase has any meaning it must apply equally to figurative artists. A Venus by Titian and a locomotive by Turner must come 'from within', otherwise they would not be a Titianesque Venus or a Turneresque locomotive. That they took shape in the artist's mind's eye under the stimulus of a direct experience of women or locomotives that originally came to the artist 'from without' is not to be denied. But it is equally impossible to envisage in any creative artist inner urges that were not stimulated from without. Only an artist with no sensory equipment at all—no knowledge of light, line, colour, warmth, cold, sound, or even silence—could claim that his creative urges originated from within. If he could live at all he would not live for long in a world in which he did not know that fire burns and light illuminates. And certainly a being with no sensory perceptions (and all sensory perceptions must be specific) would wish to produce a work of art, since he would have nothing to communicate, and a non-communicating artist is a contradiction in terms.

The abstract artist's claim that the imagery he employs comes 'from within' is therefore nonsense. If it means anything it means that the experience that comes to him 'from without' is translated into imagery during the process of communication. And that is the basis of every work of art, abstract or illusionist.

At the moment when all references to the specific disappear from the work of art, symbolism ceases to be possible. A symbol must be a recognizable clarification of an experience that would be meaningless, or, at best, uninteresting, if it were merely described. The more accurately the artist describes it the less it can be said to come 'from within'. But the power of a symbol depends on its being recognizable as a metaphor.

The abstract artist has, by definition, nothing to clarify but vague concepts like 'warm', 'cold', 'rigid', 'flexible'. And if he is to make such concepts vivid and memorable he can only do so by means of symbols whose meaning is beyond doubt. If we cannot accept the connection between 'warm' and 'vertical', then Kandinsky cannot hope to communicate a meaning. He has not clarified but obscured the state of mind he wishes to express. Art for Art's sake is all he has managed to achieve, and 'Art for Art's sake' is the complete negation of the romantic attitude. The implicit first person singular, the note of autobiography without which the romantic is lost, is impossible if the artist's only purpose is to attempt to find a visible equivalent of a concept. If there is not general agreement that his equivalent has made the concept more vivid or more memorable, he has failed in his task.

The fact that this is precisely what music succeeds in doing, and that we judge the genius of a composer by his power to produce audible equivalents that do, by general consent, make such concepts memorable, is frankly puzzling. It is difficult to answer the argument 'Planned organizations of sound must of necessity be non-figurative, and they can be as emotionally evocative as any other medium of communication. Why, then, should not equally non-figurative planned organizations of form and colour be equally evocative?'

The question seems unanswerable. Yet I believe that the answer lies in the basic difference between the uses we habitually make of our eyes and of our ears. What we *see* has gathered round itself so vast an accumulation of meanings and associations that we can no longer think of the visible world as a mere accumulation of colour and form. Our knowledge of the world of phenomena is a great storehouse of memories, each with its own complex accompaniment of associations. Not the shapes and colours of the cloud, the tree, the mountain range, or the gesture of a human being are the core of our visual experience, but the meanings that our memories weave into them. And the artist's task is to make those meanings clear.

What we *hear*, on the other hand, is hardly capable of becoming such a storehouse of memories. The sounds produced by Nature, the babble of the brook, the song of the bird, the wind in the forest, are not to be 'read' in this way, and they can never become the basis of music. The melodies and the harmonic sequences invented by the composer are evocative by virtue of some mysterious set of correspondences that are unconnected with the sound of the wind or the breaking wave. It is not part of my task to explain the composer's correspondence between experience and sound. Nor am I competent to do so. But I am convinced that there is a logic in the time-sequence of music, the building-up and the subsequent satisfying of musical expectations. These depend entirely on a time-sequence that has no parallel in abstract visual art.

Kandinsky's visual grammar in *Point and Line to Plane* is logical and convincing, but it is a grammar that can only exist in a vacuum. It can attach itself to moods: it can render those moods visible. But having done so, it cannot refer to the experiences that produced those moods. Consequently it can never make use of the storehouse of memories on which the figurative visual arts depend for the infinite variety of their appeal.

Under such conditions the abstract artist, for all his freedom of choice and invention, can only make his communication on the most elementary level. He has rejected realism because he is unwilling to wear the shackles that all realists must wear. Classicism is open to him, but his classicism is restricted to the use of Platonic mathematics, for he has turned his back on the phenomena that surround him and therefore cannot idealize them. Least of all can he be a 'romantic', for the essence of romanticism lies in its use of the autobiographical first person singular, and, without a storehouse of memories of the specific, autobiography is impossible.

He is left therefore in a desert occupied only by his own urge to create and a medium that awaits his creative commands. What happens under such circumstances is a curious situation that reminds us of the temptation of St Anthony.

The desert—the vacuum inevitably created by his rejection of whatever in the phenomenal world could stimulate his creative mechanism—is his self-imposed environment. But a vacuum must be filled or its inhabitants perish. And in the artist's case the vacuum created by his refusal to consider 'subject-matter' as his proper sustenance can only be filled in one of three ways.

He can fall back—as Ben Nicholson and Mondrian have done—on mathematical relationships of a purely Platonic kind, thereby carrying the classic theory to its ultimate logical conclusion. Secondly, he can content himself by exploiting his own creative urges and leaving behind him on the canvas a record of his own purely muscular vitality guided by nothing but a vague instinct for rhythmic pattern, which, in its turn, proves little more than that his hand has acquired a set of muscular habits. Such artists have earned the entirely appropriate term of 'action-painters'. Hartung and Pollock are possibly the 'purest' of them, and if the processes of creating 'from within' could have a meaning at all it could be applied to action-painting. Thirdly, the artist, in his self-created vacuum, can find himself face to face—like St Anthony with his tempters—with nothing but a medium that urges him to enjoy and exploit its sensuous charm. He has no alternative but to yield to the temptation, and in doing so he becomes its victim. Such is the programme of the abstract expressionist.

The normal relationship between the artist and his medium—the dictatorship he exerts over it, compelling it to obey his creative will, but only on condition that he asks no more of it than it is able to give and takes full advantage of its behaviour provided that behaviour does not *deny* his creative will—is no longer at his disposal. The two-way traffic, whereby what has to be said can only be translated into visual terms by a willing translator, is broken. The medium, once his servant, has now become his master, and he, once a creator, has become a hedonist. 'Art for life's sake' has changed, by way of an uneasy phase of 'Art for Art's sake' into 'Art for paint's sake'. And at that point the artist, enslaved, as was Huysman's hero, des Esseintes, by his own capacity for sensuous experience, can do nothing but cultivate his own sensitivity. It is an undeniably enjoyable occupation, but a selfish one, and in the end it must prove, like all forms of hedonism, sterile, and therefore powerless as a means of communication.

The *literature* of hedonism, on the other hand, suffers from no such limitation, for the writer uses a medium that draws its strength from the dictionary. He can describe as well as record his sensitivity. Certain writers—notably James Joyce—have found the dictionary inadequate for the task, and have undertaken to expand it, and, in part, to rewrite it with undeniably enriching results. And in so far as Joyce invented his own vocabulary one could say that he is a writer of abstract prose. But the writer who attempts to abandon altogether the dictionary—the agreed link between the sound of a word and its meaning—and rely on the evocative use of sound alone, is manifestly deprived of his central means of communication. Except as mildly evocative refrains, the 'hey nonny no' or the 'willow waly' or 'zimzamaroo zaradee' of the non-dictionary writer are useless to the poet, and he has never been so foolish as to rely on them except as reinforcements to his main purpose.

This would hardly need saying if the *tachiste* artist of today had not undertaken to perform the same unrewarding task in visual terms. He, too, has abandoned his dictionary—his agreed link between a form-and-colour organization and its meaning. It is, of course, true that the visual dictionary is more flexible and less precise than the verbal dictionary, but it exists, and the artist's personal comment on experience is sadly weakened if the colour-form organization that 'means' tree, cloud, sunshine, thunderstorm, cannot be used by him, however obliquely. The equivalents of a vaguely nostalgic 'willow waly' or a vaguely energetic 'zimzamaroo' are still available, and today's abstract expressionist busily exploits their potentialities. But their potentialities, though infinite in variety and unfettered in range, are sadly lacking in impact.

It is in vain that the artist appeals to the composer to back him up in his search for a type of creative activity that needs no help from the dictionary. It is true that no dictionary of *sound*-meanings exists. No musician has ever argued that a common chord 'means' peace or that the timbre of an oboe 'means' urgency. For the musician's strongest weapon is not sound, but his command of time-sequences. It is not the common chord itself but its relationship to the whole network of harmonies that follow it that makes it significant. And by means of that network he establishes rhythmic progressions that automatically build up expectations in the listener. Not what he hears but what he hopes to hear next is the essence of his listening. His expectations, let us say, are baffled by the sequence of sounds that comes to him. What he has heard disappoints him, but even while he is experiencing surprise or disappointment the sequence goes on. The momentary defeat of his expectations turns to delight as he discovers that an unexpected resolution provides a final satisfaction richer, because it had been delayed, than the one he had expected.

Music's greatest power depends on such effects. The time-sequence provides a *journey* for the ear that can have no parallel in the visual arts, which can only present one with the *end* of the journey. There can be no abstract-expressionist equivalent for, say, the opening bars of the prelude to *Tristan and Isolde*.

The two long-drawn first notes could 'mean' almost anything. They are intended as pointers to something that *must* follow, but what *kind* of something no one could guess. Their only intrinsic quality seems to be that of leisureliness. Then comes a hint of what we might hope for—a descent of a semitone that is almost certainly going to lead easily into another drop, like a ball gently rolling downhill. The hope is gratified. The downward movement continues and suddenly stops on a chord so baffling that we almost exclaim 'Surely not! How, out of anything so bitter, could even moderate sweetness be arrived at?' Then, three ascending notes lead upward as though climbing effortlessly through a bank of cloud into sunshine; and the effect is of an unexpected arrival at a desirable destination after a brief but difficult journey. How difficult the journey has been can easily be tested by stopping at the first chord and refusing to continue into the resolution; or rather, into the partial resolution, for the chord is, in fact, never resolved throughout the whole of the prelude. The defeat of expectation is intolerable.

Such effects are denied to the painter, and for that reason the painter's appeal to music in his search for a justification for turning his back on the world of phenomena is meaningless. He can easily find other justifications, the most potent of which is the freedom to invent that he enjoys once he is released from the obligation to describe.

Yet that freedom is a marginal one. The purpose of this book has been to define the limits of romanticism and not to examine the possibilities of abstract art. But if one is to make a rough division of artists into three major families, of which the romantic family is one, it is surely evident that such a division can only be made by examining the three major methods of translating specific experience into pigment; and the operative word in that sentence is surely 'specific'. For only the specific will submit to translation. To evolve form-and-colour organizations that have no traceable origin in the phenomenal world is certainly an exciting and adventurous programme. But such organizations are not translations. Therefore the artists who undertake them cannot be divided into families, and therefore to speak of classic, realist, or romantic abstraction is to invent categories that do not exist because they cannot exist. The abstract painter who bases his visual vocabulary on geometry is not in the true sense a classic artist, for the classic artist idealizes whatever he encounters. But geometry is in itself a statement about ideals and to 'idealize the ideal' is a phrase with no possible meaning.

And the abstract painter who paints in a fine frenzy with no other thought but to exploit to the full the sensuous possibilities of his medium and impose on it an eloquence denied to the figurative painter is not, in the true sense, a romantic, for he is not imposing his temperament on the seen world, nor is he using the methods of the emotional autobiographer—the sure sign of the romantic.

With the entry of pure abstraction, the possibility of splitting artists into categories disappears. For the non-figurative artist romanticism is a word without a meaning.

Index